THE STUARTS

The Stuarts

John Miller

Hambledon and London
London and New York

Hambledon and London

102 Gloucester Avenue
London, NW1 8HX

175 Fifth Avenue
New York, NY 10010
USA

First Published 2004

ISBN 1 85285 432 4

Typeset by Carnegie Publishing, Lancaster,
and printed in Great Britain by Cambridge Universtiy Press.

Distributed in the United States and Canada
exclusively by Palgrave Macmillan,
A division of St Martin's Press.

Contents

Illustrations   vii

Abbreviations   ix

Preface   xi

1   Inheritance   1

2   James I   37

3   Charles I   67

4   The Interregnum   113

5   Charles II   139

6   James II   181

7   William and Mary   203

8   Anne   225

Glossary   251

Notes   255

Bibliography   281

Index   285

Illustrations

Between Pages 50 and 51

1 James I, by Daniel Mytens, 1621

2 Anne of Denmark, the wife of James I, by unknown artist, *c.* 1617

3 George Villiers, first duke of Buckingham, *c.* 1616, probably
by William Larkin

4 Charles I, after Sir Anthony Van Dyck, *c.* 1635

5 Henrietta Maria, the wife of Charles I, after Sir Anthony
Van Dyck, *c.* 1635

6 Thomas Wentworth, first earl of Strafford, by Sir Anthony
Van Dyck, 1636

7 Prince Rupert, Count Palatine, probably by Gerrit van Houthorst,
c. 1642

8 Oliver Cromwell, by Robert Walker, *c.* 1649

Between Pages 146 and 147

9 Charles II, studio of John Michael Wright, *c.* 1665

10 Catherine of Braganza, wife of Charles II, studio of
Jacob Huysmans, *c.* 1670

11 Louise de Kéroualle, duchess of Portsmouth, by Pierre Mignard,
1682

12 Nell Gwynn, studio of Sir Peter Lely, *c.* 1675

13 James, duke of York, and Anne Hyde, duchess of York,
by Sir Peter Lely, *c.* 1665

14   James II, by unknown artist, 1690

15   Mary Beatrice of Modena, second wife of James II,
      by William Wissing, *c.* 1685

16   William III, after Sir Peter Lely, 1677

17   Mary II, by unknown artist

18   Anne, by John Closterman, 1702

Text Illustrations

Title page of *Eikon Basilike*   66

Charles II's entry into the City of London, 1660   138

Sophia, electress of Hanover, the mother of George I   202

Illustration Acknowledgements

The author and publishers are grateful to the National Portrait Gallery for permission to reproduce plates 1–18 and for the text illustration on p. 202.

Abbreviations

BIHR	*Bulletin of the Institute of Historical Research*
BL	British Library
BT	Baschet transcripts of French ambassadors' dispatches: Public Record Office, PRO 31/3
Carte MSS	Bodleian Library, Oxford, Carte Manuscripts
CSPD	*Calendar of State Papers Domestic*
CSPV	*Calendar of State Papers Venetian*
EcHR	*Economic History Review*
EHR	*English Historical Review*
HJ	*Historical Journal*
HMC	Historical Manuscripts Commission Reports
JBS	*Journal of British Studies*
NHI	*A New History of Ireland*, iii, *1534–1691*, ed. T. W. Moody, F. X. Martin and F. J. Byrne (Oxford, 1976); iv, *1691–1800*, ed. T. W. Moody and W. E. Vaughan (Oxford, 1986)
NS	New style (of dates): continental countries used a calendar ten – later eleven – days ahead of that used in England
P & P	*Past and Present*
TRHS	*Transactions of the Royal Historical Society*

Preface

The Stuart kings and queens of England are far less well known than the Tudors. Henry VIII is seen as a larger than life figure, marrying six wives, asserting England's independence of Rome and brutally eliminating all who stood in his way. Elizabeth, the Virgin Queen, sacrificed her personal happiness for the good of her kingdom, proclaiming that she was married to her people. Her reign is widely seen as a golden age, when poetry and drama flourished and England began to assert its position in the world, with English sea commanders cheekily defying the might of Spain and laying the first foundations of an overseas empire. There is some truth in these images of course, but that of Elizabeth in particular was polished and honed as part of a determined public relations exercise, designed to conceal the very considerable insecurities felt by her ministers. It was reinforced by critics of the Stuarts, either in their own time or in later centuries, who set up Elizabeth as an ideal monarch against whom her successors could be measured and found wanting.

By contrast the image of the Stuarts in the popular mind is associated with anything but grandeur or achievement. Charles I is best known for losing the civil war and his head. This has given him a certain romantic, indeed tragic, aura, but hardly makes him a great king. Charles II is best known for his many mistresses and illegitimate children. Here was a king who put pleasure before business and presided over one of the lewdest and most foul-mouthed royal courts in English history. Yet it was under the Stuarts rather than the Tudors that England emerged as a major European and world power. Henry VIII's repeated military failures against France showed that the glorious days of Henry V were long gone; and England's successes against Spain under Elizabeth were spectacular precisely because the English were such rank underdogs. The first hesitant, and generally unsuccessful, attempts to found colonies may have occurred under Elizabeth, but England's worldwide trading and colonial empire really took off under the Stuarts, particularly the later Stuarts. Elizabeth's reign is also remembered as the age of Shakespeare, but Shakespeare continued to write well into the reign of James I, producing many of his greatest works, including *Macbeth*, *Hamlet* and *The Tempest*. Indeed, the roll-call of poets and playwrights from the Stuart age is at least as impressive as that of the Tudors – and that of architects far more so.

This book is not an uncritical attempt to eulogise the Stuarts, still less to denigrate the Tudors. Rather it looks at each of the Stuart monarchs, assessing their achievements – or lack of them – in relation to the opportunities and problems that faced them. It also considers them not only in an English but in a *British* context. James VI and I was the first monarch to rule not only England and Ireland but Scotland as well. Under Anne, the Act of Union of 1707 joined England and Scotland, two ancient enemies, into the single nation of Great Britain. Many of the tensions under the Stuarts stemmed from England's relationship with the other two kingdoms, in which England sometimes used its superior wealth and resources to impose its will. But there was also a longer, slower process of Anglicisation, as English ideas, values and to some extent institutions gradually reshaped Scottish and Irish society. This can either be seen as the triumph of English standards of order and civility, over violent, clan-based societies, or as the arrogant destruction of ancient and vibrant Celtic cultures and ways of life.

Whereas the history of the Stuart era has little current contemporary relevance to the English, in Ireland (and especially Northern Ireland) the clashes between Irishman and Englishman, Catholic and Protestant are still part of the framework of everyday life. Each year the marching season in Northern Ireland reopens old wounds and re-emphasises sectarian differences. These divisions extend to Scotland, which also has its Orange lodges and marches; unlike in England, support for a football club – Celtic or Rangers, Hibernian or Hearts – in Scotland is a statement of sectarian allegiance. The revival of Scottish nationalism in the second half of the twentieth century also reopened the question of the nature of the Union and raised the question of the form in which it should continue – if at all. The recent establishment of the Scottish and Welsh assemblies – following the much earlier concession of home rule and then independence to Ireland – has meant a major reversal of the establishment of English hegemony within the larger entity of Great Britain. This began under the Tudors, with the union between England and Wales in 1539, was carried much further under the Stuarts by the Act of Union of 1707, and completed by the Union between Britain and Ireland in 1801. Looking at the Stuarts in a British context, therefore, allows us to reconsider the development and nature of 'Britain', at a time when the existence of a distinctively 'British', or indeed 'English', identity is more and more open to question.

1

Inheritance

On 24 March 1603 Queen Elizabeth I died, after a reign of almost forty-five years. She had never married or nominated a successor until, on her deathbed, she declared that she wished a king to follow her, adding 'and who should that be but our cousin of Scotland?'[1] King James VI of Scotland had much the best hereditary claim to succeed her. Henry VIII's three children – Edward VI, Mary I and Elizabeth – had all died without heirs. Henry VIII himself, a brutal and suspicious man, had executed most of those relatives who posed any threat to his throne, but one branch of the family had remained out of his reach. His sister Margaret had married James IV of Scotland, who was succeeded by James V and he in turn by Mary, Queen of Scots. Mary's strong claim to succeed Elizabeth had caused deep anxiety and embarrassment among English Protestants, because she was a Catholic. Her execution in 1587 opened the way for her son, James VI, to become the first monarch to rule over both Scotland and England; or, as he preferred to call them, Great Britain.

James was far more acceptable to the English than his mother had been, because he was a Protestant. His mother had been forced to abdicate in his favour when he was a year old, in 1567. She had fled to England the following year and remained her cousin's prisoner until her death. James was brought up a Protestant and had gradually and painfully learned the craft of kingship. After his mother's death he established discreet contact with English politicians, but Elizabeth's refusal to name him as her heir meant that his succession was never completely certain. Within hours of her death, however, the English privy council ordered that James should be proclaimed King James I of England; the proclamation had already been seen, and approved, by the new king. Messengers were soon on the road to Edinburgh and on 5 April James set out to take possession of his new kingdom.

Although in retrospect Elizabeth's death seemed the end of an era, at the time grief was muted and expectations of the new king were high. The Tudors – or to be more precise Henry VIII and Elizabeth – loom much larger in the popular imagination than any of the Stuarts. Elizabeth's reign is seen as a time of national exuberance and expansion, in the arts and on the high seas. England made the first steps towards establishing an overseas empire, the Armada was defeated and Sir Francis Drake 'singed the king of Spain's beard'. Elizabeth conducted an elaborate but chaste flirtation with her courtiers and declared herself married to her people. By the 1590s the marriage was showing signs of strain, as the queen's ever thicker make-up failed to conceal the ravages of time. Corruption was rampant at court and rival factions jostled to control the government when the old queen died. Not surprisingly, she became jealous and suspicious. Some complained that she was now a recluse, hearing 'only such tunes as her keepers sounded unto her'.[2]

The national self-confidence during her reign, so admired by later generations, was far less apparent at the time. England was a second-rate power, its resources dwarfed by those of France and, above all, Spain. Had any of the four armadas landed, the English militia would have been no match for the formidable Spanish army. In 1570 the pope had excommunicated Elizabeth and declared her subjects absolved from their allegiance. This made her vulnerable to assassination or rebellion by her Catholic subjects, and indeed there were several plots against her life. With the succession likely to fall to Mary, or uncertain, English men and women had had every reason to be anxious. Meanwhile abroad, after reaching a high point in the 1560s, European Protestantism was in retreat and, in France and the Netherlands, fighting for its life. England's prospects of surviving as an independent, Protestant nation seemed less than encouraging.

James's accession was greeted with relief and rejoicing. Uncertainties about the succession seemed a thing of the past, as the new king already had two young sons. He was broad-shouldered and slender, with a square-cut beard and piercing blue eyes. He was learned and eloquent, a faithful husband and a diligent ruler. He seemed more decisive and less elaborately formal than his predecessor. His generosity was a welcome contrast to the late queen's parsimony. As he made his way slowly south, he was delighted by the reception he received and by the wealth and plenty that he found everywhere. He knighted many of those who came to see him and even on one occasion a piece of beef: 'Arise, Sir Loin!' cried the king. The festivities and rejoicings continued when he reached London, but soon sober reality began to intrude. For James had to face a task faced by none of his predecessors on either side of the border: that of ruling three very different kingdoms, England, Scotland and Ireland.

Such 'multiple kingdoms' were far from unusual in seventeenth-century Europe. The French kings ruled a disparate collection of provinces, with different laws, languages and institutions and a strong sense of provincial identity. The lands ruled by the kings of 'Spain' (in reality Castile) were still more diverse. In comparison, Scotland and England were homogeneous and well-integrated kingdoms. True, there was a degree of linguistic diversity in both. In the borders, Lowlands and north east of Scotland, where the majority of the population lived, the people spoke Scots (a language similar to, but distinct from, English). In the Highlands and Islands most of the population spoke Gaelic. In England, apart from a dwindling minority in Cornwall, the people spoke English, albeit with a variety of local pronunciations and dialects. Most people in Wales, however, spoke Welsh as their first or only language, so the Church of England brought the Bible and the Prayer Book to the Welsh in their own language. Institutionally Wales had been absorbed into England in the 1530s, with English systems of law and local government (based on counties and justices of the peace). Welsh representatives were added to the House of Commons at Westminster and 'Welsh' bishops (usually Englishmen appointed to Welsh dioceses) sat in the Lords.

In most other respects, England was far more of a nation state than 'France' or 'Spain'. It was already being ruled as a single entity at the time of the Norman Conquest. The imposition of Norman forms of social organisation and law created a greater level of homogeneity than had existed under the Anglo-Saxon kings. By the end of the twelfth century, despite retaining a multiplicity of local customs, England had a national system of 'common' law. Although other systems of law (notably ecclesiastical law) continued to exist alongside the common law, its pre-eminence became established. This process accelerated in the reign of Henry VIII, partly through his assault on the autonomy of the church, but also thanks to the curtailing of 'liberties and franchises'. Medieval kings had granted out 'public' functions, for example the administration of justice, to private individuals or groups (such as town corporations, guilds or universities), who were granted jurisdiction over their members – the right to hold courts, resolve disputes and impose punishments. In the 1530s most of these rights of jurisdiction were taken away. A few survived – notably the church courts and the bishopric of Durham, where the bishop still had his own courts. In addition, the Tudors (and Stuarts) continued to grant to town corporations the right to hold property, dispense justice and manage their own affairs. But in general the common law and the king's justice had become all-pervasive by the end of the sixteenth century, making England a uniform and coherent state.

By 1603 England had also become more orderly. Medieval kings had granted 'public' functions to private individuals because they had lacked the power in the localities to maintain order and to collect revenue. At the heart of the feudalism of the Normans and Plantagenets was the granting of land in return for service – primarily military service, but also assistance in securing obedience and order. Effective governance depended on cooperation between the king and the great landowners, the nobles, who possessed the local power over men that the king lacked. In the Marcher lands, near the borders with Scotland and Wales, selected nobles were also responsible for defence. In the north, great families like the Percies or the Nevilles had private armies. Managing such men required skill. They were proud, often truculent, and operated within codes of honour which placed a man's loyalty to his immediate lord above his allegiance to a distant king: the Percies had almost a tradition of rebellion. Apart from their household retainers and numerous tenants, these lords also developed extensive clienteles of lesser landowners, who served the lords (in warfare or local government) in return for protection and reward.

The problem for the king was to use the influence of the nobles without becoming embroiled in their rivalries; to make their potentially disruptive power a force for order. One valuable instrument in this process was Parliament. In France the national representative body, the Estates General, enjoyed only a fitful existence, and did not meet between 1614 and 1789, while several provincial assemblies (or estates) continued to meet regularly. Such regional assemblies never developed in England, but a national Parliament had evolved from the late thirteenth century. Throughout western Europe late medieval rulers struggled to develop bodies – preferably national bodies – which could provide consent to new laws and new taxes, and so make it easier to ensure that laws were obeyed and taxes paid. Both the English and the Scottish kings succeeded in creating such national assemblies, and it was through Parliament that Henry VIII secured the union of Wales to England and eliminated most of the liberties and franchises. Parliamentary legislation played a key part in the development of the Tudor state.

It was one thing to pass laws, quite another to enforce them. The maintenance of order in the localities depended on the cooperation of the nobles. While some were violent and unruly, most felt obliged to serve the king and assist in maintaining order. They owed their estates and fortunes to service to the crown and especially service in war, which was not only the *raison d'être* of the nobility but could be extremely profitable. They expected, however, that their service would be fairly rewarded (with lands or offices for themselves and their clients), that they would be consulted on issues that mattered to them (particularly the conduct of war), that their rights and interests would be respected, and that the king would do justice between them (through his courts or mediation and arbitration). When kings failed to act as 'good lords' to their nobles, the nobles might rebel – especially if there was a plausible rival claimant to the throne.[3]

They would also take steps to help and protect themselves. Under the well-meaning but weak Henry VI, a small clique of nobles had exploited their favour with the king to shut other nobles out of the king's counsels, to monopolise rewards and to pursue their feuds, confident that the king would protect their followers from punishment. Lesser landowners, unable to trust in the king's justice, sought the protection of greater; greater landowners protected themselves, taking advantage of their clients' influence as magistrates and jurors. With a vacuum of authority at the centre, self-help and self-defence became the order of the day. Those with their own law courts used them to advance their own interests. Others did all they could to bend the machinery of the king's courts their own way.

By 1603, the misgovernment of Henry VI and the 'overmighty subjects'

of the Wars of the Roses were a distant memory. The Tudors had
brought the English nobility under control. Circumstances had helped
them. Developments in infantry and artillery made the nobles' cavalry
skills less relevant. Price inflation forced changes in estate management.
In the north, especially, nobles had leased out land in small parcels to
the same families, from generation to generation, building up traditions
of mutual loyalty. This made military, but not economic, sense. As prices
rose, small farmers struggled to produce a marketable surplus and were
unable to pay increased rents. To sustain their incomes, landlords
lumped small farms into more viable units, leased to the highest bidder:
profit was more important than traditions of loyalty.

Even the Percy earls of Northumberland succumbed to this pressure.
In the fifteenth century it was said that their tenants 'knew no lord but
a Percy', but when the seventh earl rose against Elizabeth in 1569 few
of his tenants followed him. In 1642, at the start of the civil war, the
tenth earl summoned his tenants; they ignored him.[4] But the taming of
the nobility owed much to the crown too. Henry VIII began the practice
of ennobling men who were administrators – in other words civilians
– rather than soldiers. He also made it clear that nobles who posed any
sort of threat to him – especially his blood relatives – were likely to lose
their heads.[5] Parliament passed Acts to limit retaining and royal armies
ceased to be composed of the private retinues of noblemen; the officers
who commanded them were servants of the crown. Successive Militia
Acts established that military service was a general obligation; nobles
and gentlemen commanded the county militias, as lords lieutenant and
deputy lieutenants, by virtue of commissions from the crown. Elizabeth's
government undermined the power of the great northern Marcher
families and discredited the honour culture on which their regional
power had depended. Henceforward no loyalty to any lord was to come
before every subject's allegiance to the crown.[6]

The establishment of order was a slow process. Habits of self-help
and violence died hard, especially in Wales and the far north of England.
In Cumberland, even after 1660, kidnapping and feuding continued
sporadically, and judges needed an armed escort.[7] Nevertheless, the
standards of law and order which prevailed in south-east England, and
the habit of settling disputes through the law courts or by arbitration,
rather than by force, spread slowly through the rest of the country. By

now, the English were not an 'ungovernable people', although peasants and townspeople were seen as alarmingly prone to riot and rebellion.[8] Writers described the people as a hydra, a 'many-headed monster', that once aroused was almost impossible to suppress. Driven by animal instincts – greed and lust – the propertyless masses posed a constant threat to the propertied elite. Only the flimsy police resources of the state and the clergy's repeated insistence that obedience to authority was a Christian duty somehow kept them in check.

Fear and loathing dominate descriptions of 'the people' in early seventeenth-century pamphlet literature.[9] It is not hard to see why. England had a long tradition of peasant rebellions, which were widely remembered. A declaration by the king in 1642 referred to the peasant leaders Wat Tyler (1381) and Jack Cade (1450) without further explanation.[10] Norwich corporation still celebrated its deliverance from Ket's rebellion of 1549 over a century later.[11] The savage reprisals ordered by the government after the rebellions of 1536, 1549 and 1569 showed how frightened it had been.

Disorders continued into the seventeenth century. In 1607 there were widespread riots against agrarian change in the east midlands. Schemes for clearing forests in the south west (extinguishing common rights in the process) provoked disorders over several decades, while violent protests against the draining of the fens continued throughout the seventeenth century.[12] There was also more ritualised (and predictable) violence in the cities, especially London. In more than half the years between 1603 and 1640, London apprentices gathered on Shrove Tuesday to attack brothels or playhouses, while the rivalry between the Inns of Court sometimes led to pitched battles involving large groups of students and servants.[13]

If there is no denying that riot and rebellion were common, there is room for debate about their significance: did they really pose a threat to property and the social order? Generally speaking, the answer is 'no'. Rebellions and riots were not mindless or generalised expressions of class hatred, although they might express anger against 'the rich' or 'the landowners' (or the lawyers). They were protests not against the existing distribution of power in society but against the *abuse* of power. High bread prices were blamed on farmers or dealers who kept grain off the market in order to force prices up, or transported grain to London where consumers were prepared to pay more. Landlords who enclosed common land for their own profit or converted arable land into sheep pasture (reducing the demand for labour) were condemned for profiteering at the expense of the poor – and not just by their victims. After the 1607 rising James I wrote that, having punished the 'diggers', the government should punish the enclosers.[14]

The same was doubly true in the forests and the fens. The forests were cleared and the fens drained mainly by outsiders, often with connections to the royal court and the City of London. The forest-dwellers and fenmen had long enjoyed extensive common rights – in the case of the latter, lush grazing, fishing and wildfowling. These rights were overridden by the businessmen and drainers, with the full support of the king. In these circumstances, economic protest shaded into political protest, just as in 1536 or 1549 those protesting against religious innovation called for the removal of the 'evil counsellors' who had advised these changes.

Several points emerge from this. First, rioters and rebels were generally protesting against change, not trying to bring it about. Secondly, they appealed to systems of values that were widely shared among the elite. This was especially true of the explanation of high food prices in terms of human greed, which lay at the heart of the orders given by the crown to magistrates in times of dearth.[15] When Ket and his men destroyed enclosures, they were anticipating the work of a recently established royal commission against enclosure. Religious conservatism was certainly not confined to the poor in the sixteenth century. Similarly, although it was far from unknown for people to invent ancient rights or customs, there was no doubt that many of the rights claimed by the forest-dwellers and fenmen *were* ancient, most strikingly those set out in an indenture kept in the parish church at Epworth, Nottinghamshire; and the methods used against the commoners provoked protests from the local gentry and clergy.[16] Thirdly, rebellion and riot were usually a final resort, after appeals to the authorities had failed. Food riots at Maldon, Essex, in 1629 occurred only after repeated representations from the town corporation and the county magistrates to the privy council that it was provocative to ship grain out of the port when local clothworkers were desperately poor and hungry.[17] Finally, riots generally involved a minimum of violence – often none at all – and rioters showed considerable respect for the law. As the legal definition of a riot was of three or more people assembling to commit an unlawful act, crowds that gathered to pull down fences often broke up into groups of two. Food rioters would simply stand in the way of grain convoys to prevent them leaving town. Violence tended to be directed against objects (fences, drainage works, the effigies of entrepreneurs) rather than people. This was less true in the fens, partly because many of the drainage workers were Flemish and spoke no English, so that violence was the only language they would understand. But even in the fens, where the riots were larger and more sustained than elsewhere, only two people were killed in the whole seventeenth century, both in questionable circumstances.[18]

It will be apparent that rioters and rebels, far from challenging the existing order, reaffirmed it by protesting at what they saw as infractions of accepted norms. (The same could be said of popular shame punishments of deviants, such as women who beat or cheated on their husbands.) They generally focused on individuals – grain-dealers, enclosing landlords, fen-drainers – and not on the ruling elite as a whole, or the government. Tudor rebels appealed to the monarch to do justice or ignore evil counsel and did not challenge his authority or right to the crown. The one 'rebellion' that made such a challenge explicitly – the attempt in 1553 to make Lady Jane Grey queen – failed abysmally. Other rebellions with a dynastic agenda – Wyatt in 1554 and the Northern Earls in 1569 – significantly kept it hidden.

Looking at the rebellions and riots of the sixteenth century, it is easy to gain the impression that this was a deeply unstable and divided society. It would be truer to see them as a form of negotiation, a demand for justice within a framework of values that was widely shared between rulers and ruled, even if those in positions of power sometimes flouted those values for their own profit.

It is also worth pointing out what did not happen in the sixteenth century. First, after the massive protest against the laughably misnamed 'Amicable Grant' of 1525 (a tax of unprecedented severity), there were no major tax revolts until the 1640s. French peasants and townsmen lynched tax-collectors and mutilated their corpses. The English poor did not, for the simple reason that they paid little or no tax. Secondly, there was no civil war. If the Wars of the Roses can be blamed in large part on noble resentment at the manifold inadequacies of Henry VI, that resentment led to civil war because of divisions in the royal family about the succession. This last problem returned following the death of Henry VIII in 1547, thanks to his complicated marital history. For the next forty years, each ruler faced a potential rival of the opposite religion: Mary under Edward VI, Elizabeth under Mary, Mary Queen of Scots under Elizabeth. Surely here was a perfect recipe for a religious civil war of the sort that convulsed France for nearly forty years. This might not have been a danger if, as historians used to claim, the triumph of Protestantism had been swift and complete. But it now seems that Catholic England took a long time to die and that the imposition of Protestantism was slow and vigorously contested. So why was there no religious civil war?

To answer this question we need to look deeper into the English polity and, in the process, reconsider the impression of the English people given by focusing on riot and rebellion. If England was a much-governed country, who did the governing? Looking at the counties, one could argue that the 'rulers' were a small elite of landowners (peers and gentry), who served as magistrates (justices of the peace) and commanded the county militias; they also held the lion's share of the seats in the two Houses of Parliament. To these could be added a few rich merchants from London and the major provincial towns, plus the more senior lawyers and clergy (the bishops sat in the House of Lords). But the magistrates did not rule alone. They were assisted by many lesser officials, whose responsibilities covered only a part of a county or a single parish, together with a multitude of jurors. These lesser officials – for example parish constables, churchwardens and overseers of the poor – were often elected and served for a limited period. During the seventeenth century parish officials came to be supervised by vestries – parish councils which were in theory elected, but in practice came to be self-selecting. As for juries, besides deciding criminal cases at the quarter sessions or assizes, or assisting in coroners' inquests, they drew to the attention of the authorities matters in need of redress: defective highways and bridges, obstructions and nuisances, disorderly women and disorderly alehouses, vagrants and squatters. Similar patterns applied in corporate towns, the larger of which had several layers of government – parish, ward and borough.[19]

If participation in local government and law enforcement was widespread it was not universal. Women played little or no part and the participation of men was far from equal. Some offices, such as parish constable, were unpopular and burdensome; there were other responsibilities (such as service on juries or in the militia) that the rich and well-connected tried to dodge. But other offices were eagerly sought. The gentry competed to be appointed justices of the peace (at least before the later seventeenth century), while the parish offices that conferred real power (churchwarden, overseer of the poor) tended to be dominated by a relatively small group of wealthier farmers and craftsmen. These would be men of standing, usually literate (they needed to keep records and accounts) and respected by their neighbours: 'the better sort' in both economic and moral terms. Such men would also feature prominently in the vestry. Similarly, in corporate towns aldermen and councillors would be selected from among the wealthier businessmen and professionals. Although villages and towns might seem at first sight to be little democracies, they turn out on closer inspection to be ruled by oligarchies of the self-styled 'better sort'.

But was this a problem? It is easy to assume that oligarchy breeds corruption and oppression, as councillors plunder municipal resources and feast at the taxpayers' expense. This sometimes happened, notably in towns that possessed extensive resources in terms of town lands (for example, Coventry) or economic privileges (Newcastle-on-Tyne). But most towns did not have such resources and councillors served for nothing; indeed service on the council cost them money, so one has to assume that they served either because it brought prestige or out of a sense of civic duty. In most towns and parishes there was little competition for office, which was burdensome and time-consuming. The interests of rulers and ruled did not necessarily diverge. They lived in close proximity and often shared the same values. In towns all would agree on the need to keep the streets clean and lit, the deserving poor relieved, and harbours and waterways navigable.

In town and parish the respectable could also agree on the need to discipline and punish the 'loose, idle and disorderly' poor, not least by denying them poor relief. Officials and respectable opinion shared an ethic based on hard work, sobriety, thrift, responsibility and obedience to authority. Those who failed to subscribe to that ethic needed to be punished, for their own good, before they slid down the slippery slope into drunkenness, crime or prostitution. The extent to which the English

had a predisposition to submit to discipline was shown by the extraordinary village constitution drawn up in Swallowfield, Berkshire, in 1596.
Because of an administrative anomaly, there were no justices of the
peace nearby, so the 'chief inhabitants' set down a set of rules to govern
the community. These provided both for the relief of the 'honest' poor
and for the punishment of the disorderly, including those who failed
to observe the Sabbath.[20]

The Swallowfield articles show that, although they were in many ways
an orderly people, the English were far from passive. Nor were they
easily divided into rulers and ruled. This was partly because of the extent
of participation and self-government at several levels, partly because the
rotation of office meant that the power which one man exercised over
another one year might be reversed the next. Nor did power necessarily
follow social status: gentlemen accused of violent crime found themselves judged by juries of farmers and craftsmen. Participation in
government and law enforcement encouraged people to see government
and the law as a resource, which could be used in seeking redress and
resolving disputes. Criminal prosecutions were normally started by the
victims, or their kin, often after failing to secure redress in other ways.
Civil litigation was often initiated as part of a process of bargaining to
secure redress. Although inter-personal disputes and violence were common – the English were notoriously quarrelsome, especially when drunk
– the multiplicity of law courts offered means of resolving differences
and there was frequently pressure to do so from within the community.
The English respected the law (if not the lawyers) largely because they
participated in the legal process and knew that it worked. Law was not
something imposed on them arbitrarily from above.

It must be stressed that the English experience of the law was characterised by *active* participation, not passive acquiescence, and embraced
a strong sense of justice. If men (and women) felt that the law had been
flouted or misapplied, they would petition, protest, riot or rebel. One
of the most striking examples of self-help in the sixteenth century was
the Bond of Association of 1584. Driven to distraction by Elizabeth's
refusal to execute Mary Queen of Scots, or debar her from the succession, many Protestants, including privy councillors and senior clergy,
undertook to kill anyone harming the queen's person. This was a
compact of rebellion, legitimated not by existing law but by the shared

conviction that the queen's death would lead to the destruction of Protestantism. As it was assumed that Mary would be implicated in any design against Elizabeth, the signatories undertook to kill her or at least prevent her accession to the throne.[21] And this in a kingdom where for nearly half a century the clergy had relentlessly taught that rebellion was a sin against God, akin to parricide.

The English habitually obeyed the law, but obedience had its limits, seen most frequently in riot. Familiarity with the law bred a strong sense of right and wrong, which was applied to the actions of kings as well as those of lesser mortals. Although rebellion was not normally a viable option – it was seen as wicked and subversive of the established order, and the penalties for failure were severe – the king's dependence on the cooperation of his people in government meant that, if that cooperation was withdrawn, government could grind to a halt. This would be especially dangerous in wartime, when the king needed them to raise extra revenue and to fight. The king could deal severely with individual dissidents, but he found it much harder to deal with mass disobedience, as shown by the failure of the Amicable Grant and by the tax strike of 1640. He could get away with numerous acts of petty tyranny or illegality, but in the long run government worked better if (as Charles II was told in the 1670s) he 'fell into the vein of his people'.[22]

Scotland and Ireland also became more orderly in the sixteenth and seventeenth centuries, in part as a result of the extension of English influence into the other two kingdoms and Lowland influence into the Highlands. In both countries, the nobles exercised a strong control over the peasantry, from whom they demanded money, provisions and service. This was partly a function of power. These were violent societies: in return for obedience and service, the lords provided protection. The obligation that this created was often reinforced by a sense of family loyalty to the lord as head of the clan. Vestiges of this survived even in England, in the 'names' (clans) of Cumberland and Westmorland, and in Wales. In Ireland and the Borders, Highlands and Islands of Scotland clan loyalties remained strong. In Ireland as late as the wars of 1689–91, landowners mobilised their tenants, who would fight for them but for no one else.[23] Apart from protection, lords offered justice, through arbitration or their own law courts. The power of the Scottish nobility, even in the Lowlands, owed much to 'heritable jurisdictions', inherited rights to hold courts, which were sources of both power and profit. While perhaps providing justice in disputes between tenants, they offered tenants scant hope of redress against their lords. When the English radical William Cobbett visited Scotland in 1830, he was shocked by the servile dependence of the peasantry.[24]

The near-absolute power that many Scottish and Irish nobles exercised over the peasantry was compounded by military power. By 1603 the English nobility had become a predominantly civilian elite. They built unfortified country houses rather than castles, and the great halls in which they had entertained their retainers had been divided up into more private, and more comfortable, rooms. Their military role was now confined to occasionally exercising the county militia. Their armouries contained weapons that were old and only for show. By comparison, their Scots and Irish counterparts were armed to the teeth. Feuding and cattle rustling remained common in the remoter parts of Scotland and Highlanders came down into the Lowlands in search of booty. In Ireland brigandage was endemic and lords and gentry lived by extortion and plunder. In the wars of the 1640s and 1689–91 this brigandage escalated to a horrendous level, involving what were notionally regular armies as well as local warlords and peasant bandits. The country was utterly devastated and over one third of the population may have died between 1641 and 1652.[25]

The militarisation and violence of Irish and Scottish society posed severe problems for their kings. Scotland had never been conquered by the English, but in some respects it had developed similarly to England in the middle ages.[26] This owed something to the church, the great unifying force of Western Christendom, and much to a series of capable kings in the twelfth and thirteenth centuries, who had imported Norman, or Anglo-Norman, institutions and modes of government in order to strengthen their rule. These kings helped unite a variety of tribes into a single kingdom and encouraged the development of towns. Feudalism added cohesion and order to the Lowlands and the north east. The fact that Norman influence did not penetrate into the north west led to the development of a society different to that which existed elsewhere in Scotland, Gaelic-speaking and based on clans.

At this stage, relations between Scots and English were not unduly hostile. Ties of family and self-interest counted for more than nationality and frontiers were fluid. From 1286, Edward I's attempt to subordinate Scotland to England, and his ferocious brutality, created a Scottish nationalism defined in terms of hatred of the English. From the late thirteenth until the mid sixteenth century, hostilities continued in the form of either actual warfare or cross-border raids and cattle-stealing. As England was the wealthier kingdom, the English generally took the offensive, exploiting divisions among the Scottish nobility under a series of weak or underage kings. Their aim was to neutralise Scotland or to establish a friendly regime in Edinburgh, rather than to conquer the whole country, which, given the terrain and the ferocious hostility of the people, was probably beyond their capabilities. They may well also have felt that Scotland was too poor and backward to be worth conquering. One commentator in the 1650s called it 'the fag-end of the Creation' and, at a time when there were numerous schemes in England for the colonisation of Ireland, there was no such scheme for Scotland.[27] This did not mean that the English had no interest in plundering the towns of the south and Lowlands, which had the additional aim of deterring opposition to English power. In 1545 the earl of Hertford sacked seven abbeys, sixteen castles, five towns and 243 villages. The previous year he had sacked Edinburgh and carried away over 20,000 cattle and sheep.[28]

It was during these Anglo-Scottish wars that the House of Stuart gained the crown of Scotland. The family originated in Brittany and came to Scotland via the Anglo-Welsh border, where one of their number, Walter Fitzalan, was recruited by the Normanising king David I in the 1130s. The family had a tradition of expertise in estate management and six generations served as high stewards to Scottish kings – hence the name Stewart (or Stuart, which was the French spelling). The high steward became the most prestigious and powerful office under the crown. When David II died without heirs in 1371, his steward was crowned as Robert II. He was succeeded by his son, Robert III (he had changed his name from John, which was believed to be unlucky), and then by five kings named James. Most succeeded to the throne as minors and many met bloody ends. Margaret Tudor's husband, James IV, was killed at Flodden in 1513. James V fared little better, dropping dead with shock on hearing of the defeat of his army at Solway Moss in 1542.

Yet the dynasty survived. Between 1371 and 1542 every Stuart king left a male heir, giving it unquestioned legitimacy and continuity, in contrast to the contest between Lancaster and York in England. It could also draw on centuries of royal tradition, which was emphasised to stress Scotland's independence of England. Robert II claimed to be the one hundredth successor of the legendary founder king, Fergus Mor mac Erc. The Stuarts also claimed descent from the equally legendary Banquo. Shakespeare had more than one eye on James I when he had the witches show Macbeth the line of Banquo's descendants, stretching on until doomsday. Despite suffering repeated English attacks and plundering, Scotland and its royal house survived. The Stuarts married into some of the best families in Europe, including the French royal house, and in 1603 James VI inherited the throne of Scotland's oldest enemy.[29]

An additional reason why the English never conquered Scotland was the 'Auld Alliance' between the Scots and the French. During and after the Hundred Years War, the French were quick to exploit the danger that Scotland posed to England's rear, which was greater than the threat from Ireland because Scotland and England were separated only by a land frontier. The French (like the English) sought to install their supporters in the royal government as well as sending over military advisers and (less often) military help. In 1542 Mary, the daughter of James V, succeeded to the throne at the age of one week. She was betrothed at the age of one to the future Edward VI (which, given the way they developed, would have been a marriage from hell, had it come to fruition). Instead she married the son of the king of France, who succeeded to the throne as Francis II, when his father was killed in a jousting accident in 1559. Mary became queen of France as well as of Scotland and sent an army to crush the nascent Protestant Reformation in Scotland.

Francis died of consumption in December 1560. By the time his young widow returned to Scotland, all French troops had been expelled, thanks to the military and naval support given by Elizabeth's government to the anti-French nobility. This cooperation initiated an exceptional outbreak of good relations between Edinburgh and London, reinforced by an emerging common Protestantism. The movement towards Protestantism, the in-fighting among the nobility and the scandals surrounding her own private life led Mary to flee to England in 1568, leaving her young son, James, as king.

Mary's arrival evoked mixed feelings on Elizabeth's part. She had by far the best hereditary claim to the succession. She would, however, be the natural focus for any Catholic rising, which became more likely after the excommunication of 1570; the Catholic Church regarded Elizabeth as illegitimate, because Henry had divorced his first wife in order to marry her mother, Anne Boleyn. It was therefore advantageous for Elizabeth to have Mary in her power, under surveillance, rather than in Scotland or France making trouble. It was also in her interest to keep Mary alive. In an age of religious wars and rebellions, she was reluctant to shed the blood of a fellow monarch. In addition, Mary's vastly superior hereditary claim would make it difficult for Mary Tudor's widower, Philip II of Spain, to pose plausibly as the Catholic candidate to replace Elizabeth. Last but not least, as James VI grew to maturity, Elizabeth could see the advantage of having the heir presumptive as a prisoner who could not easily act as a focus for a 'reversionary interest', in opposition to the current queen.

In 1587, after Mary's execution, Elizabeth's refusal to acknowledge James as her heir created a certain coolness in their relationship. Even so, after generations of war, the *détente* that began in 1560 proved durable. Cross-border cooperation reduced, but did not eradicate, border raids and rustling. Anglo-Scottish friction (together with royal weakness and minorities) had been a major contributor to Scotland's endemic violence. Lacking effective royal leadership, and threatened with raids from England or the Highlands, much of Scottish society had had to be in a continual state of military preparedness. This required castles and fortifications, but also forms of social organisation that would allow for speedy mobilisation.

Kinship and family played a substantial part in creating cohesion, but these were reinforced by forms of feudal organisation (the granting of land in return for service) imported from Normandy via England. Feudal ties were strongest in the Lowlands, where they were strengthened by landlords' heritable jurisdictions and by bonds of manrent, voluntary agreements (similar to those in fifteenth-century England) whereby lesser landowners bound themselves to serve magnates in return for protection and reward. But feudal concepts slowly penetrated the Highlands as well, including the practice of primogeniture, whereby land and leadership passed automatically to the eldest son;

in Gaelic society, leadership tended to pass to the bravest and clever-
est (or the strongest and most cunning) of the former chief's male
kin. By the sixteenth century, differences between Highlands and
Lowlands were becoming blurred: both kinship and feudal ties were
important.

If these forms of organisation were encouraged by the need for
self-defence, they could also be used to plunder the English or the
vulnerable: booty was one motive for entering into bonds of manrent.
As noble networks grew larger in the fifteenth century, their leaders
maintained a degree of discipline among their followers, but when
leaders clashed disorder could develop on a massive scale. Feuding and
plunder were endemic, accompanied by almost casual slaughter (including women and children). One chief was described as 'a very active man,
he burnt and harried Sleat for his pleasure'.[30]

In seeking to manage their nobility, the Stuart kings were handicapped
by their youth and by the inherent weakness of the Scottish crown. The
nobles had considerable respect for the monarchy in theory, but they
expected the king not to interfere in their spheres of influence and tried
to use his power for their own benefit. In the sixteenth century, even
in the Lowlands, magnates used force to a degree that was rare in
fifteenth-century England. The powers of the Scottish crown were much
more limited than those of the English monarchy. Its means of coercion
were derisory, largely because its income was minute, even by English
standards. There was also a far less developed system of law and royal
courts, much of the machinery of everyday justice being in the lords'
hands. The machinery of local administration, such as it was, was
controlled by the magnates as fully as in England in the darkest days
of Henry VI.

As he grew, James VI learned that governing Scotland consisted in
considerable part in managing the nobility, playing one off against
another, making what capital he could out of loyalty to the crown; when
he needed to coerce or to punish, he relied on the nobles' military
power. Establishing order was a painfully slow process, but it bore fruit
first in the Lowlands and then in the Borders and the Highlands. With
it came a gradual penetration of Lowland ways, English dress and the
English language, which complemented – and then replaced – Scots.
Underlying the process of creeping anglicisation was the perception that

England offered a model of order and prosperity that Scotland would do well to emulate. The gradual spread of English modes of thought and behaviour, from Lowland England to the English uplands and the Scottish Lowlands and then to the Scottish Highlands (and from the area of original English settlement around Dublin to the rest of Ireland), owed much to coercion and government pressure, but also to a growing belief within these societies that they offered tangible advantages.[31]

James had other assets. In Parliament the lords sat in the same chamber as the representatives of the burghs (towns) and influenced many burgh elections. Nevertheless, Parliament did provide a voice for those with a vested interest in peace, notably the burgh representatives, the lesser landowners (or lairds) and the lawyers. Moreover, James developed a committee, controlled by his supporters, called the lords of the articles, which drew up the bills that came before Parliament: parliamentary legislation was to provide an important means of bringing greater order to Scotland.

Another asset, potentially, was the church. Whereas the English Protestant Reformation, and what passed for a Protestant Reformation in Ireland, were driven by royal authority and implemented by Acts of Parliament, the Scottish Reformation happened independently of the crown. The Tudors (having repudiated papal authority) were careful to keep the rest of the ecclesiastical structure intact and under their control: the 'election' of bishops by cathedral chapters consisted of endorsing the monarch's nominee. The church's organisation – its hierarchy, its law courts, its network of over nine thousand parishes – provided a valuable adjunct to the royal administration. Not only did the parish become a vital arena of local government (notably in the administration of the poor law) but the church was a powerful force for indoctrination and discipline. Its courts punished moral lapses, and the clergy, at the behest of the crown, continually reminded their parishioners that obedience to established authority was a moral duty and that rebellion was a sin. Wary of the subversive effects of religious division, Elizabeth tried to control what was taught in the parish churches (and the universities) and to prevent unauthorised extra-parochial activities, even suspending an archbishop of Canterbury who did not share her view that such activities were dangerous.

In Scotland, by contrast, church government by bishops (episcopacy) was swept away and a Presbyterian system, modelled on those of Geneva and Huguenot France, was established. Power flowed up from the parishes, at least in theory. In each parish, the preacher (or pastor) was assisted in the 'kirk session' by lay elders (in maintaining moral discipline) and by deacons (in relieving the poor). Parishes elected representatives to local presbyteries or *classes* and to regional synods. These functioned as courts, endorsing the decisions of kirk sessions and imposing punishments, and elected representatives to the general assembly of the Church of Scotland.[32] The general assembly, however, exploited its position as arbiter of disputes to impose its will on the local assemblies and parishes. It developed into a formidable body, because of the power it wielded over the clergy and the people. Apart from the moral authority that the clergy possessed as pastors and preachers, they also, through the kirk session, maintained a parish-based system of moral discipline which was reinforced from above. In England, moral discipline was mainly the preserve of the church courts. Scottish parish-based discipline was effective, because the most powerful men of the parish were involved, as elders; the deacons' control over poor relief also enabled them to bring the disorderly poor to heel. And the system had teeth. In Scotland, unlike England, excommunication brought real legal and civil disadvantages, as well as social stigma.[33]

Given the kirk's power over the people, it had the potential to become a formidable force for order. Preachers denounced violence and rapine and encouraged the practice of Christian values. From this point of view, the kirk could be a powerful ally in the king's search for order. But the Presbyterian clergy had their own agenda, of godly reformation, and did not see themselves as mere auxiliaries to the king. On the contrary, they saw it as the king's duty to do their bidding. In England there was no doubt that the church was subordinate to the crown: the monarch was (by the grace of God) supreme head, or governor, of the church. In Scotland, according to Andrew Melville and other high Presbyterians, church and state were separate. The church concerned itself with spiritual matters and the state with temporal. But, where there was a spiritual dimension to temporal issues, the king should follow the advice of the church, as expressed through the general assembly; for the assembly was qualified, as the king was not, to interpret the word, and the will, of God.

What might seem at first sight a matter of separate but equal spheres, temporal and spiritual, proved on closer inspection to involve the subordination of the former to the latter. As James wryly remarked, the claims of the general assembly to oversee and advise rulers had more than a little in common with those of the papacy. Both created a potential conflict of allegiance of a sort that was much less likely in England. There the clergy paid lip-service to the principle that subjects should obey God rather than man, but in practice assumed that those in lawful authority would command nothing contrary to the will of God, so subjects should obey the monarch. The Scottish general assembly made no such assumption and so posed a threat to James's ability to direct the government.

James had no general assembly to contend with in Ireland, but in other respects Ireland was even more difficult to govern. Following the Anglo-Norman conquest in the thirteenth century, a small English colonial elite maintained a precarious hold over much of the island, its power being most effective within the Pale, around Dublin. Medieval English kings did what they could to anglicise Ireland, including setting up a Parliament. But much of the country continued to be ruled by Gaelic chieftains, who maintained a rudimentary order. Some of the settlers of English descent fraternised and intermarried with the Irish and proved almost equally unruly. Lacking effective power in Ireland, the English kings relied (as they did in the remoter regions of England) on local magnates, notably the Fitzgerald earls of Kildare. They in turn relied on military force, and strings of castles, and played one noble off against another.

Although there was friction between the Irish and the English, who thought themselves superior to the natives, there was nothing like the ferocious hatred that the Scots came to bear the English. Whereas Scottish national identity was forged in the crucible of bloody wars against England, there was as yet only a limited sense of Irish nation-hood. The English crown and nobles of English descent (known by 1603 as the Old English) were additional players in the complex kaleidoscope of power politics among the Irish chieftains, in which family was more important than ethnicity. There were strong links between the clans of Ireland and Scotland – the Macdonnells of Ulster and Macdonalds of the western Highlands, for example. The English crown made use of Old English magnates out of necessity but was unwilling to trust them too far, either as individuals or in Parliament. Under Poynings' Law of 1494, no bill could be introduced into the Irish Parliament unless it had been approved by the English privy council.

Until the early sixteenth century, English 'rule' over Ireland was loose and limited. Kings were content to avoid trouble and to prevent Ireland becoming a base for dynastic rivals or pretenders. They ruled their two kingdoms separately, using different institutions and indeed different titles: medieval kings were 'lords of Ireland'. With the breach with Rome and the Protestant Reformation, to a relatively unproblematic ethnic divide was added a potentially explosive division over religion. As England became Protestant, Ireland remained resolutely Catholic. It did not help that, unlike their counterparts in Wales, the bishops of the Protestant established church, the Church of Ireland, stubbornly refused to translate the Bible or prayer book into Gaelic, the language of the overwhelming majority of the people, on the grounds that it was a barbarous language.

The Irish also rejected Protestantism because it was identified with what they saw as an increasingly tyrannous English regime. Even before the advent of Protestantism, the secession of Henry VIII's England from the international Catholic Church created a potential clash of allegiance for Catholics in Ireland, Old English as well as native Irish. Whom should they obey first – king or pope? As England became more Protestant, their dilemma became more acute. The Old English thought of themselves as English, loyal to the crown. The Irish nobility had also been willing to recognise the suzerainty of the English king: he was far away and his influence could prove useful as they pursued their feuds and interests. Henry VIII assumed the title of king of Ireland in 1541, in an attempt to strengthen his claim to the allegiance of the Irish nobility. He encouraged them to surrender their lands to him in order to have them regranted under English land law, which involved a more explicit promise of fidelity and gave the king a claim to act as guardian to any heir or heiress whose father died while they were under age. But as Europe became increasingly divided along confessional lines, English rulers became less prepared to trust in the loyalty of Catholic magnates, fearing that Catholic Ireland might serve as a base from which a hostile

Catholic power could attack England from the rear. And indeed a Spanish force landed there in 1601.

If the threat posed by Catholic Ireland was to be contained, the English crown needed to strengthen its grip on the country. But Ireland was full of powerful nobles, well-fortified castles and a populace used to fighting. The roads were poor, the climate was inhospitable and the terrain was difficult, ideally suited to guerrilla warfare. Rebel armies gathered quickly and equally quickly melted back into the civilian population. If medieval kings had been satisfied with a loose control over the island, this was because they lacked the resources (and perhaps did not see the need) for a complete conquest. Queen Elizabeth's government accepted the need to establish more effective English rule, but feared the opposition that this would provoke and baulked at the cost of a full military conquest. Nevertheless, a small elite of 'New English' Protestants – soldiers, lawyers and civil servants – called for a vigorous programme of anglicisation. One of the most vehement, the poet Edmund Spenser, claimed that Ireland could be a rich and peaceful kingdom, were it not for the Irish, who were lazy, insubordinate and violent; the peasants had no incentive to work hard, as the fruits of their labour were taken by their lords. The Irish needed to be brought up to English standards of order and to share the benefits enjoyed by the English: settled arable agriculture, in place of rootless, footloose pastoral farming; English law, written, sophisticated and certain, in place of the more fluid, customary Irish law; structured English forms of government, rather than informal arbitration and coercion by chieftains; the English language; and, of course, Protestantism.

This programme was couched in terms of a 'civilising mission' that would also save the peasantry from their predatory lords; much the same arguments would later be used in the wilder corners of empire, such as the North-West Frontier. But there was also the concern for English national security and these New English 'servitors' – like so many young men who later went out to India – were looking to make a quick fortune, which they could do only at the expense of the natives. Although Elizabeth and her ministers accepted the servitors' basic analysis, they feared that to proceed too far too fast could provoke rebellion, at a time when war with Spain was first a danger and then (from 1585) a reality. Nevertheless, the New English proceeded as quickly as they could. Leaving aside Ulster, still predominantly Gaelic, they extended English influence beyond the Pale and Leinster, south into Munster and west into Connacht. They gradually (as in Wales) extended English institutions of local government, based on counties, with sheriffs and justices of the peace. In Wales, the process had been peaceful and willingly embraced by the Welsh. In Ireland, it was essentially military, based on at least the threat of force, with local commanders raising money (the cess) from the native population for the subsistence of their men.[34]

The servitors tried to weaken the power of the Catholic lords over the peasantry, arguing that the Old English were as corrupt and predatory as the Irish. They sought to increase the amount of land in English hands (including their own). Some sought out 'concealed' crown lands, which they then rented cheaply, as well as using force and fraud to deprive Irish landowners of their estates. The most successful and ruthless, like Richard Boyle, first earl of Cork, amassed vast fortunes. Some of the Irish played into their hands. An invasion sponsored by the pope in 1579 triggered a series of rebellions in Munster, which were put down with great brutality. A young Walter Raleigh played a leading role in massacring the garrison at Smerwick, an atrocity which merits comparison with Cromwell's at Drogheda and Wexford. Much of Munster was left devastated and many of those who escaped starvation were slaughtered by the English soldiery. The rebellions offered a pretext for wholesale confiscations: some of the New English claimed that all the leading Catholics of Ireland had been implicated in the conspiracy. After a hasty survey, large tracts of Munster were declared forfeit and allocated to Englishmen, who undertook to bring over English settlers.[35]

The Munster 'plantation' was on a vastly larger scale than those undertaken under Elizabeth in the New World. It was not a complete success. Some whose lands had been confiscated appealed to the English privy council and got them back, so that the lands of the settlers were intermixed with those of the native inhabitants. Relatively few English farmers and labourers were enticed over to Ireland, even though times were hard in England. The Irish were seen as bloodthirsty savages, and papists to boot; English settlers could expect to meet with hostility and violence. As the process of anglicisation advanced, the hostility of the Catholic population grew. The Old English, who were used to directing

the government, were elbowed aside by the New English, who proclaimed that Catholics' allegiance to the pope made it impossible for
them to be loyal to the queen.[36] The New English argued that, by
remaining Catholic, the Old English had gone native and forfeited any
claim to Englishness. The Old English complained that much of the
conduct of the New English was illegal and arbitrary, especially the
expropriation of Catholic landowners and the cess. Local officials and
military commanders imprisoned or summarily executed those who
challenged them, often claiming to act under martial law. The Old
English claimed that subjects in Ireland should enjoy the same legal and
constitutional rights as their counterparts in England, a claim that in
principle Elizabeth accepted. Their wrath boiled over in the Irish Parliament of 1585–86, in which the Dublin authorities tried – and failed –
to extend to Ireland the English laws requiring everyone to attend
Protestant parish churches. Parliament was not called again until 1613.

The Old English had no thoughts of rebellion, but some of the Gaelic
Irish sought to take advantage of England's war with Spain to recover
what they had lost and perhaps throw off English rule altogether.
Discontent was especially rife in Ulster, where the New English were
beginning to make inroads. Philip II sent arms and ammunition. The
first, relatively minor insurrections took place in 1593, but the key figure
in the province, the earl of Tyrone, played a cunning game, alternately
undertaking military operations and negotiating with Elizabeth's government, which was uncertain whether diplomacy or force offered the
better means to keep the rebellion from spiralling out of control. The
English military effort in Ireland was bedevilled by indecision and
incompetence, notably under the ill-fated earl of Essex, until Lord
Mountjoy took over as viceroy in 1600. The belated arrival of a Spanish
army in Kinsale was insufficient to shore up Tyrone's war effort. The
Nine Years War, as it is usually known, a series of conflicts, mostly in
Ulster and Munster, was the most serious challenge yet to English rule.
The Munster plantation was temporarily destroyed and everywhere there
was brutality, brigandage, devastation and death. Eventually, exhausted,
Tyrone surrendered to Mountjoy, six days before news arrived of the
queen's death.[37]

Although Elizabeth had jibbed at the cost and disruptiveness of military conquest, her government had been forced to it in the end. The

English military presence rose from about 2500 in the 1570s to 21,000 in the latter stages of the war, which cost the crown nearly two million pounds, an enormous sum.[38] The relatively localised nature of the rebellions meant that this was not a thoroughgoing 'national' conquest, but by 1603 it was clear that the loose, informal methods of the early Tudors would no longer suffice for the government of Ireland. A small elite, defined in terms of religion and nationality, was gradually imposing its values and its will on a resentful majority. The New English governors had greatly increased the problem of ruling Ireland, now not only a distinct but also an alienated kingdom. It remained to be seen how much further the process of anglicisation could be carried without provoking further, bloodier rebellions, which might end with Ireland throwing off English rule altogether.

When James VI came to the English throne in 1603 the two kingdoms of England and Ireland, united only by their common ruler, became three, creating the 'British Problem'.[39] The Protestant Reformation had added to the crown's difficulties in managing Ireland. The accession of a Scottish king in England complicated matters further. James, unlike his predecessors, was to rule three separate kingdoms, each with its own administration and Parliament. Each possessed its own distinctive system of law, although the New English were seeking to extend the use of English law in Ireland. And each had its own majority religion: Episcopalian in England, Presbyterian in Scotland, Catholic in Ireland.

There were also religious minorities, with more in common with majorities elsewhere than the majority in their own kingdom: Catholics in England and Scotland, and Presbyterians in England and (later) Ireland. Godly Protestants in England looked towards Scotland for a model of a church more fully reformed than the Church of England. Although the Protestants of the three kingdoms shared a visceral fear and hatred of Catholicism, their own divisions meant that they were unable to come up with a common response to the perceived threat from 'popery'; to make matters worse, Protestants increasingly used the language of anti-popery in disputes with fellow-Protestants.

None of this meant that it was impossible to govern James I's three kingdoms and indeed one can argue that he governed them with considerable skill. But it was undoubtedly difficult. If sensitivity and understanding were needed to govern any one kingdom, greater sensitivity and understanding were needed to govern all three. Above all, it was vital to appreciate that they *were* different, in terms of institutions, law, social organisation and religion; the dominant elements of each valued their distinctiveness and defended it fiercely. Just as kings of Spain faced revolts when they tried to impose Castilian ways on Catalonia or Portugal, kings of England would be wise to avoid imposing English ways on Scotland or Ireland – unless they had power sufficient to cope with a hostile reaction. James VI and I was not likely to fall into such a trap, but the same was not necessarily true of his successors.

When James I came to London in 1603, he believed that he was exchanging poverty for plenty, noble violence for public order, and cantankerous Presbyterians for obedient bishops. A sophisticated and long-established system of law courts offered a peaceful means of resolving disputes. The agencies of local government, in county, town and parish, enforced an increasingly complex and demanding corpus of parliamentary legislation: England was a far more *governed* country than Scotland or Ireland. Yet James found England more difficult to rule than he had expected, and his long experience of ruling Scotland proved of only limited use to him south of the border. England's greater size, and the complexity of its government, created problems of governance which were subtler, but no less demanding, than the more rudimentary struggle to maintain basic law and order in Scotland and Ireland. In particular, the involvement of so many of the king's subjects in local government, and the development of Parliament as a forum in which the king could negotiate with his people, created firm expectations as to *how* the king should govern. In early seventeenth-century Scotland, as in fifteenth-century England, politics centred on the king's relations with the great nobility. In early seventeenth-century England, the king had to contend with a much wider 'political nation'.

The issues which mattered most to members of the informed public were first, 'liberty and property' and, secondly, religion. Liberty and property were seen as the 'birthright' of the 'freeborn Englishman' and were secured by Parliament and juries. New laws and new taxes were legal only if approved by Parliament The jury system, and the procedural safeguards of the common law, protected the citizen against arbitrary imprisonment or illegal confiscation of his property. It was widely believed that, in less fortunate countries, the king could tax and imprison people at will. The English king could not and his subjects watched vigilantly for any attempt to do so.

Compared to France or Spain, the Tudor monarchy was financially weak. England had a much smaller population, but its crown was also less effective in tapping the nation's wealth. Like most medieval monarchies, it derived much of its revenue from the king's personal resources – his landed property and the dues he received as head of the feudal system. This had largely ceased to function as a form of military organisation, but it still gave the king a claim to payments from his richer subjects, notably livery (when a son succeeded his father in an estate) and wardship (whereby the family of an under-age heir purchased his guardianship). It was hard to keep income from feudal dues rising in line with inflation, not least because they fell on the most politically influential members of the population, who were strongly represented in Parliament.

As the scale and costs of war escalated, continental monarchs sought to raise more money from taxes, levied on property, commodities or transactions. Taxes were far more effective than feudal dues in tapping the nation's wealth, but in England they had to be voted by Parliament. MPs were far from eager to burden themselves, and their neighbours, with new taxes and operated on the principle that those who benefited from particular services from the king should pay for them. Thus the cost of the navy and the protection of trade were supposedly met from taxes on trade (tonnage and poundage – customs duties on a variety of imports), while the costs of local government and defence were to be covered by local rates. Tonnage and poundage constituted the only permanent tax voted by Parliament and under the Tudors it had become so uncontentious that each new monarch was granted it, for life, in the first Parliament of their reign. Monarchs were then expected to 'live of their own', to demand no further taxes without a very good reason, which usually meant war or the immediate prospect of war. Elizabeth was given several grants in peacetime, but parliamentary grants of taxation remained difficult to secure and brought in less than was needed. The breach with Rome and the Protestant Reformation added to the fear of rebellion, so Henry VIII, Edward VI and Elizabeth, rather than ask for too much in taxation, made ends meet by plundering the church, starting with the monasteries.[40]

Plundering the church could not go on forever and did not address the fundamental problem that the crown was underendowed – poorer, in real terms, than it had been in the fourteenth century. Moreover, the royal revenue suffered badly from the price inflation of the sixteenth and early seventeenth centuries and from the wiles of taxpayers. Nevertheless, the frugal Elizabeth had coped well until the financial equilibrium of her regime had been destroyed by the cost of the wars against Spain and in Ireland. Wary of borrowing and reluctant to ask Parliament and people for too much in a time of high prices and harvest failure, she made ends meet by selling crown lands, which raised ready cash at the expense of future income. James I was to do the same.

When the Commons could be persuaded to vote taxes on land, or subsidies, the yields were disappointing and became steadily more so. Subsidies were assessed and collected by commissioners, local gentlemen appointed by Parliament. Each landowner was required to give in an estimate of their annual income from land – after making deductions for 'necessary' expenses, and not on oath. Underassessment became more and more flagrant: Elizabeth's lord treasurer, Burghley, declared an income of £133 (on which he managed to build Burghley House!). Commissioners accepted the assessments of their fellow gentry, hoping that they would return the favour at a later date. As a result the sums voted by Parliament were so inadequate that the early Stuarts must have wondered whether they were worth bargaining for.[41]

But was there any alternative? The revenue potential of feudal dues was limited, the crown lands were a rapidly wasting asset. What the crown needed was to generate much more income from taxation. The subsidies ought to have provided that income, but they did not and the Commons refused to grasp the nettle of underassessment. So what was the king to do? He could squeeze a little more out of some hitherto unexploited feudal rights, but his real need was for taxation that did not require the consent of Parliament. James found this first in impositions, additional customs duties which were supposedly intended to discourage imports by making them more expensive. In a carefully staged test case in 1606 (Bate's case), the judges declared that, if that were the intention, impositions were legal; they would not be legal if they were levied in order to raise money. But, as the king was the sole judge of his own motives, who could tell? Soon many new impositions were levied, despite the Commons' protests.[42] They were to be followed by a variety of other fiscal devices which enabled the king to raise money without the consent of Parliament.

Anxieties for the security of liberty and property, not unknown before 1603, became much more intense under the early Stuarts, and so did anxieties about religion. By 1603 England was a Protestant country; Catholics were a small minority, sporadically persecuted and generally quiescent. But throughout Elizabeth's reign there had been bitter debates about the nature of English Protestantism. Unlike the Calvinist churches of Scotland or France, England retained a hierarchical system of church government, based on bishops. The most militant early Elizabethan Protestants had qualms about serving in a church with bishops, but most eventually decided that forms of government mattered less than preaching the Gospel and carrying through a godly reformation.

The biggest obstacle they faced was the queen. She insisted that the services prescribed in the 1559 Book of Common Prayer, which included certain ceremonies, should be followed to the letter. The zealous Protestants, who became known as puritans, regarded such ceremonies as the sign of the cross over the baby's head in baptism, and the wearing of a clerical gown (surplice), as unscriptural and popish. They denied that the clergy could be forced to use any ceremonies not required by the Bible. They also disliked set forms of prayer and service, which made worship mechanical and unthinking. They believed it was the duty of pastors to edify and to warn, to touch the hearts and stretch the minds of their people. But Elizabeth feared that unchecked preaching and discussion could lead to division and subversion. In Scotland, the Netherlands and France, Calvinist writers justified rebellion against ungodly (Catholic) monarchs. She preferred printed homilies, officially approved, to improvised sermons, and restricted preaching as much as she could.

The puritan vision of the church centred on evangelism and godly moral discipline, and aimed to create people who based their lives on the precepts of the Bible, were hard-working, sober and frugal, and kept the Lord's day holy. Elizabeth saw the church as a means of social and political control, whose main function was to inculcate obedience and tell the people their duties. She favoured set forms of service and a modicum of ceremony, not only because they were safer, but also because ceremony aided devotion and made it easier for those with conservative religious leanings to conform to the new church. By the 1580s the latter consideration no longer applied, but there had developed a sentiment among the clergy and people that one could call 'Anglican' (although the term was not used at this time). Most early Elizabethan Protestants regarded the Prayer Book as 'unperfect', at best a first step along the road to a full godly reformation. By the end of the reign many had become accustomed to its services and had developed a real affection for them. What puritans saw as its disadvantages became its strengths. The predictability of services enabled even the illiterate to follow them. The elements of question and response and the habit of taking communion at Easter emphasised community – this was *Common Prayer*.[43] And the elements of ceremony added to the sense of edification created by the architectural grandeur of parish churches; even without the images which had been removed or whitewashed over, they still drew eyes and thoughts heavenwards. The prayer book was not created in response to any pre-existing 'anglican' sentiment, but in time it helped to create such a sentiment.[44]

The English Reformation, unlike that of Scotland, was a royal reformation. As head of the church, Elizabeth prevented it from going too far. Despite the agitation of preachers, MPs and privy councillors, the prayer book remained unchanged. Puritans might wring their hands in despair, but there was nothing they could do. So long as Mary Queen of Scots was alive, Elizabeth's survival was vital for the survival of Protestantism. Active resistance could benefit only the Catholics, so the puritans' only option was to go on trying to persuade her to change her mind. Meanwhile, puritan clergymen adapted Prayer Book services, failed to wear the surplice and omitted ceremonies that they disliked. How many failed to conform is impossible to tell. Church court records reveal those who got into trouble, but others did not, because their bishop did not impose conformity, or because their parishioners did not report them, or because they had powerful lay patrons and protectors.

By the 1590s the puritan movement had become quiescent: an attempt to build a Presbyterian system from below was swiftly crushed.[45] Ministers got on quietly with ministering to their flocks. With the execution

of Mary, the spectre of a Catholic successor receded. By the end of the
decade, when the threat from Spain had also waned, the English Catholics seemed resigned to minority status and Protestantism seemed
secure. After all the religious battles of Elizabeth's reign, James inherited
a church that was far from uniform but enjoyed a slightly uneasy peace.

That peace continued for most of James I's reign and became less
uneasy. James had been raised as a Calvinist and, unlike Elizabeth, had
a genuine interest in theology. He promoted the Authorised (or 'King
James') Version of the Bible, which became one of the foundations of
English Protestant piety. He did not share Elizabeth's deep suspicion of
preaching, so those bishops and ministers who wished to preach frequently were able to do so. As for the puritan parish clergy, the level
of conformity required was relaxed: an undertaking to use the Prayer
Book was usually sufficient.[46]

James's achievement in maintaining peace within the church was all
the more impressive given the divisions that were developing among the
clergy. Their origins can be traced back to the latter part of the previous
reign. A small number of clerics and academics began to argue, not that
the Reformation had not gone far enough, but that it had gone too far.
The removal of most of the visual elements from the service had destroyed
vital aids to edification and devotion. In seeking to destroy the despotic
power which Catholic priests were alleged to exercise over their people,
the distinctiveness and the spiritual authority of the clergy had been
reduced almost to nothing. The continuities with the pre-Reformation
church, which puritans found so distasteful and embarrassing, became
something to celebrate. Bishops (accepted reluctantly by puritans as one
of several possible means of running a church) were eulogised as essential
to a true church. Drawing on legends that the English church had been
founded independently of Rome, some claimed that it had a continuous
succession of bishops to match Rome's claim of a continuous succession
of popes. It therefore had as good a claim as Rome to be a true 'visible'
church: both could trace their origins back to Christ Himself. Moreover,
unlike the Roman Church, which had spread its false practices to England
in the middle ages, the Church of England was a *reformed* true church.
As such it was unique. Puritans emphasised their common ground with
Reformed churches in Scotland, on the Continent and in New England.
Those who espoused this new view of the church did not.

Such views were advanced by only a few writers in the 1590s, but became more widespread. They suggested a form of service with more emphasis on ceremony and holy communion, which implied that communion was of deep spiritual significance and that the priest who consecrated the bread and wine enjoyed special spiritual powers. This was emphasised by the way in which communion was celebrated. Although Elizabeth's government sent out conflicting signals, in most parishes people received communion seated around a table placed in the body of the church, decently and reverently, but without kneeling or in any way suggesting that the bread and wine was anything other than bread or wine. In other words, they replicated, and commemorated, the Last Supper, as Christ had required.[47]

Under James some clergy moved the table to the east end of the church, placing it 'altar-wise' and railing it off, creating a sacred space into which the priest came to consecrate the bread and wine in a manner reminiscent of the Catholic mass. The people were to come up to the rails to receive communion, on their knees. Many also placed more exclusive emphasis on the prayer book services, often ceasing to preach altogether. Where there had been gradations of conformity under Elizabeth, the clergy were now becoming polarised into two camps, one emphasising preaching, the other the visual and the sacraments.[48] The latter were at first somewhat defensive. A stained-glass window of 1629 depicts the taking down of Christ's body from the cross, based on a fifteenth-century painting; at the bottom is written 'the truth hereof is historical, divine and not superstitious'.[49]

Views also differed as to how Sunday should be celebrated. For puritans, it should be given over to God. Apart from going to church and listening to the sermon, families should read the Bible, pray and digest the message of the sermon. At the other extreme, some clergy were tolerant of 'innocent' Sunday recreations: honest, manly sports like archery and wrestling (but not football, which was an excuse for a brawl). Such clergy were also more tolerant of sociability linked to the church: parish feasts (especially following the walking of the parish boundaries), church ales (drinkings, to raise money for parish funds) and wakes.[50]

One key difference between puritans and non-puritans was that the former directed their ministry at the individual, urging him (or her) to read the Bible and live according to its teachings. Non-puritans empha-sised the collectivity, the community of the parish, with the people as the obedient flock and the 'priest' (puritans would have said 'minister') as the shepherd. Implicit in this difference was a difference of theology. The Thirty-Nine Articles, the founding theological statement of the Church of England, were not entirely consistent, but included a clear statement of double predestination, a doctrine associated with Calvin. This stated that God, since the start of the world, had decided who was to be saved and who was to be damned and there was nothing that anyone could do about it. This was intended to rebut the Catholic teaching that salvation came through good works, penance and partici-pation in the church's sacraments; but it had alarming implications. One might wonder what sort of God would bring so many people into existence in order to consign them to eternal torment. It was a stark and potentially depressing doctrine: people made themselves ill worrying whether they were saved or damned. It was also divisive: Calvinist preachers tended to suggest that the elect, God's chosen, were few, a handful, very different from their fellow men and women. And it was pastorally difficult, because it disconnected salvation from conduct. Why should one follow God's commandments if it could have no effect on one's chances of being saved?

Puritan pastors had to guard against the twin perils of overconfidence and despair among their parishioners. They tried to tread a middle path, using 'the manipulation of anxiety'. Nobody could be sure that they were saved, the pastors warned, as no one could know the mind of God, but the chances were that those who lived godly lives were God's chosen.[51] Moreover, although nothing could save the ungodly from the perdition which God had decreed for them, it was the duty of godly magistrates and parish officials to ward off the dreadful punishments which God in His wrath might impose on communities (plague, fire, harvest failure) by punishing drunkenness, promiscuity, sabbath-breaking and other ungodly behaviour. John White, the pastor of Dorchester, launched a programme of moral regeneration in the town after the church spire was struck by lightning in 1613, triggering a catastrophic fire – literally, fire from heaven.[52]

If predestination was hard for preachers to cope with, it was also hard for the people. Those who accepted it were liable to think of themselves as different from their less fortunate and less godly neighbours. Attempts by the godly to impose their standards of conduct on the ungodly added to this sense of difference. Those who were less zealous would recoil at a doctrine that proclaimed that they were probably damned. However hard puritan preachers laboured the point that good works could not bring salvation, human nature and the most limited acquaintance with Christ's teachings – 'Love thy neighbour as thyself' – encouraged the belief that good works were pleasing in the sight of God. This was highlighted in the requirement that those who took communion at Easter should first ensure that they were 'in charity' with their neigh-bours, by resolving quarrels. Puritan preachers often lamented that their preaching had only a limited effect and that the bulk of their flocks still believed that salvation could be achieved by doing no evil and by living on good terms with the neighbours. Many found puritan preaching intellectually too demanding (and often, one suspects, incomprehen-sible), but also morally repugnant. Many also, it seems, found non-puritan worship, with its reassuring familiarity and repetition and its emphasis on community and the visual, both more accessible and more edifying.[53]

James therefore inherited a kingdom which was divided in religion and there were signs that those divisions were growing. Received wisdom at the start of the seventeenth century suggested that divisions of religion threatened the security of a state. Yet England had moved from Cath-olicism to Protestantism without serious civil strife and the English were much less inclined to rebellion by 1603 than they had been a hundred or two hundred years before. James's was a difficult inheritance, but not an impossible one. It remained to be seen how well he coped with it.

2

James I

The most familiar image of King James dates from his last years. It is of a man who had aged prematurely, unsteady on his feet, leaning on the shoulder of his favourite, the duke of Buckingham; indeed his legs were so weak that he often had to be carried.[1] His tongue was too large for his mouth, so he tended to slobber when he spoke. His personal cleanliness left much to be desired: he rarely washed or changed his clothes, which he tended to wear until they fell to pieces. His skin was sensitive and he scratched himself and fiddled with his clothing, especially around his groin. He was rarely completely drunk but, as he drank steadily through the day, he was rarely entirely sober either.[2]

This image owes much to one man, Sir Anthony Weldon, who wrote and later published a *Character of King James.* Weldon had been dismissed from a lucrative court office for writing a description of Scotland that was full of derogatory remarks and bad jokes. Scotland, he wrote, was short of most things necessary for life, except 'fowl': 'foul houses, foul sheets, foul linen ...' The women were ugly and the thistle was the nation's fairest flower.[3] Weldon was a spiteful and embittered man, but the picture he gave of the ageing king, as physically decrepit and the worse for drink, was confirmed by the French ambassador and others.[4] By contrast, when James first came to England in 1603, he made an overwhelmingly favourable impression. He was thirty-six, physically fit, with a fair complexion. He was affable, quick-witted and articulate, with an excellent memory and he seemed pleased with his new kingdom and eager to learn.[5] He also had two sons, which, after all the uncertainties about the succession under the Tudors, was very reassuring.

The favourable impressions on both sides did not last. James and the English quickly became disillusioned with one another. Historians have generally been critical of the Stuarts as a family, seizing on aspects of James's character and conduct that seemed authoritarian or in other respects un-English. Even James's scholarship was turned against him: he was dismissed with a sneer as 'the wisest fool in Christendom'.[6] He is best known now for his books on witchcraft and the evils of tobacco, but his works on political theory – on the nature of kingship, on papal power, on the unjustifiability of tyrannicide – were at the time seen as scholarly contributions to contemporary debates, and were answered by some of the greatest writers in Catholic Europe.

James's homosexual inclinations have generally been mentioned with distaste. It is uncertain to what extent his relationship with his favourites was physical. James referred ambiguously to 'the time which I shall never forget at Farnham where the bed's head could not be found between the master and his dog [Buckingham]'.[7] Other letters, especially when Buckingham was away in Spain, talk often of love and hint at a physical relationship – one refers to 'a new marriage' – but, given James's physical condition in 1623, one wonders if this could have been any more than talk.[8] He had complained in 1615 that his previous favourite, the earl of Somerset, had refused repeatedly to lie in his chamber, but as he always slept surrounded by three other beds (from fear of assassination) it seems unlikely that he was seeking an intimate assignation.[9] It is perhaps significant that when James issued a general pardon in 1610, it excluded those convicted of sodomy.[10]

On the other hand, James made no secret of his affection for his favourites. 'I act like a man', he told an astonished privy council 'and confess to loving those dear to me more than other men. You may be sure that I love the earl of Buckingham more than anyone else ... Christ had His John and I have my George.'[11] The two of them, with Prince Charles, formed a bizarre *ménage à trois*, with its own private language peppered with baby talk. James called himself Buckingham's 'dad and husband', Buckingham was James's 'dog', 'sweet heart' or 'sweet child and wife', and the heir to throne, even in his twenties, was 'Baby Charles'.[12] Such language, and his habit of kissing his favourites in public, made contemporaries wonder what they got up to in private. The hostile Weldon declared, of the king's affection for Buckingham, 'the king was more impatient than any woman to enjoy her love'.[13]

James never showed much interest in women and he often spoke of them with dislike or contempt,[14] especially in his later years, when ill-health made him more bad-tempered than usual.[15] But for much of

James's life there was little evidence of homosexual predilections either. Apart from an adolescent crush on his cousin, Esmé Stuart, the first sign came in 1607. One of his Scots pages, Robert Carr, broke his leg. James nursed him back to health and he became the king's constant companion. James showed his affection openly, leaning on his arm as he walked.[16] He also tried to teach Carr Latin, in the hope that they could study together, but intellectually Carr proved a disappointment. Nevertheless, James made him earl of Somerset, and, in effect, his personal private secretary.

Somerset was supplanted in 1615 by a rival, put forward by an unlikely alliance including the archbishop of Canterbury and the queen. George Villiers came from an obscure Northamptonshire family, but he had charm and good looks in abundance and danced divinely.[17] He was far more intelligent and ambitious than Somerset (whose reputation was soon ruined by his involvement in a poisoning scandal). He rose rapidly through the peerage, becoming duke of Buckingham in 1623: there had been no duke without royal blood since the execution of the fourth duke of Norfolk in 1572. According to Weldon, from 'a pretty harmless, affable gentleman', Buckingham 'grew insolent, cruel and a monster not to be endured'.[18] As well as the object of the king's affection, he became (in practice if not in name) his first minister and, on the eve of the king's death, it was a moot point whether England's foreign policy was being directed by the king or by the duke. Such was James's fondness for Buckingham that he even showed affection for the womenfolk and children of his favourite's family – in his later years he was not very tolerant of children either – who were described as swarming around the court like rabbits and dancing up and down like fairies.[19]

Although one could argue that both Somerset and Buckingham helped James to rule, by taking some of the burden of government off his shoulders, there can be no doubt that both met an emotional need. James was in many ways a lonely man. Once the brief honeymoon between the king and his English subjects had ended, James fled the responsibilities of kingship, and the very public life of the court, for the hunting field, finding solace in the chase and a small group of Scottish hunting and drinking companions. His wife, Anne of Denmark, had little to offer him. James was an intellectual, who enjoyed discussing theology and who remarked that if he had not been king he would have liked to have been a university man.[20] Anne was no scholar: she liked clothes, jewellery and dancing, and became interested in the fine arts. When she converted to Catholicism (for reasons which seem to have had little to do with theological conviction), she collected reliquaries and other attractive devotional objects. James generally treated her kindly, although he occasionally lost his temper with her – he always had a short fuse. Anne did her duty as a royal wife, bearing him two sons and a daughter. But, if James's was less unhappy than some royal marriages, it could hardly be described as made in heaven. As Bishop Godfrey Goodman delicately put it: 'The king of himself was a very chaste man and there was little in the queen to make him uxorious. Yet they did love as well as man and wife could do, not conversing together.'[21]

Of James's three children, his favourite was his daughter, Elizabeth, who was charming and intelligent, the apple of her father's eye. In 1613 she married Frederick, Elector Palatine, and left to live in Germany. The elder son, Henry, was in many ways a model prince, but unfortunately a model against whom his father could be measured and found wanting. He was sober, paid his bills promptly and maintained an orderly house-hold. James's court tended to be anything but orderly. Perhaps the most notorious episode was when James entertained his brother-in-law at Theobalds House in Hertfordshire. King Christian IV was a hard drinker and most of those present followed his lead. As a result, by the time a masque was to be enacted for the kings, many of the participants, women as well as men, could not remember their lines and in some cases were barely able to stand. The women who represented Faith and Hope were found 'sick and spewing in the lower hall' and Peace belaboured with her olive branch anyone who got in her way.[22] Henry was also brave and warlike. James, although he hunted recklessly, was a self-confessed coward. His years in Scotland had left him fearful of kidnap and assassination, and he wore a padded doublet that was supposed to be dagger-proof.[23] Henry had no time for his father's intellectual pursuits, declaring that leading his people in war was a king's most important responsibility.[24] But he never got to be king. He died in 1612 and his brother, 'Baby Charles', became Prince of Wales.

Charles, a small sickly boy with short legs (the result of rickets), had always lived in his brother's shadow. He learned to walk and to speak very late; by adulthood he was fit and active, but suffered from a stammer.[25] His elder brother had told him that, when he was king, Charles could be archbishop of Canterbury, so that his robes could cover his rickety legs.[26] Such remarks can have done little to build up Charles's self-confidence. He was shy, prim and priggish. He lacked the intellect to converse with his father and was repelled by the clamour and crudity of the court. He remained a sad, peripheral figure, until Buckingham, sensing the need to establish a rapport with the heir to the throne, sought his friendship.[27] Buckingham, with his charisma and boundless self-confidence, was the antithesis of the withdrawn, lonely Charles. Charles looked up to Buckingham as if he were an adored elder brother and, through Buckingham, he grew closer to his father and began, haltingly, to make his mark on policy.

James's initial confidence that he would prove a successful king of England was based on a solid record of success as king of Scotland.[28] From childhood he had learned the hard way that, while the Scots magnates respected the institution of monarchy, they had a cavalier attitude towards the person of the king. Nobles had vied to gain possession of the young James in order to govern in his name. He also had to contend with the lectures of Andrew Melville and the high Presbyterians, who told him that he was 'God's silly vassal' and that he should submit to their direction.[29] But James was intelligent and learned fast. He invoked the aid of the more amenable magnates to punish the disorderly nobles and lairds of the Lowlands and Borders. In the Highlands he favoured a few 'loyal' clans, like the Campbells, whom he used to police and punish the others, giving them *carte blanche* to do what was necessary; feuding was a way of life in the Highlands, but this policy brought to it a modicum of coherence and structure.

While he could never challenge heritable jurisdictions, he tried to ensure that the rule of law was made more effective, a process in which the legal profession, eager for business and profit, cooperated willingly. His Scottish privy council (like Star Chamber in England) tried cases of riot and violent assault and punished feuding lords and chieftains. The council derived much of its authority from the presence of the greatest nobles. These were too powerful to be called to account. James learned to treat them courteously, to avoid showing too much favour to any individual or faction, and to maintain a careful balance among them. One of his great skills was dealing with people on a face to face basis. He was a shrewd judge of character and was quick to respond to nuances of mood and behaviour. He was able to neutralise the threat from those of the nobles who were potentially dangerous, while punishing the disorders of lesser (but still disruptive) lords. Habits of violence were far too engrained in Scotland to be removed overnight, but when James died Scotland was a considerably more orderly country than it had been sixty years before.[30]

In trying to extend the rule of law, the Scottish Parliament played a significant part. As mentioned earlier, certain elements within Parliament – lairds, townsmen, lawyers – stood to gain from a more ordered society, where they could trade and practise in peace. James enhanced his prospects of managing Parliament by the creation of the lords of the articles, who prepared all the bills that were submitted to Parliament. Just as he proved able to persuade nobles to do as he wished, so he addressed both the lords of the articles and the Parliament in person, arguing his case – he was an astute debater. He also on occasion addressed the general assembly and in 1606 established a measure of control over it. Melville was exiled and bishops were re-established, albeit with limited powers, as chairmen of synods, rather than autonomous rulers of their dioceses. A series of Acts of Parliament reduced the independence of the general assembly, which now met only when summoned by the king; its proceedings were managed by the privy council. In 1618 the assembly was pressured into endorsing the Five Articles of Perth, which allowed for the celebration of Christmas and other festivals that had been abolished as popish. These articles were permissive, not compulsory, but (together with the revival of episcopacy) they showed that James was extending his control over the Scottish church – and bringing it more into line with that of England. Between 1618 and 1638 the assembly did not meet. James proceeded cautiously, allowing the Scots to become accustomed to one change before moving on to the next and, where possible, maintaining an element of ambiguity. He was careful to avoid giving the impression that he was imposing English ways and institutions on Scotland and indeed his campaign to extend his influence over the church had begun well before 1603.[31]

Although he boasted, when in England, that he now ruled Scotland with a stroke of the pen, he was too aware of the realities of Scottish life to risk moves that were precipitate or provocative. Although his absence from Scotland – he returned just once, in 1617 – inevitably reduced his personal impact on its government, he had learned much before leaving for England and had a reliable team of privy councillors. Managing the nobility from England was not much of a problem either. As king of England he had far greater rewards to bestow than he had had before 1603, when he sometimes had not had enough to eat. A bevy of Scots lords accompanied him to England and profited mightily from his generosity. Even those who did not take up residence in England found it advantageous to travel to London in search of favours. And the fact that James was in England removed any danger that a Scottish magnate faction might try to seize his person. There were complaints that James neglected Scotland, that it was out of sight and out of mind. But if he did, it was an informed and salutary neglect. James was too experienced and canny to embark on measures that could threaten the equilibrium that he had created.

James's English subjects probably knew little of his record in Scotland, but they seem to have accepted his claim that he was an experienced king. Their criticisms of James focused on what he did in England. The traditional explanation for this has been that James brought from Scotland alien concepts of absolute monarchy that clashed head-on with the ambitions of an increasingly assertive and self-confident House of Commons, eager to dictate royal policy. There were those who held one or other of these perceptions, but neither was necessarily correct. James certainly believed in the divine right of kings, a belief that was widely shared. The divine attributes of kingship were emphasised in the coronation ceremony, in which the king (or queen) was crowned by the archbishop of Canterbury and anointed with holy oil.

It had also long been widely believed that the king could cure scrofula (or the King's Evil) by means of the 'royal touch'. Scrofula was brought on by the swelling and degeneration of the lymphatic glands and the sufferer's face became covered with putrid and foul-smelling sores. The repulsiveness of the symptoms highlighted the charity of the monarch in physically touching these people, while those cases in which they were healed showed the sacred nature of monarchy. The practice of the royal touch was common across Europe in the middle ages and beyond, and continued in England under the Stuarts. It was carried out with considerable ceremony and those who were touched (including Dr Johnson, who was touched by Anne) received a special medal to mark the occasion. It might seem that by the seventeenth century this was an archaic and stage-managed ceremony, kept alive in a vain attempt to maintain an already outdated view of monarchy, rather like the monarch's washing the feet of poor people on Maundy Thursday (in obvious imitation of Christ). It is clear, however, that the demand to be touched was enormous and spontaneous. When Charles II returned from exile in 1660 he touched 23,000 people in four months; and during his reign there were frequent collections in parish churches to enable poor scrofula sufferers to travel to London to be cured by the king.

When James I told the Commons in 1610 that God had created monarchy he was saying nothing startlingly new, although he was on less familiar ground when he enumerated the attributes of God that kings allegedly shared. He went on, however, to stress that although they had originally been absolute, in settled kingdoms with established laws kings were obliged to rule according to law. If they did not, they ceased to be kings and became tyrants (which implied that they forfeited their right to rule, as God had created authority for the general good).

No doubt those who heard this speech were struck less by familiar references to the obligation to rule according to law than by the unfamiliar and sweeping claims of royal power.[32] Moreover, James's understanding of the law sometimes differed from that of many lawyers or MPs. James was convinced that impositions were legal because the judges had said they were (provided they were levied to discriminate against imports – and James had little trouble convincing himself that they were). To many of his subjects this seemed a dangerous step down the road to arbitrary taxation and the elimination of Parliaments. It seems improbable that James was consciously seeking to establish a more absolute form of monarchy. At most he wanted to reduce the level of criticism by Parliament, much of which he regarded as ill-founded, by calling Parliaments as rarely as possible. It is, however, understandable that many of his subjects *did* suspect him of aiming to impose absolutism.

As early as 1610 MPs expressed fears that the collection of impositions might leave the king sufficiently solvent to have no need to call Parliament.[33] To fears of arbitrary taxation were joined fears of arbitrary imprisonment. James was unimpressed by the claim of the great lawyer Sir Edward Coke that only professional legal practitioners, with their specialist training and vast collective experience, could fully understand the common law. When he believed that the judges' opinions ran counter to common sense or natural justice he put pressure on them to see things his way, consulting them individually and dismissing Coke for persistent criticism.[34]

In addition, James made more extensive use of the court of Star Chamber. This comprised the privy council, assisted by one or two judges; it did not use juries and its procedures were quicker and simpler than those of the common law courts. Star Chamber had been developed as a way of dealing with those too powerful to be punished by the common law courts, magnates with the power to bribe judges and sheriffs, or to overawe local juries. It had become popular with litigants because of its fairness and its willingness to defend the weak against the powerful. But its impartiality became open to question in cases where the king's interests were involved and James used it to silence critics and those who evaded the censorship of the press. Increasingly the king's perception of law and justice diverged from that of the political nation.

There was a similar difference of perception about Parliament. Many historians have claimed that the Commons were becoming more ambitious and powerful, pointing to clashes between Elizabeth and her Parliaments and demands by the Commons for freedom of speech. But the reason they demanded freedom of speech was that Elizabeth tried to impose novel restrictions on what they could discuss. She declared that questions of her marriage and the royal succession (including that of Mary Queen of Scots), together with religion and foreign policy, were beyond their competence. But these were the issues that the Commons most wanted to discuss. With the survival of Protestantism depending on Elizabeth's life, it seemed to many Protestants wildly irresponsible for her to refuse to settle the succession. Even Henry VIII, in many ways a monster of egotism, had done all he could to secure an orderly succession.

On these key issues the sympathies of Elizabeth's privy councillors were far more with the Commons than with the queen. They were her loyal servants, but as Protestants they would have to live with the consequences of a Catholic succession, including perhaps a religious civil war; their alarm was expressed in the bond of Association of 1584. The Commons' clashes with the queen reflected not ambition, or entrenched and opposite points of view, but anguished discussions between those who thought they were on the same side about how best to achieve shared objectives.

Only in the 1590s did the atmosphere become more adversarial. The succession and Protestantism seemed more secure, so there was no longer the same sense of common danger. The ministerial team that had served for most of the reign died off and court and administration became increasingly divided into factions, led by Burghley's son Robert Cecil and the earl of Essex. As the queen's grip weakened, both sides tried to attract clients and supporters. The rewards, or patronage, at the crown's disposal had never been lavish, but in the war years of the 1590s the crown was more strapped for cash than usual. The faction leaders, desperate to reward their followers, persuaded the old queen to authorise grants which were widely seen as unethical and illegal, notably patents and monopolies.

The crown often issued patents, empowering private individuals to perform public works, such as harbour or river improvements, collecting the necessary money from the local ratepayers. These often attracted unscrupulous 'projectors', looking for a quick profit; some carried the project through on the cheap, others collected the money and did nothing. Similarly, the crown could grant monopolies to those who had invented new products and processes, or who brought new industries into England. In the 1590s, monopolies were granted on many items of everyday consumption. The price of patents and monopolies was paid by the ratepayer and the consumer; the profits were reaped by sharp-witted City entrepreneurs and their allies at court, who procured the grants. Competing faction leaders swallowed their scruples (if they had ever had any). Standards of public conduct plummeted and a sour smell of corruption hung over the royal court.[35] The growing public anger was reflected in Parliament. That of 1601 was the most adversarial and ill-tempered of the reign; recognising the strength of feeling, Elizabeth promised to revoke the most obnoxious of the monopolies.

The row over monopolies should not be seen as evidence of hostility towards the monarchy. Contemporaries did not see the interests of crown and Commons, or crown and people, as opposed or incompatible.

MPs represented the people, but most also served in the royal administration, as magistrates, militia officers or civil servants. Apart from
voting taxes, Parliament passed a great deal of local and private legislation. Nowadays, most of Parliament's time is taken up with government
legislation, which is pushed through the Houses by the whips of the
majority party. The few private members' bills can find parliamentary
time only if the government agrees. Under Elizabeth and James, the
majority of bills were introduced by backbenchers; 'government'
measures were often limited to money bills. There were no parties, and
so no coherent majorities. Votes were avoided where possible, being
seen as divisive; the Houses preferred to talk their way through to a
rough consensus. As the statutes passed at Westminster were enforced
in the localities by officials similar to the MPs who had shaped them,
this made considerable sense. In France, royal edicts were drafted and
promulgated by the king, who might then choose to amend them in
the face of representations from the law courts. In England, most laws
were drafted and amended by members of the two Houses; the monarch's only input was to grant or deny the royal assent to what the
Houses had agreed.

If legislation was characterised more by negotiation and consensus
than by confrontation, in a wider sense the Commons offered a forum
for dialogue. The House contained an important cross-section of the
nation's elite, men of extensive experience in local government. The
monarch's councillors explained the thinking behind royal policy and
the reasons for taxation and drew on MPs' local experience of how well
existing legislation was working and how it could be made to work
better.[36] The great Poor Relief Acts of 1598 and 1601 owed much to the
experience of London, Norwich and other towns of dealing with urban
poverty. Under the Tudors both crown and Parliament grew stronger.
Parliament legislated on topics it had never touched before, like the
church or the succession, and moved into new areas of social policy,
and much of its legislation strengthened the crown, for example the
establishment of the royal supremacy over the church.

Given the level of subjects' participation in government, this spirit of
cooperation should not come as a surprise. Kings had called Parliaments
into being to assist in government, by providing the necessary framework
of laws and the necessary money; Parliaments saw it as their duty to do

so. But although Parliaments were important their role was limited. They provided, through legislation, a framework for government, but they did not govern – that was the job of the monarch, whose control over the executive was virtually never challenged before 1641. They were rarely in session; under Elizabeth they met on average for a few weeks every three years – less frequently than in the fifteenth century. The membership of the Commons changed considerably from one Parliament to the next; what continuity there was came from royal councillors, rather than from backbenchers. Councillors gave a lead in the Commons because their access to the monarch's person, and the expert knowledge that this conferred, earned them the respect of MPs.

It does not follow, of course, that MPs were incapable of criticism or complaint; they were representatives as well as royal servants. So long as the monarch's demands on the people seemed reasonable, avoiding measures which seemed extortionate or unfair, criticism was likely to be restrained and constructive. The most trenchant complaints faced by Elizabeth came in 1601, when the queen was blamed for unleashing predatory projectors on her subjects; for many MPs, their concern as representatives here outweighed their loyalty as servants. The extent to which their concern was shared was shown in elections. Usually these were stitched up in advance by the local gentry, but in Norfolk (and perhaps elsewhere) elections were fought on issues relating to patents and other misuse of royal power; thousands of freeholders came to vote.[37] MPs were loyal to the crown, but not blindly so; if they were anxious, or angry, they said so. Criticism was intended to persuade the monarch to abandon unpopular policies and to rebuild trust between monarch and people.

A wise monarch recognised this. Elizabeth abandoned her monopolies with as much grace as she could muster. At times, James showed similar tact and good sense, but at others he responded angrily to criticism, condemning it as ill-mannered, ill-informed and malicious. He called only one brief Parliament between 1610 and 1621. His son was to prove still more intolerant and still more inclined to provoke confrontation. Both came to suspect that some of their critics aimed to undermine the king's ability to rule by challenging or denying essential royal prerogatives. As with the perception that James was bent on establishing absolutism, his perception that a minority of MPs were conspiring against him was misconceived, but there was enough objective evidence to make it plausible. The result was a spiral of distrust on both sides that reached a peak in the early years of Charles I's reign.

When James came to England, he had a limited political agenda. He accepted that England and Scotland were different and that each had to be governed according to its own rules. But he also hoped that his accession to the English crown would complete the reconciliation between his two kingdoms. It seemed logical to him that the union of crowns should lead to a political union, a union of the two Parliaments and systems of law, as had happened with Wales. But Scotland, unlike Wales, was a sovereign kingdom. Its system of law, in some ways less developed than that of England, was very different.[38] The Scots clergy saw the kirk as more truly reformed than the Church of England. It would have been impolitic to suggest an ecclesiastical union, so James opted for a very gradual convergence.

Not all were against some form of union. Those Scots who accompanied James found England agreeably wealthy. But for this very reason the English were generally hostile, noting that when a poor kingdom was yoked to a rich one there was only one way the money would flow. In the eyes of the English, the Scots were not only poor but verminous, afflicted with 'the itch'. MPs made derogatory remarks about Scotland and the Scots, stressing how many Scottish kings had met untimely deaths and implying that the Scots might cut the throats of the English.[39] James was deeply offended, both because he was proud of being a Scot but also because he had a genuine ideal of bringing to an end centuries of fratricidal conflict. Rebuffed by the Commons, James had to be content with proclaiming himself king of Great Britain. The hostility and contempt shown by the English towards Scotland made him all the more eager to seek sanctuary among his Scottish hunting and drinking companions.

The response to his calls for union was not the only reason why James became disillusioned. Scotland was a much less governed country than England. Ruling Scotland depended on the inter-personal skills at which James excelled. England was bigger, its political elite was much larger, and its administration was much more complex. The king played a remote, withdrawn role. Instead of debating in Parliament or elsewhere, he made formal speeches and then withdrew.[40] He also had to play a more formal public role; he was expected to process through the streets, to receive people formally, to sit still and to look regal. But James hated sitting down. He also hated paperwork and long council meetings about complex matters of administration and finance.[41] These did not seem to him to be the business of kings, which ought to comprise matters of high policy – above all foreign and ecclesiastical policy. He fled to the woods to hunt and left Robert Cecil, now earl of Salisbury, to carry the burden of administration, which wore him out. He died, not yet fifty, in 1612.

England was also much richer than Scotland, but that was a mixed blessing. The royal revenue was much larger than that of the Scots crown, but so were the demands on it. James was unused to dealing with requests for favour on that scale. He found it difficult to practise the frugality that came naturally to Elizabeth. True, she had perhaps been too frugal, and, as a married monarch with children, his expenditure was bound to be higher than hers. But the fact remained that James had little experience of managing money and was not good at it. He found it difficult to grasp quantities: at one point Salisbury, exasperated, produced £5000 in gold, in order to show how much it was.[42] James did not learn. He was a generous man and did not like to disappoint people, especially those he liked, such as his Scottish friends, Somerset and Buckingham. The Scots profited enormously, although James claimed that they benefited from his personal largesse, not from public offices. James Hay, earl of Carlisle, received rewards over thirty years to the value of over £400,000, including such titbits as Barbados. (The king's annual revenue was well under a million and the richest peer on the eve of the civil war had an income from land of about £23,000 a year.)[43] His generosity to Carlisle was exceeded by his bounty to Buckingham, which was compressed into a shorter period. Recklessly extravagant himself, Buckingham also needed money for his seemingly endless supply of needy friends, clients and relations.

Not only did more and more rewards pass into or through Buckingham's hands, but some showed a cynicism reminiscent of the 1590s. Again there were dubious patents and monopolies, 'like a sort of idle dreams that vanish away.'[44] These were procured by Buckingham or his cronies and implemented by shady operators from the City. A

1. James I, by Daniel Mytens, 1621. (*National Portrait Gallery*)

2. Anne of Denmark, the wife of James I, by unknown artist, *c.* 1617. (*National Portrait Gallery*)

3. George Villiers, first duke of Buckingham, *c.* 1616, probably by William Larkin. (*National Portrait Gallery*)

4. Charles I, after Sir Anthony Van Dyck, *c.* 1635. (*National Portrait Gallery*)

5. Henrietta Maria, the wife of Charles I, after Sir Anthony Van Dyck, *c.* 1635. (*National Portrait Gallery*)

6. Thomas Wentworth, first earl of Strafford, by Sir Anthony Van Dyck, 1636. (*National Portrait Gallery*)

7. Prince Rupert, Count Palatine, probably by Gerrit van Honthorst, *c.* 1642. (*National Portrait Gallery*)

8. Oliver Cromwell, by Robert Walker, *c.* 1649. (*National Portrait Gallery*)

patent to license alehouses (to ensure that they were orderly) quickly degenerated into a protection racket, in which those who failed to take out licences had their premises smashed. A patent was issued for a lighthouse on Dungeness (for which a syndicate charged passing ships fees); the 'lighthouse' turned out to be a candle on the headland.[45] These grants provoked a storm of protest in the Parliament of 1621. James claimed not to have known how dubious many of them were. Contemporaries were sceptical, but it may have been true. He agreed to the lighthouse scheme when he was seriously ill ('as is pretended') and in December 1620, having decided to call Parliament, he set up a commission to investigate 'grievous' patents and monopolies. When Parliament met, James compared the nation to a garden covered with weeds that needed cleansing.[46] Lord Keeper Bacon was impeached (prosecuted by the Commons and tried by the Lords) for sealing the patents; he was convicted of corruption, as were two of the most notorious monopolists. These were the first impeachments since 1450. James issued a proclamation annulling eighteen monopolies and patents and in 1624 he gave his assent to an Act banning most forms of monopoly.

In allowing Bacon's impeachment to go ahead – he could have aborted it by dissolving Parliament – and in agreeing to the Monopolies Act, James showed that he could be tactful and conciliatory. There were other occasions when he showed similar tact. In 1604 he helped resolve a row about disputed elections by agreeing that they should be decided by the Commons. In 1606, after the Gunpowder Plot, he made a gracious speech in which he said that he was proud that the plotters had wished to kill him in the midst of his Parliament.[47] But in general his sense of public relations was poor. His court was disorderly – the drunken shambles at Theobalds was an extreme example, but not unique – and he failed to project an image of majesty.[48] The practice of selling peerages – even compelling purchasers to buy them – was encouraged by Buckingham, but it undermined the dignity of both monarchy and nobility.[49] James was also extravagant. His subjects did not expect him to live or dress like a peasant – pageantry, then as now, cost money – but they did not appreciate his lavishing money and gifts on those who were seen as undeserving (Scots or Buckingham), especially when they flaunted the fruits of the king's bounty. One extreme example was the 'double banquet' given at court by Carlisle, in which a lavish spread was laid out and then thrown away and the 'real' banquet was produced. When Carlisle went as ambassador to Paris, he spent £2200 on a feast, 'being rather a profusion and spoil than reasonable or honourable provision'. Later the king, although desperately short of cash, gave Carlisle £20,000 towards the cost of his embassy.[50]

For a king pleading poverty – and who rarely paid his bills on time – this was politically unwise: how could he claim that the crown was underendowed when he gave away so much? MPs were always quick to find reasons why they did not need to vote money. The sense that James could not be trusted with money underlay the failure of the Great Contract of 1610. Salisbury proposed that the king should give up wardship and other feudal rights in return for £200,000 a year, plus £600,000 to pay off his debts. On the face of it, this was a reasonable proposal. Feudal dues were very expensive to collect – it was estimated that two thirds of the revenue from wardship was spent on administration – so this would save those who were liable to it more than the king was to receive in its stead. But there were snags. The king was reluctant to trade away ancient rights of the crown and refused to bring in accounts. He was afraid that whatever the Commons voted would prove too little, especially in view of the repeated shortfall on the subsidies. The Commons felt that they were being asked to vote too much, especially to pay off the debts: how could they justify voting such a huge sum to their neighbours? Lacking accounts, they could not be sure that they were not signing Parliament's death warrant, especially in view of the resentment and suspicion aroused by impositions. Discussions that had once looked promising petered out and James reverted to finding revenue where he could.

In 1610 James dissolved the Parliament that had first met in 1604. He was bitter: the Commons had insulted his country, 'perilled and annoyed our health, wounded our reputation, emboldened all ill-natured people, encroached upon many of our privileges and plagued our purse with their delays'.[51] He claimed that most MPs were loyal, but that they had been misled by a 'puritan', 'popular' minority.[52] The pejorative use of the word 'puritan' may seem surprising, given the moderation shown by most English puritans at this time, but James tended to equate puritanism with disobedience.[53] His use of 'popular' was equally pejorative: these members were trying to stir up his people against him. He would rule for the common good, he said, but not according to the common will.[54]

He wondered aloud how his predecessors had allowed an institution like Parliament to come into being. The answer, of course, was that they had actively encouraged it, as a means of mobilising consent. It had helped the Tudors to enhance their power over church and state. But James could see no useful purpose in such an institution. He tended to see truculence as defiance and to take rudeness personally. His disinclination to call another Parliament was reinforced when his councillors persuaded him to call one in 1614. He dissolved it after a series of rows, including another about impositions; it was nicknamed the 'Addled Parliament', because it failed to pass any legislation. At the dissolution James tore up the uncompleted bills before the members' faces.[55]

If James's relationship with Parliament had gone from bad to worse, he was far more successful in his capacity as supreme head of the Church of England, despite the deep divisions among clergy and laity. Anti-puritanism grew, as communities were divided by the attempts of puritan pastors and magistrates to regulate the conduct of the ungodly and suppress church ales and Sunday sports. James I was well aware of these divisions and did his utmost to contain them, appointing as bishops men from both wings of the church. By the 1620s the divisions had also acquired a theological dimension. Many were unhappy with predestination and felt that good works should play some part in salvation; the anti-puritan stress on communion had similar implications. A few clergy had also attacked predestinarian theology, but the most coherent and plausible alternative was devised by a Dutchman, Arminius, whose system became known as Arminianism.

Arminius provoked the wrath of orthodox Calvinists by arguing that, while saving grace came from God alone, people could accept or reject it. His teachings were condemned by the Dutch Reformed Church at the Synod of Dort (1618), to which James sent a delegation. This would suggest that James remained a Calvinist; the articles approved for the Church of Ireland in 1615 were also thoroughly Calvinist. Nevertheless there were growing numbers of critics of Calvinism among the English clergy, who came to be known as 'Arminians', a term of abuse which tended to be extended to anti-puritans generally.[56] James always showed some favour towards the Arminians, but only in his last years did he seem to lean more towards them, perhaps because zealous puritans were urging him to intervene on the Protestant side in the Thirty Years War.

James had a very personal interest in this conflict because of the involvement of his daughter Elizabeth and her husband. As Elector Palatine, Frederick was one of the seven German princes with the right to elect the Holy Roman Emperor. The majority were Catholic, but Frederick was a Protestant. In 1618 the Protestant nobles of Bohemia expelled Ferdinand, son of the Holy Roman Emperor, recently chosen as their king, and invited Frederick to become king in his place. Frederick accepted and he and Elizabeth spent a winter in Prague before being driven out by the armies of Ferdinand, who had now succeeded his father as emperor. Worse followed. Spanish and Bavarian forces overran his hereditary principality, the Palatinate, on the middle Rhine, and Frederick, Elizabeth and their growing brood of children were forced to take refuge in the Netherlands. Meanwhile, following Frederick's expulsion, the Bohemian Protestants were routed at the White Mountain. Flushed with success, Ferdinand set out to convert the kingdom to Catholicism and to eradicate Protestantism throughout the Holy Roman Empire.

English Protestants watched these developments with acute alarm. The great days of Protestant expansion on the Continent had long passed and now the liberties of subjects and the Protestant religion seemed everywhere on the defensive against the growing power of absolute monarchy and Counter-Reformation Catholicism. In France, the privileged position enjoyed by the Protestants since the Edict of Nantes of 1598 was effectively destroyed by 1629; now they were dependent on the king's goodwill. In Germany and eastern Europe Protestantism was in retreat against the forces of the Habsburg emperor and his allies. Meanwhile, after a twelve-year truce, the war of independence of the Protestant northern provinces of the Netherlands against Spain resumed, with victory for the north far from certain. Faced with what seemed the final struggle between Protestant and Catholic, good and evil, many English Protestants were concerned that James seemed unaccountably reluctant to take up the leadership of the Protestant cause. The anxiety created by his seemingly lukewarm commitment to Protestantism was compounded by fears that he harboured plans to establish absolute monarchy, to dispense with Parliament, impose taxes without consent, and imprison his critics without due process of law. The two anxieties were linked: absolute monarchy was identified, in the English Protestant mind, with popery. Both were authoritarian, dependent on coercion and on keeping the people ignorant; and the leading absolutist powers on the continent were Catholic.

James watched events in Bohemia and Germany with mixed feelings. He felt that Frederick should not have accepted the Bohemian crown, because the Protestants there had had no right to offer it to him. Bohemia was part of the hereditary lands of the Austrian Habsburgs. But equally James felt that Frederick should not have been expelled from the Palatinate and sought to recover it for him. His strategy centred on the relationship between the Spanish and the Austrian branches of the royal house of Habsburg. Although Spanish troops had conquered the Palatinate, James chose to see them as acting for Ferdinand rather than Spain. There was a tendency in the west to underestimate the Austrians and to see the Spanish as the senior partner, partly because of their huge territories in the New World, from which they imported massive quantities of gold and silver. Although Spain was no longer as powerful as it had been under Elizabeth, its armies were still formidable and both James and his English critics assumed that, if Spain called for Frederick's reinstatement in the Palatinate, the emperor would comply.

To persuade Spain to cooperate, James relied on friendship. Since bringing Elizabeth's war with Spain to a speedy end in 1604, he had cultivated good relations with Madrid, and he had something tangible to offer in a proposed marriage of Charles to the 'infanta' (princess) Maria, the sister of Philip IV, who succeeded to the Spanish throne early in 1623. This was not a strategy that commended itself to James's Protestant subjects. By 1620 the plight of Frederick and Elizabeth had become part of the wider question of whether Protestantism would survive on the Continent. Many of his people looked to James to lead the international Protestant cause in its hour of need, but James was not a warrior. He was, however, shrewd enough to appreciate that Spain might embrace the marriage with Prince Charles more eagerly if there were a less palatable alternative. He needed to be able to show that if the proposal were rejected he would be able to make war on Spain instead, for which he would need money. In 1621 he recalled Parliament, which could be relied upon to be hostile to Spain.

The Commons needed some prodding. While carefully avoiding the thorny question of impositions, they investigated other grievances, including patents and monopolies. The fact that James seemed willing that the guilty should be punished gratified the Commons, but they were preoccupied with domestic issues. Eventually, spurred on by clients of Buckingham, the Commons were persuaded to discuss the situation on the Continent. They made suitably anti-Spanish noises, but denounced the plan to marry Charles to the infanta. This may have seemed logical: if Spain was the greatest threat to Protestantism, how could the prince of Wales marry a Spanish princess? But James was furious at the Commons' attempt to meddle in the personal affairs of the royal family. He sent an angry message (from Newmarket) saying that such matters were outside the competence of Parliament. The Commons drew up a 'protestation', defending their right to discuss foreign policy. When he returned to London, James tore the offending page out of the Commons' journal with his own hand.

It might seem that this had been another 'addled' session, but the Commons had voted subsidies at the outset, as a gesture of goodwill, which James's reaction to the monopolies investigation could be seen as reciprocating. Even though James was said in 1622 to be 'distasted with [the Commons'] tedious manner of proceeding',[57] the continued uncertainties abroad made it likely that he would soon need to call another Parliament. To dispense with Parliament would be a confession of impotence and would mean that his initiatives could be ignored. For the time being, James reverted to the Spanish marriage, and so did Buckingham and Charles. Charles convinced himself that he loved the infanta madly, slept with her portrait beside his bed, and began to learn Spanish.

As the wily Spaniards spun out the negotiations, Charles and Buckingham became impatient. The latter had little time for the tortuous niceties of diplomacy, but it was Charles who devised a bizarre and foolhardy plan to cut through the delays. On 17 February 1623 the two of them took ship under the names of Tom and Dick Smith, wearing false beards and accompanied by only one servant. After a series of picaresque adventures as they travelled through France, they reached

Madrid, where Charles planned to demand the infanta's hand. But the
Spanish negotiators found one pretext after another for delay and
Charles and Buckingham made one concession after another in the hope
of bringing the negotiations to a conclusion. Charles was impatient to
win his beloved, Buckingham was impatient to get home, fearful that
his position at court was being undermined. At last, after the Spaniards
demanded one concession too many, the two young men realised that
they had been made fools of and returned to England in high dudgeon,
threatening revenge.[58]

The progress of their negotiations had been watched with great anxiety
in England. If the negotiations succeeded, would England become a
satellite of Spain? If they failed, might the heir to the throne be held
hostage? When they returned to London there was a huge surge of relief;
bonfires blazed throughout the capital.[59] Buckingham had been highly
unpopular when he left; when he returned, calling for war against Spain,
he was a hero. James was delighted to see his 'boys', but very anxious
about the talk of war. His suspicions of the troublemakers in the
Commons persisted; he feared that they wished to embroil him in war
and then extort concessions in return for money, stripping him of his
lawful powers and leaving him a mere figurehead.[60] Buckingham pooh-
poohed these fears. His already considerable self-confidence had been
inflated by the hero's welcome he had received, and he was sanguine
about his ability to manage Parliament. He overbore the querulous king,
who insisted that it would all end in tears and told his son that he would
live to have his bellyful of Parliaments.[61] When Parliament met, Buckingham persuaded James to seek its advice on foreign policy (a complete
reversal of his stance in 1621) and to agree to pass an Act against
monopolies. James also agreed that he could make it known that any
money voted could be 'appropriated' (tied) to war against Spain: the
Commons need not fear that any money they gave would be diverted
elsewhere.

It might be tempting to see the discussions on foreign policy, the
Monopolies Act and the appropriation of money as evidence of the
Commons' aggression and ambition. It makes more sense to see them
as ways in which Buckingham wooed the Commons, whose support he
needed not only to embark on war but also to overcome the king's
opposition. James was old and fond, and put up only limited resistance.

Lionel Cranfield, earl of Middlesex, the lord treasurer, offered more formidable opposition, on the sensible grounds that James could not afford war. So Buckingham's clients, supported by Charles, promoted Cranfield's impeachment on charges of corruption; he was convicted and dismissed. James did little to protect him, offering the accurate but unhelpful comment that all good lord treasurers were unpopular.[62]

Buckingham pressed on, securing a grant of money, but offering serious hostages to fortune. First, while securing the Commons' support for a war, he did not make it clear what sort of war he had in mind. The Commons believed that Spain could be brought to its knees if the English targeted its merchant ships and especially the annual bullion fleet. If that happened, ran the argument, the Spaniards would have no choice but to pull out of the Palatinate. Buckingham, for once, was more realistic. He believed that only a military expedition to the Palatinate could bring about Frederick's reinstatement. Secondly, although the Commons voted money, it was not nearly enough. Buckingham shared James's inability to appreciate the value of money and never let sordid considerations of accountancy stand in his way. He remained confident of his ability to manage the Commons and was sure that money would somehow appear when needed. Thirdly, after the failure of the Spanish match, Buckingham went to Paris to seek a French bride for Charles; if England were to make war on Spain, it would make sense to have the Spaniards' traditional rivals as allies. The French government, which had domestic problems aplenty with the Huguenots, had no wish to be sucked into a major war, especially at the behest of the English. But Buckingham's confidence was sky-high – he even made a pass at the French queen.[63] He was determined to return home with a marriage treaty and promised the French that, after the marriage took place, English Catholics would be allowed a measure of freedom of worship. Unfortunately, at the same time James assured Parliament that he would not allow Catholics greater freedom. Having relaxed proceedings against them in 1623, James in 1624 ordered that the penal laws should be enforced, only to order a further relaxation at the end of the year.[64] It would be impossible to keep both promises.

These assorted chickens would not come home to roost for a while yet. For the moment, Buckingham strutted the English and European stage with a magnificent disregard for life's little practicalities. Early in

1625, buoyed up by Parliament's endorsement and a modest grant of money, he organised an expedition to the Rhineland, commanded by an experienced mercenary, Count Ernst von Mansfeld. But the French would not allow his motley and ill-disciplined army to march through France, so they had to travel via the Northern Netherlands. Most had died or deserted before they reached the Palatinate and the dream of restoring Frederick remained unfulfilled.[65] The problems encountered by the expedition damaged Buckingham's credit with the king and there were rumours that he would fall from power, but James's affection (if not his trust in Buckingham's judgement) remained unshaken.

By early 1625 the English public viewed the policies of James's government, at home and on the Continent, with a mixture of alarm and incomprehension. By contrast, there were few complaints about its conduct in Ireland. The bloodshed, suffering and destruction of the Nine Years War highlighted the incompatibility between the Catholic majority (Irish and Old English), on one hand, and the anglicising New English, on the other. The latter had behind them the power of government and law and were able, in the final analysis, to draw on the wealth and military power of England to impose their will. The former had numbers, as Catholics still held by far the greater share of the land, and land, reinforced by kin loyalties, conferred power over men. The rebellion had shown that Catholic resistance could be overcome only with a military effort on a scale that the London government would prefer to avoid. If English rule in Ireland was ever to be made secure, it would be necessary to shift the balance of landed power from Catholics to Protestants, undermining the power over men of the Old English and (especially) the Gaelic Irish.

The rebels' surrender in 1603 might have seemed to offer an opportunity to confiscate the estates of those who had been in arms, but neither the authorities in Dublin nor the new king in London felt sufficiently secure to risk measures that could provoke further rebellion. Instead, Mountjoy allowed Tyrone and his allies to surrender on terms that left their power in Ulster virtually intact; one of Tyrone's leading lieutenants, Rory O'Donnell, was created earl of Tyrconnell.[66] In the longer term, however, the authorities in both Dublin and London recognised that a shift in the balance of landed power was necessary to secure English, and Protestant, rule over Ireland. Both also recognised that this had to be a gradual and piecemeal process, to avoid provoking armed resistance. As under Elizabeth, those in Ireland were the more impatient and took the initiative.

James I liked to portray himself as a peacemaker, seeking to heal the rifts between Catholics and Protestants in continental Europe, which, in his view, posed the greatest threat to international peace. There was less evidence of such eirenic intentions in his own kingdoms. He wrote in 1603 that he regarded Rome as a true but corrupted church and that persecution was a mark of a false church. The Jesuits, it was true, were subversive, but he thought that generally Catholics should not be persecuted if they remained quiet.[67] But in 1605 a group of maverick English Catholics tried to blow up the king and the Houses of Parliament and new legislation was brought in against them. A new oath of allegiance described the power that the pope claimed to depose kings as impious, damnable and heretical. Most English Catholics had no intention of rebelling against their king, but were reluctant to say so in such terms. In addition, the recusancy laws were strengthened: to the obligation to attend one's parish church every Sunday (on pain of a fine of one shilling a week or £20 a month) was added the obligation to take communion, according to the rites of the Church of England, once a year. These measures made it harder for Catholics to equivocate on the questions of allegiance and church membership.

In Ireland, far from trying to build bridges between Catholic and Protestant, James presided over a regime that took further the policies of Protestantisation and anglicisation that had started under Elizabeth. The London government tried to restrain the authorities in Ireland from persecuting Catholics, but it endorsed the transfer of land from Catholic to Protestant and the increasingly systematic exclusion of Catholics from positions of power. The simplest way of depriving Catholics of land was by confiscation, but that required that they be guilty of rebellion or some other crime rendering their property liable to forfeiture. Few Catholic landowners were prepared to oblige the Dublin government in this way. The major exceptions were the earls of Tyrone and Tyrconnell, who in 1607 fled abroad. Their power in Ulster, safeguarded by the terms of their surrender in 1603, had been systematically undermined by the authorities, and they feared that it would be reduced to nothing.

Their lands, mostly in counties Tyrone and Derry, were declared forfeit to the crown. The next year, following a revolt led by Sir Cahir
O'Doherty, the assizes declared that most of the land in six counties
was also forfeit.[68]

The crown encouraged various individuals and corporations to develop the land. Derry city was assigned to the City of London; from that
day to this, the name given to the city is a question of allegiance, with
Unionists calling it Londonderry and Nationalists Derry. The planters
were required to bring over and install substantial numbers of settlers.
In the existing plantations – in Leinster, and in Munster, where the
plantation was renewed after its destruction in 1598 – the land was
generally farmed by Catholic tenants and labourers and the 'settler'
presence was confined to a small elite of landowners. The estates of
settlers were intermingled with those of Catholic proprietors and there
was considerable social mixing and even intermarriage.[69]

In Ulster, the land was divided into smaller units, with the intention
of creating a denser Protestant settlement, of farmers and craftsmen,
who would add to the potential body of armed Protestants in Ireland.
As in Munster, it proved difficult to persuade English settlers to
come. Ireland was still seen as dangerous and backward, and Ulster
was the poorest of the four provinces in terms of soil and climate –
as well as being the most Gaelic. Such considerations proved less of
a deterrent for wretchedly poor peasant farmers from south-west
Scotland. Farming conditions, and levels of brigandage, in Ulster
were no worse than those that they were used to, perhaps better.
Thousands made the short sea trip across the North Channel and
settled in counties Antrim and Down. Further west, in counties Tyrone
and Derry, most of the land (as in Munster) was farmed by Catholics
who paid rent to English proprietors. The Scottish settlements were
solidly Protestant; Catholics were driven out. The settlers were Presbyterians, who brought their pastors with them, and they were fiercely
anti-Catholic. They formed self-consciously alien and isolated communities, little oases of Protestantism in a hostile land. The roots of
the siege mentality that became so characteristic of Ulster Unionism
may be traced back to these early Scots settlers, of whom there were
as many as 50,000 by 1640.[70]

If little land outside Ulster could be secured through forfeiture, the

Dublin authorities had to find other means of depriving Catholics of their land, through the law. Much of Ireland was pastoral, with wealth measured in sheep and cattle, rather than clearly delineated tracts of land. Land 'ownership' was fluid. As in Scotland, inheritance customs were less formal than in England, with clan leadership passing to the strongest of the male kin and 'ownership' being in part a function of power. Even where effective control over an area of land was long established, it was unlikely to be susceptible of documentary proof. Irish law was in many respects oral, relying on traditions passed down from generation to generation. English society and law – thanks in large part to the order and method of the Normans – relied on written documents, such as charters, title deeds and estate surveys. The imprecision of Irish land law meant that many landowners were unable to demonstrate 'ownership' according to English standards of proof. The judges who sat in the courts in Dublin Castle, or who toured the provinces, were Englishmen, trained in English law. Native Irish landowners (especially) were unable, when challenged, to prove their title to their lands, which rendered them liable to forfeiture.

Sometimes they were indeed declared forfeit, but more often they were not. Instead they were offered a variation of the practice of surrender and regrant used under Henry VIII. Then the aim had been to persuade landowners formally to surrender their estates to the king; he then granted them back, with solid titles under English law, which recognised the king's feudal authority over the owners. This had the benefits (for the king) of formalising their allegiance and of securing the guardianship of sons whose fathers died while they were under age. Such young men could be brought up at the English court and anglicised, thus spreading English values through the Irish landed elite. The most important of these young men was to be James Butler, earl and eventually duke of Ormond, a member of a great Old English family, who converted to Protestantism and who, for half a century, was the most prominent servant of the Stuarts in Ireland.

Under James I, surrender and regrant was used very differently. A commission to enquire into 'defective titles' was set up in 1606. Landowners who could not prove their titles to their land were invited to surrender them to the king, who would then grant back some of the land, with full English legal title, but paying a considerable rent to the king.

The land retained by the king could be rented out to Protestants for plantation. Meanwhile, as under Elizabeth, individuals sought out 'concealed' royal lands, which were also granted out, occasionally to Irishmen, but far more often to New English Protestants. The grants were often of smallish parcels, in order to break up the large holdings of Irish lords and reduce what the English described as the 'slavish dependency' of the peasantry.[71]

This was not a quick process. The legal hearings took time, witnesses and juries had to be summoned, documents (where they existed) had to be produced. But it was effective. Proceeding through the processes of law, even an alien law, was less likely to provoke resistance than more arbitrary measures. It also targeted landowners one at a time, making concerted resistance unlikely. And the fact that most landowners retained some of their lands made them less likely to protest or rebel than if they had lost all of them. Besides, if they rebelled they would lose everything. Gradually, more and more land passed into Protestant hands. By 1641 the only substantial unplanted areas in Ulster and Leinster were County Monaghan and parts of counties Dublin and Wicklow. In Munster the picture was more patchy and there were as yet few plantations in the westernmost province, Connacht.

This process did not rely entirely on the law. Economics also played a part, as Catholic landowners fell into debt and sold out to Protestants. And it was far from complete in 1640. Any figure for the proportion of land in Catholic hands has to be conjectural, as there was no national survey before the 1650s, but an informed contemporary estimate for 1641 put it at 60 per cent, considerably less than in 1603. The fact that this transfer had occurred without serious disorder showed the advantages of using the law to carry out the policy of plantation. There are suggestive similarities, indeed, with the caution and patience which James had shown bringing the Scottish nobility to heel. In the context of English rule in Ireland, the policy of plantation made sense and James pursued it consistently. Charles I failed to do so and seriously destabilised Ireland.

The main victims of the legal offensive against Catholics' land titles were the native Irish. The Old English, the bulk of whom lived in Leinster, where Anglo-Norman influence had been strongest, were more likely to have written titles to their land. They also, traditionally, held the majority of offices, administrative, legal and municipal; and they held the majority of seats in Parliament, which in 1586 had vigorously opposed anglicisation. When Parliament met again in 1613 (Parliaments were neither regular nor frequent in Ireland) they no longer had that majority. Numerous small boroughs had been enfranchised, mostly in Ulster, which duly returned Protestant members. Even so, the Irish Houses were too unreliable (from the point of view of the government) to try to push through legislation accelerating the processes of investigating titles and surrender and regrant. The extension of English law in Ireland owed nothing to Acts of Parliament and rested ultimately on the royal prerogative. Indeed, as the judges in Dublin handed down one judgment after another that transformed Irish land law, they usurped the role of the Irish Parliament in making law.[72] The Old English opposed this as much as they could, but their opportunities for opposition diminished. Condemned to minority status in Parliament, they were also squeezed out of public office. Magistrates in county and town were now all Protestants – even in Dublin, where there were many wealthy Catholic merchants, who had traditionally played a large part in the city's government.

Catholics were not severely persecuted. In England by 1610 there was a formidable array of laws, with heavy penalties, against all aspects of Catholic behaviour, including the possession of Catholic books and devotional objects – it was an offence to have rosary beads. The recusancy laws attempted to force Catholics to attend Protestant services, but (thanks to the opposition of the 1586 Parliament) they were not extended to Ireland, where the laws against Catholics were less extensive and only fitfully enforced. The authorities showed little interest in converting the Irish, who were seen as too degenerate and foolish to be worth saving; they could go to perdition in their own way. The Church of Ireland clergy, supported by tithes paid by an overwhelmingly Catholic peasantry, ministered in the parish churches to a handful of Protestants, while the Irish worshipped in barns and fields; only in Dublin and a few other towns were Church of Ireland Protestants numerous. The limited interest shown by the New English elite in suppressing Catholic worship or promoting Protestantism showed that their main concerns were political – to erode the landed power and to break the political power of the Catholics, both Irish and Old English. As one Catholic was to write in 1695, 'they took more pains to make the land turn Protestant than the people'.[73]

The king was now old and frail. On 27 March 1625 he died, having suffered a stroke and a severe bout of dysentery. Buckingham was with him to the last, giving him medicines with his own hands, which later gave rise to rumours that the duke had poisoned his master. In many respects James died a disappointed man, full of foreboding about the future. He had found ruling England more difficult than he had expected. The backbiting, intrigue and carping criticism of the English were harder to cope with than the violence and occasional duplicity of the Scots. He had learned to understand the Scots but he never fully understood the English. He had had to cope with a system of government that was more complex than he was used to and which he found temperamentally alien; he soon convinced himself that it was bad for his health. And when he sought companionship that would alleviate his sense of isolation and alienation it became the subject of malicious gossip. In Buckingham, he had let loose a genie, a gambler who played for higher and higher stakes and who was totally unabashed by failure. James's relationship with Parliament was fraught on both sides, but it never quite broke down. As in Scotland, James was restrained by innate caution, a canny sense of the practical. He could lose his temper and make tactless claims; but he could also apologise and be tactful and gracious. He could become involved in confrontations, but he would never push things to the brink. Underlying the occasional bombast, the ringing statements about the godlike attributes of kings and the flashes of temper lay a fear of extremes, which could be put down to cowardice, but it would be more generous to recognise that he genuinely loved peace, a rare attribute in a warlike age. This was recognised even by Weldon. 'He loved good laws and had many made in his time … he lived in peace, died in peace and left all his kingdoms in a peaceable condition.'[74] The same could not be said of his son.

The Explanation of the EMBLEME.

Ponderibus *genus omne mali, probriſq; gravatus*,
Vixq; ferenda ferens, Palma ut Depreſsa, *resurgo*.

Though clogg'd with weights of miſeries
Palm-like Depreſs'd, I higher rise

Ac, velut undarum Fluctûs Ventiq;, *furorem*
Irati Populi Rupes immota *repello*.
Clarior è tenebris, *cœleſtis ſtella, coruſco*.
Victor et æternum—felici pace triumpho.

And as th'unmoved Rock out-brave's
The boiſtrous Windes and rageing waves:
So triumph I. And shine more bright
In sad Affliction's Darkſom night.

Auro Fulgentem *rutilo gemmiſq; micantem*,
At curis Gravidam *spernendo* calco Coronam.

That Splendid, but yet toilſom Crown
Regardleſsly I trample down.

Spinoſam, *at ferri facilem, quo* Spes mea, Chriſti
Auxilio, Nobis *non eſt* tractare *moleſtum*.

With joie I take this Crown of thorn,
Though sharp, yet eaſie to be born.

Æternam, *fixis fidei, semperq;—beatam*
In Cœlos oculis Specto, Nobiſq; *paratam*.

That heav'nlie Crown, already mine,
I View with eies of Faith divine.

Quod Vanum eſt, ſperno; quod Chriſti Gratia præbet
Amplecti studium eſt: Virtutis Gloria merces.

I slight vain things; and do embrace
Glorie, the just reward of Grace.

G.D.

Τὸ Χ⟨ρ⟩ ᾱδὲν ἠδίκησε τὴν πόλιν, ᾱδ᾽ τὸ Κάσσια.

Title page of *Eikon Basilike*.

3

Charles I

Few kings of England have provoked more conflicting opinions in succeeding generations than Charles I. For centuries Charles was the 'royal martyr', whose execution was solemnly commemorated, with prayers, fasting and humiliation, every 30 January. This was largely the product of one exceptional work of propaganda, *Eikon Basilike* ('The Image of the King'), which consisted of religious meditations and prayers that Charles had allegedly written in prison. Its frontispiece, which appeared with many variations, showed the king at prayer, his gaze fixed on heaven, a crown of thorns in his hand and an open Bible in front of him. At his feet lay his earthly crown, 'glorious but heavy', while his eyes beheld 'a blessed and eternal crown'. After the Restoration, he was venerated almost as a saint: when a chapel was consecrated in the new spa town of Tunbridge Wells in 1678, it was dedicated to 'Charles the Martyr'.

This sympathetic image was compounded by the van Dyck portraits of the king, which were widely reproduced. They showed Charles as dignified, indeed truly regal – sometimes on horseback, to hide the shortness of his legs. There was a solemnity, even sadness in his large brown eyes, as if he somehow knew the fate that awaited him. When the sculptor Bernini saw van Dyck's triple portrait of the king, he exclaimed that this was a man born for tragedy. Van Dyck also depicted him as a family man, the devoted father of six children; there was to be no uncertainty about the succession in his time. Van Dyck may have flattered his royal subject – few who painted the great and good did not – but much of what he portrayed was true. Charles was very conscious of the need for dignity and his court was far more orderly than that of his father. Cardinal Richelieu recommended it to Louis XIII as a model that the French court should emulate.[1]

Charles also became a devoted husband. His marriage to Henrietta

Maria of France did not start well. She made little secret of her contempt for the English or her devotion to Catholicism, going barefoot with her ladies to Tyburn where many Catholic 'martyrs' had been executed. She was wilful and petulant, at one point getting into a blazing row with her husband about whether it was raining. The friction between them was encouraged by Buckingham, who feared that Henrietta Maria's influence over the king might eclipse his own. But once Buckingham was dead, Charles fell in love with Henrietta Maria and she with him. Theirs was a large and happy family, without the slightest whiff of scandal; in this Charles I was unique among the Stuart kings. And so he remained in popular memory, a king who had perhaps made mistakes, but who was more sinned against than sinning. In one of the most popular plays of the 1870s, the plight of Charles and his family reduced audiences to tears. When the Prince of Wales came to see it, a few radicals in the audience hissed the king, but they were drowned out by those who cheered.[2] In the words of that wonderfully gentle satire on popular views of English history, *1066 and All That*, Charles and the Cavaliers were 'wrong but wromantic', while Cromwell and the Roundheads were 'right but repulsive'.[3]

The list of Charles's positive attributes can be extended.[4] He was the most important royal patron of the arts since Henry VIII, attracting great continental painters to England (Rubens as well as van Dyck) and buying shrewdly. Perhaps his greatest coup was the acquisition of the collection of the duke of Mantua, which included the series of enormous paintings of 'The Triumphs of Caesar', by Mantegna, now at Hampton Court. As with his father's intellectual prowess, Charles's connoisseurship was not universally appreciated by his subjects, many of whom condemned Catholic religious art as idolatrous. Charles was also pious, not so much in the sense of possessing a deeply articulated religious understanding, but in the sense of deriving spiritual fulfilment from acts of worship – a further expression of his highly developed aesthetic sense. And he had a strong sense of honour and conscience, which led him to do what he regarded as right, without equivocation or compromise.[5]

His piety and conscience were not appreciated by many of his subjects either. His brand of piety was seriously out of step with the religious ideals of both the puritans and those one might call 'prayer-book anglicans' or 'parish anglicans'.6 Moreover, Charles combined a strong commitment to conscience with a habit of behaving in ways which others regarded as devious and dishonest. Utterly convinced of his own rightness, he could not imagine that any honest person could see things differently. If they disagreed with him, they were either wrong or malicious; either way he did not need to take account of their views. In Charles's moral universe, everything was wrong or right, black or white – there were no shades of grey. If he was convinced he was right, he saw nothing wrong in using underhand methods or telling half-truths (or lies) in order to achieve his justified ends. If he was forced against his will to make unreasonable concessions, he saw nothing wrong in reneging on them afterwards, because promises made under duress were not binding. He also had an unsettling habit of reinterpreting agreements, to a point where some came to question whether there was any point in negotiating with him.7

Like his father, Charles was confident that he knew what was best for his subjects. Unlike his father, Charles was not restrained by a sense of the practical. Faced with opposition, he pressed on. If opposition grew to a point where he could advance no further, he beat a tactical retreat, determined to resume his forward march when circumstances allowed. It never occurred to him that his critics' opinions should be taken seriously. Charles was a tidy-minded man who craved order. In his mental world, kings ruled and subjects obeyed. Nowhere was this seen more clearly than in his view of the church. Charles expected that on Sundays the people would go to church, where they would sit quietly, worship reverently and be told their duties; seemliness was far more acceptable to Charles (and to God) than fiery sermons or agonies of faith and conscience. His vision of the church largely coincided with that of the Arminians, whom Charles supported wholeheartedly. Increasingly, only anti-puritans were appointed to bishoprics and Charles gave full backing to the attempts of William Laud, archbishop of Canterbury from 1633, to impose anti-puritan values on the Church of England. Whereas James had tried to balance the two wings of the church, Charles backed one side's efforts to impose its will on the other.8

Laud offers ammunition to those who claim that academics should not be allowed out into the real world. He was obsessed with orderliness and appearances and sought to impose the same standards on country parishes that he had imposed as president of St John's College, Oxford, where he tried to make students keep their hair short and stay out of alehouses. He also suffered from his own energy, at one point rupturing himself when swinging a heavy book for exercise. His concern for neatness complemented Charles's highly developed aesthetic sense in a drive to make the 'beauty of holiness' the defining characteristic of the church. Neither Charles nor Laud had much tolerance for boorishness or boisterousness, for rustics who seemed to regard Sunday services as a social occasion, who gossiped in church, slept or played with their children or dogs. Nor did he have any time for English puritans or Scots Presbyterians, who preached sermons which could stir up or confuse their hearers and showed no appreciation of the beauty of holiness. Charles had no great understanding of theology, although he distrusted Calvinists and puritans on political grounds. He regarded theological debate as inflammatory and divisive and tried to suppress it.[9] His vision of the church was benevolent but deeply condescending towards the laity. It reflected his view of subjects as essentially passive, needing to be guided and led, incapable of thinking for themselves. Experience suggested that when people did think they were likely to come up with the wrong answers.

Under Charles and Laud the shift from preaching to the sacraments and the placing of communion tables altar-wise ceased to be a matter of individual initiative and became official policy. Proper standards of worship had to be observed everywhere: it was not acceptable to baptise babies in buckets or to serve communion wine in a beer flagon.[10] Communion tables were to be railed in (partly to keep the congregation's dogs away), with a proper chalice and altar cloth; the church fabric was to be repaired, surplices were to be worn, and pigs were to be kept out of graveyards. Diversity was not to be tolerated. The de facto connivance at moderate nonconformity that had existed under Elizabeth and James was to end.[11] Everyone had to conform, including the 'stranger' churches founded by Calvinist refugees from France and the Netherlands, and even English congregations in the Netherlands and New England.

Laud's programme was enormously ambitious and would have taken many years to implement. While some bishops embraced it enthusiastically, others were lukewarm or hostile. Puritans were outraged, crying shrilly that Laud was leading the church towards Rome or even bringing in popery. But many non-puritans, who liked and valued the prayer book services, raised similar criticisms; this was not the church that they had come to know and love.[12] If they valued the liturgy, they also valued sermons and were repelled by 'popish' innovations such as bowing at the name of Jesus. (Some of these practices had been officially required under Elizabeth, but as they had not been observed they were seen as new.)

There were other grounds for resenting Laud's programme. It cost money, which many small parishes did not have, and it seemed fussy, meddlesome and unnecessary.[13] Laud was totally unconcerned by lay reactions to his commands, as shown by the question of pews. Pews varied in size and grandeur, with grandest being built or rented by members of the gentry, visible and prized marks of status. With the new-found emphasis on communion, Laud decreed that it was necessary for everyone to be able to see the altar. Pews that blocked people's view should be removed or cut down to size, a very public affront to those to whom they belonged. But Laud and his henchmen were no respecters of persons. Bishop Wren of Norwich, after a long dispute with the city's corporation, secured an order from the privy council that the mayor and aldermen should attend the cathedral rather than one of the city churches. They were given seats in an unprestigious part of the cathedral, beneath a gallery. Some citizens amused themselves by spitting on the aldermen's heads and someone dropped a prayer book, which broke the mayor's glasses. It was a humiliating experience that left the aldermen smarting for revenge.[14]

Reponses to Laudianism varied. Many puritan families emigrated to New England, preferring to take their chances in a 'howling wilderness' where they would be able to worship freely. As the number of preaching ministers diminished, puritans sought out the few who remained, 'gadding' for miles for a good sermon. As puritans from several parishes converged on those with preaching, so they withdrew from their own parishes and formed a new community of the godly. Often they brought lunch and made a day of it, discussing the sermon, reading the Bible and praying together.[15] In many parishes the distinction between puritans and non-puritans widened. As puritans came to regard the church as not just imperfect but dangerously corrupt, they sought to have as little as possible to do with those who attended its services. The godly were urged to distance themselves from the ungodly. Asked if it was acceptable for a godly wife to make love to her ungodly husband, one writer advised that it was, provided she did not enjoy it.[16] Their alienation led to a revival of calls for radical reform of a sort that had not been heard since Elizabeth's reign. As the bishops were seen as chiefly responsible for the changes that were taking place, there were demands for episcopacy to be abolished: drastic ills required drastic remedies.

Laud's attempted counter-reformation in the Church of England was easily linked by his opponents to the prominence of Catholics at court, especially in the circle of Henrietta Maria. It was alleged that the authorities were lenient towards Catholic recusants, although in fact the laws against them were enforced.[17] It was also linked to the ongoing wars on the Continent, which the English saw in religious terms, and to more secular understandings of 'popery' – the perceived threat to Parliaments and the onward march towards royal absolutism. The belief that these various developments amounted to a popish plot against Protestantism and English liberties was shared by many non-puritans – and there was no shortage of evidence to give it credibility.[18]

By 1640 many communities were divided by religion, into puritans and non-puritans, or anti-puritans, and these divisions help explain patterns of popular allegiance in the Civil War.[19] Laud's religious policy had also alienated many from the king and his government. Many were not alienated to the extent that they were prepared to take up arms against the king, but some were. One 'cause' of the civil war was that a significant minority was prepared to fight either to prevent the imposition of 'popery' or to bring about, at last, a thorough Protestant reformation. That they were ready to do so is a searing indictment of Archbishop Laud and Charles I. Both had long believed that 'puritans' were 'rebels'. The Laudian programme in the church was to make them so.

Charles's vision of order and tidiness embraced all of his three kingdoms. Unlike James, he was profoundly convinced of the superiority of England and Englishness. Where Scotland and Ireland differed, they should be brought into line with England. This was especially true of their established churches: it is significant than the only person he consulted about all three kingdoms was Laud.[20] Religious resentments were to unite many of his subjects against him in all his dominions. The other major source of contention centred on money and the law. Charles, like James, believed firmly in the rule of law and accepted that he was morally obliged to rule according to law. Like James, he had a distinctly subjective view of what law was and had little difficulty in convincing himself that whatever best suited his interests must be lawful. Charles said that he would follow his judges' advice – when they did not speak in riddles.[21] He sometimes consulted them individually.[22] Several were dismissed, although it is not always clear that this was because they had given unpalatable legal opinions.[23] On the other hand, the pressure on judges was far less crude than it was to be in the 1680s, the use of judicial torture was discontinued,[24] and there were no political executions (in England) in the 1630s. But Charles did imprison his political enemies, invoking the privy council's right to imprison those suspected of treason, without showing cause. This was used most flagrantly in 1627, when five knights were gaoled for refusing to pay a forced loan; there were accusations, in this case and others, that the king and his law officers engaged in sharp practice verging on flagrant illegality.[25]

Charles also extended the use of Star Chamber. It continued to enforce press censorship, punishing with the loss of their ears the authors of books attacking the bishops, although gentlemen (which these authors were) were normally not liable to corporal punishment.[26] It also backed up entrepreneurs favoured by the king; fenmen accused of riot were imprisoned and released only if they agreed to abandon their claims to common rights. As the earl of Clarendon noted, Star Chamber increasingly became a court of revenue.[27]

The misuse of law was in fact most apparent in the raising of revenue. Charles believed that his subjects were morally obliged to provide the money he needed to govern. If by any chance the English Parliament failed to grant money that was rightfully due to him, he believed that he was morally justified in collecting it anyway. Having convinced himself that certain revenues were due to him by right – and he usually did not take much convincing – Charles dismissed criticism of these revenues as misguided or subversive.

In 1625 the Commons tried to reopen the issue of impositions by granting tonnage and poundage to the new king for a year, rather than for life, which had become the norm under the Tudors. If this was a ploy to bring the king to negotiate a compromise on impositions, it failed. The Lords did not pass the bill, but Charles continued to collect tonnage and poundage, so he was now collecting the full range of import duties without the consent of Parliament. The Commons were outraged, but impotent. Their ability to grant or deny money was their main bargaining weapon in dealing with the king; if they refused to grant money and the king collected it anyway, what could they do? This lesson was repeated in 1626, when the Commons agreed in principle to vote subsidies but failed to complete the bill. This king raised a similar sum by means of a forced loan.

In the 1630s, the king revived the traditional device of ship money, whereby coastal counties were expected to contribute to maritime defence in the face of piracy or possible invasion. In itself, this was uncontentious, but Charles extended it to inland counties and converted it into an annual levy, creating the interesting concept of a regular emergency. Those who refused to pay, notably the Buckinghamshire squire, John Hampden, argued that this was illegal. In a famous trial, the judges decided that Hampden was wrong: there were ample precedents for the raising of ship money in an emergency and only the king could decide what constituted an emergency. As with impositions, the key issue was the king's motives, or his judgment, and the judges did not wish to question his veracity; if he said so, there must be an emergency, so people were obliged to pay. Although the sums demanded were quite small, once the principle had been established there was nothing to prevent their being increased. Because each county and town was given a quota to meet, there was no scope for evasion and under-assessment: the bulk of the sum assessed came in each year until 1640.[28] By the year of Hampden's trial, 1637, the crown had created a system of import duties, and a tax on property, which did not depend on Parliament, whose future looked extremely bleak. Why should the king call it if he did not need to ask for money?[29]

Apart from developing forms of non-parliamentary taxation, Charles facilitated (and profited from) schemes to exploit undeveloped natural resources, notably forest clearance and fen drainage. Charles helped developers to crush the resistance and destroy the common rights of the local peasantry. His attempts to portray himself as a friend to the poor fall apart if one investigates his role in the draining of the fens. Charles's legal and revenue advisers showed imagination and ingenuity in the means they found to bring revenue to the king and profit to themselves; Clarendon claimed that the advisers profited far more than the king.[30] They dug deep into the murky morass of the monarchy's ancient feudal rights to a point where they were scraping the bottom of the barrel.

William I had set aside large areas as royal forest, in which to hunt. To protect the habitat of the deer, it was forbidden to build or till the ground in these forests. This caused some friction, but the forest laws were sufficiently ancient and known to command general acquiescence – until the king's researchers discovered that the royal forests had once been much more extensive than anyone had realised. This enabled the king to prosecute all sorts of people for encroaching on the royal forest. Fines were imposed, ranging as high as £20,000 in the case of the second earl of Salisbury, the son of James's lord treasurer. Like many of those fined, Salisbury 'compounded', paying only a fraction of the fine. In Essex there were threats to pull down all fences on the lands of those who were fined in order to 'persuade' them to compound.[31] These prosecutions came within the letter of the law – it was clear that these areas had indeed once been royal forest – but they seemed extremely unfair. Similarly, the king's lawyers had discovered that long ago men who held land from the king under feudal tenures had been obliged to receive knighthoods, or pay a fine. The aim was to ensure that the king could mobilise enough cavalrymen in war, but that need had long passed. Many who held land (at least technically) from the king were now summoned to be knighted, often at impossibly short notice, and were fined when they did not appear.[32]

Fines were imposed for other offences as well. The laws against enclosures that destroyed common rights or converted arable into pasture had been enforced only sporadically. Now they were enforced systematically by commissioners who toured the country, imposing fines. This might seem to imply sympathy for the victims of enclosure, but the commissioners showed no interest in removing the fences, because they wished to return in a few years and fine the enclosers again. Other 'fines' bordered on extortion. The City of London was fined £70,000 by Star Chamber for its failure to comply fully with the terms of its contract for Derry plantation. It was later faced with other legal challenges and threatened with the loss of its charter. In the end, it paid a much reduced sum and kept its charter, but the sour taste remained.[33] Civil servants accused of charging excessive fees were allowed to compound for their 'offence'.[34]

Nor were economic 'projects' forgotten. The 1624 Monopolies Act had made an exception of corporations whose function was to maintain standards of quality, to ensure that craft guilds did not fall foul of the Act. This clause provided a pretext to create new monopolies, granted to specially created corporations, whose ostensible purpose was to ensure quality, in the interests of the consumer. The most notorious was the soap monopoly. The monopolists organised demonstrations, before an audience of peeresses and laundresses, to show that the monopolists' soap really did wash whiter. The queen's laundress (among others) declared that she used only Castile soap, but the privy council pronounced the monopolists' soap good. To make matters worse, most of the monopolists were Catholics, which made some fear that their soap might harm the soul as well as the body.[35]

The traditional legal rights of the English had not yet been destroyed, but they were being eroded. Law was failing to regulate the relations between subject and king. In a series of cases, notably Bate's case in 1606 and Hampden's case in 1637, the judges effectively endorsed the king's right to levy taxes without Parliament's consent. Taken to its logical conclusion, the ship money judgment 'left no man anything which he might call his own'.[36] The 'legality' of impositions and ship money depended on the king's intentions. Was he levying impositions in order to keep out undesirable imports? Was he collecting ship money because he judged that there was a danger of invasion or coastal raids? In other words, was the king telling the truth? This was a moral or political issue, rather than one to be resolved through the analysis of precedents, which was how the judges usually reached their judgments. They also had to consider that they were the king's judges, the law courts were the king's courts, and the king was the fount of justice; it was a maxim of the law that the king could no wrong. Hence they felt obliged to give him the benefit of the doubt; but many of his subjects did not.[37] They believed that their property rights and personal liberty were in danger and that danger seemed to be growing. These were law-abiding people, but the law was failing to protect them.[38] At the heart of their anxieties lay concern for the future of Parliament. MPs claimed that England was the last country in Europe to retain its ancient rights and liberties. 'This is the crisis of Parliaments;' one declared in 1628. 'We shall know by this if Parliaments live or die.'[39] Such anxieties increased in the 1630s, as it seemed as if Parliament might never meet again.

Sordid, predatory and questionably legal money-raising devices were not confined to England. In Scotland Charles opened his reign by declaring his intention to recover crown and church lands alienated 'illegally' since 1570. His aim was partly to ensure that the church was properly endowed, partly (as in Ireland) to reduce the peasants' dependence on their landlords and so weaken the landlords' military power. As in England, the king wished landowners to compound, rather than lose their lands, but the results were disappointing Even though the 'revocation' was confirmed by an Act of the Scottish Parliament in 1633, its most lasting consequence was to create insecurity among Scottish landowners.[40] Charles also showed himself intolerant of criticism. A leading Scottish peer, Lord Balmerino, was tried for treason for possessing a paper complaining that Parliament could not express its views freely. He was found guilty, but not executed.[41]

In Ireland, Sir Thomas Wentworth proceeded even more brutally. Wentworth had been a leading critic of the king's policies in the English Parliament in the 1620s, but subsequently he became the leading figure on the Council of the North, bringing order to what was still the most turbulent region of England. In 1633 he was appointed lord deputy and instructed to do the same to Ireland. He dealt ruthlessly with his critics. Lord Mountnorris was sentenced to death by a court martial, but subsequently imprisoned, because he had complained to the king of Wentworth's management of the Irish revenue.

Wentworth intensified the legal challenges to the titles of Irish landowners, reviving plans (shelved since the 1580s) to extend the policy of plantation into Connacht. In the first three counties he visited, he declared that the king's title to the land was incontestable and so no investigation was needed, but in Galway he met serious resistance. The Old English were strong in Galway, many landowners had good proof of their titles, and the local magnate, the earl of Clanricarde, though a Catholic, was in favour at the English court. A jury composed of substantial gentlemen refused to recognise that the king had any title to the land. Bound over to appear in court at Dublin, the jurors sent several of their number to England to complain to the king. Although the jurors received a hearing, they failed to persuade the king and returned empty-handed to Ireland. They were tried in the Irish equivalent of Star Chamber for conspiracy and wilful refusal to recognise the king's title, fined £4000 each and imprisoned. In 1637 a new jury found that the king's title was good. Four-fifths of the land in County Galway was declared forfeit to the crown, but tenants proved hard to find.[42]

One reason why tenants were so reticent was that Wentworth alienated all strands of opinion in Ireland. Although he continued the policy of plantation, he had also held out the prospect of concessions to Catholics. In 1626, desperate for ready cash for his war against Spain, Charles had entered into negotiations with some of the Old English. (He embarked on similar negotiations with English Catholics at much the same time.)[43] In return for money, he offered a series of concessions that became known as the Graces. These included freedom of worship and renewed access to office. They also would extend to Ireland the statute of limitations recently passed by the English Parliament. This stated that proof of sixty years' possession of land was sufficient to establish legal title. This the Irish would find much easier than producing documentary proof of ownership. Had it been established in Ireland, the policy of confiscation and plantation would have slowed down dramatically and very many Catholics would have been secured in the ownership of their land. The Catholics made the first of three agreed payments but Charles failed to deliver his side of the bargain. Wentworth, suspicious of the New English, initially wooed the Old English by reopening negotiations, but again failed to deliver on the major points.

Wentworth's overtures to the Old English alarmed the New English. He began to threaten their legal titles to land as well, especially those who (like the corporation of London) had not brought over as many settlers as they had promised. Urged on by Laud, his friend and political ally, Wentworth seized and returned to the church ecclesiastical property confiscated at the Reformation. Together with the similar measures in

Scotland, this alarmed the owners of former church lands in England as well as in Ireland. Wentworth and Laud agreed on the need for 'thorough' government, the imposition of the king's will without fear or favour. Wentworth's personal commitment to the beauty of holiness may be doubted, but he did not hesitate to introduce a Laudian style into the Church of Ireland, because he knew that it was the king's will. He also, like most English officials in Ireland, spared few pains to increase his own fortune; self-service and service to the king were, in his eyes, perfectly compatible.

The Irish Church had been at least as Calvinist as the Church of England, probably more so. Its main statement of doctrine, the Articles of 1615, were more unequivocally Calvinist than the English Thirty-Nine Articles. By 1633, Charles, encouraged by Laud, had decided on the need for uniformity between his three kingdoms. The Irish Articles were unacceptable because of their content and because they differed from those of the English church. In 1634, despite the opposition of the primate, James Ussher, archbishop of Armagh, the Thirty-Nine Articles were introduced into Ireland, together with canons (laws) recently passed by the English Convocation, in which the Church of Ireland was not represented.[44] These developments angered the New English, many of whom came from the puritan end of the religious spectrum. They saw themselves as being in the front line of the struggle against popery and abhorred innovations which smacked of Rome, but which also distanced the Church of Ireland from the Ulster Scots, with whom they felt considerable affinity. This was compounded in 1639 when Wentworth ordered the Ulster Scots to dissociate themselves, on oath, from the actions of their Presbyterian brethren in Scotland.

In 1633 Charles I paid the first and only visit of his reign to Scotland, to be crowned. The fact that he waited eight years before doing so did not go unnoticed and reflected accurately the place of Scotland in his scale of priorities. Charles was shocked by the lack of 'decency' in the coronation ceremony, in St Giles's cathedral, in Edinburgh. He and Laud resolved that the order and seemliness that Laud was bringing to the English church should also be established in Scotland. After some discussion with Scottish bishops (and little or none with the Scottish nobility), Charles ordered in 1637 that a new prayer book should be introduced in Scotland. He never seems to have doubted that he possessed the necessary authority; he simply assumed that he possessed a supremacy over the Scottish Church similar to that which he enjoyed in England.[45] He does not seem to have anticipated opposition, assuming that his commands would be obeyed.

In a few places they were. In Brechin Cathedral the bishop read from the new book with barely a murmur of complaint from his flock, but the bishop had taken the precaution of ostentatiously bringing two loaded pistols into the pulpit.[46] Elsewhere there were riots, especially in Edinburgh. The book was denounced for introducing 'popish' ceremonies into the pure Reformed Church of Scotland, but it was also deeply resented as English and therefore alien. In issuing the book, Charles united against himself the most powerful forces in Scottish society, the nobles and the clergy. The nobles, apart from disliking the contents of the book, resented the fact that they had not been consulted. The clergy were the most powerful formers of opinion, whose control over the machinery of church discipline gave them a great hold over the people. They were furious at what they saw as the conspiracy, by the Scots bishops and their English counterparts, to foist a corrupt, decadent form of service on their church.

The prayer book provoked a national wave of revulsion and resistance. This found its most cogent expression in the Covenant, a promise to defend true religion (in the form of the Calvinist Scottish confession of faith of 1580) against errors and corruptions, which were enumerated and included several features of the new liturgy. The preamble to the printed version stated that changes in religion would be valid only if approved by both the Scots Parliament and the general assembly of the kirk.[47] (The latter had not met since 1618.) Every adult male was expected to take the Covenant. Some refused, and others took it under duress, but there can be no doubt that in early 1638 it reflected the general opinion of the Scottish Protestant nation. The word 'Covenant', with its echoes of God's special relationship with the Jews, implied that the Scots too were God's chosen people. Charles rightly saw the Covenant as a challenge to his authority and to that of the bishops through whom it was exercised, but he was uncertain about how best to respond. He was persuaded to call a general assembly, but this declared that episcopacy was an unlawful form of church government, which should therefore be abolished in Scotland – and (by implication) in England. Charles's efforts to bring the Church of Scotland into line with the Church of England had driven the Scots to call for the English church to be brought into line with that of Scotland.

The revolt (for that is what it was) against the prayer book marked the first serious defiance of the king's commands in any of his kingdoms; the assembly ignored the king's orders to disperse. In Ireland Wentworth united the disparate elements against him to a point where a deputation of New English Protestants, Old English Catholics and one Irish Catholic travelled to London at the end of 1640 to ask the Westminster Parliament to redress their grievances. But there was no serious resistance in Ireland, because Wentworth had at his disposal the only standing army in any of the three kingdoms.

England too had been quiet in the 1630s. Charles's reign had started with a series of tense and angry parliamentary sessions. The Commons were concerned at the king's growing use of non-parliamentary taxation and furious at Buckingham's incompetence as a war leader.[48] The first military expedition that he organised, an attack on Cadiz in 1625, was a deliberate echo of Sir Francis Drake's attack on the city, but degenerated into a fiasco. The ships arrived after a rough voyage; the sailors and soldiers were exhausted and ill from eating and drinking victuals and beer which were even more unfit for human consumption than usual. When they landed, hungry and thirsty, the first thing they found was a large store of wine. They broke in, drank their fill and were soon too drunk to fight, except among themselves. Their commanders had little choice but to load them back on to their ships and withdraw. They arrived home half-starved and sick.[49]

Unabashed Buckingham tried again. His next expedition rested on convoluted and, to some, impenetrable logic. Charles's marriage to Henrietta Maria had been intended to lead to an Anglo-French alliance against Spain, but Louis XIII and his ministers were preoccupied with the subjugation of the Huguenots. Buckingham tried to persuade the rulers of the great Huguenot port of La Rochelle to revolt against the king, which Buckingham believed would force Louis to ally with the English (whose stronger fleet would then help to put down the Huguenot rebels). The rulers of La Rochelle rejected Buckingham's suggestion that the Huguenots should lay their lives on the line for the benefit of the English, so an expedition was sent to encourage them to rise. The intention was to storm the citadel on the nearby Ile de Ré, but when the soldiers got there they realised that their scaling ladders were ten feet too short. After some scratching of heads the officers settled down for a siege, but when Louis's troops arrived the English commanders retreated, marching their men back along a narrow causeway, silhouetted against the sea. The French picked them off like ducks in a shooting gallery and they withdrew with heavy casualties. One contemporary declared that this was the most humiliating defeat the English had suffered since the loss of Normandy in 1453, but there were reports of popular rejoicing in London that Buckingham had been defeated.[50]

Still unabashed, Buckingham prepared for another expedition to La Rochelle, which had now embarked on a rebellion which was to end with the demolition of its fortifications. Parliament and the wider public looked on in disbelief. The French had indeed declared war, but against England rather than Spain. Getting embroiled in wars against both Spain and France was the equivalent of incurring the hostility of both the United States and the Soviet Union at the height of the Cold War. As one humiliating failure followed another, observers struggled to understand why the king alone seemed unaware that Buckingham was a disaster. Some blamed it on witchcraft; hence the murder of the duke's astrologer, Dr Lamb.[51] It was simpler than that. Buckingham remained sublimely confident in his own abilities. He blamed bad luck and the niggardliness of Parliament. He was sure that the next throw of the dice would see him vindicated and triumphant, and then the people would cheer him as they had after the failure of the Spanish match. And so long as the duke was confident, the king was too.[52] He accepted Buckingham's explanations for failure and continued to be swept along by the older man's breezy ebullience. If this was a partnership, the king was the junior partner. Some joked that the king was in great favour with the duke. On one occasion, when the king was at a play, Buckingham appeared at the start of the second act. Without consulting the king, the players performed the first act again for the duke's benefit.[53]

Charles's perception of Parliament owed much to Buckingham. In 1624 the duke had managed Parliament with some success. He had cast his patronage net widely and enrolled people of diverse religious and political views as his clients. As criticism mounted, he became angry and impatient, and concentrated his patronage on those who were unswervingly loyal to him, especially after his impeachment in 1626. Charles saw criticism of his ministers as aimed at himself. He declared that he would not allow his servants to be questioned in Parliament, especially one so great as the duke.[54] Like his father after 1610, Charles became convinced that a group of 'popular' and 'puritan' MPs was determined to destroy the authority of the monarchy. He saw criticism as conspiracy – a Presbyterian and republican plot, a mirror image of the popular belief in a popish and absolutist plot.[55] Such a view might seem paranoid; it could more plausibly be argued that MPs feared desperately for the future of Parliaments. But there was evidence that seemed to support Charles's view. There was the revival of impeachment, which was used first against alleged criminals, but then to remove leading advisers of the king. James showed some complicity in this in the cases of Bacon and Cranfield, but Charles dissolved Parliament in 1626 to put an end to the proceedings against Buckingham.

While impeachment threatened to deprive the king of his power to choose his own ministers, the Commons refused for the first time in well over a century to grant tonnage and poundage for life to an incoming king. For Charles this showed a clear intention to deny him the money he needed to rule the country – and to fight the war against Spain that the Commons had supported in 1624. (The Commons had in fact envisaged a rather different war and expected it to be competently run.) In addition, from 1621 the Commons had set up investigative committees, which claimed the right to summon witnesses and demand documents, and to imprison those who refused to testify. No House of Commons had claimed such rights before, so this represented a novel interference in the processes of the king's government.[56]

By the end of 1626 Charles was thoroughly disillusioned with Parliament. In the next two years the spiral of mutual distrust accelerated to a point where it seemed out of control. The forced loan, collected in lieu of the subsidies that the 1626 Parliament had intended to grant, added to fears of arbitrary government, but so did the debates within the council on how the loan should be collected. These debates were leaked, and found their way into the newsletters, with a frequency that suggests that those opposed to more arbitrary methods were deliberately appealing to a wider public.[57] In the 1626 session there had been more food for thought for those who feared for Parliaments. Charles told the Commons that he would call Parliaments only if they were 'fruitful' and advised them to 'encourage' him to continue with them. One of his spokesmen warned against provoking the king to embark on 'new counsels', pointedly remarking that on the Continent assemblies that had not cooperated with their kings had disappeared; there were rumours that the king intended to use armed force against Parliament.[58]

Further evidence of 'new counsels' emerged in debates in the council on how to treat those who refused the forced loan; some, including followers of Buckingham, urged that they be imprisoned, conscripted for the army or even hanged.[59] Some councillors argued that subjects were obliged to contribute to the king's needs, adding that in a land without fortresses, and with an obedient people, there was no danger of rebellion.[60] Arminian clergymen preached that unquestioning obedience to the king's commands was a religious duty; in wartime, all that the subject possessed should be at the king's disposal.[61] After the 1626 Parliament there was a proposal that the freeholders of each country should be assembled and asked to 'vote' the king the money that the Commons had intended to grant – Parliaments, it seemed, had to be earned, through obedience.[62]

When Charles was persuaded to call a new Parliament, in 1628, it met in a state of high anxiety. The remnants of the forces raised for the La Rochelle expedition had been quartered in the south east over the winter, where they had been very unruly and aggressive towards civilians. There were fears that Buckingham might use military force to coerce Parliament; it was reported that strange 'engines' had been brought into the Tower. Charles told the Houses that if they did not do their duty, by voting money to fight the common enemy, he would have to use other methods. They should not take this as a threat, he added, 'for he scorned to threaten any but his equals'.[63] The Commons bewailed their failure to make the king understand them and decided to present a Petition of Right, which claimed to restate old laws, but in fact sought to make new. It included a condemnation of martial law – how else, the king might ask, could he maintain discipline among his forces, when the common law did not recognise mutiny and desertion as criminal? It also stated that the council had no power whatever to commit people to gaol without showing cause.

From the king's point of view this last statement was historically wrong and an assault on his prerogative, one which would deprive him of the means to deal with traitors and assassins. It confirmed his belief in a conspiracy to reduce him to a cipher, a king in name only. He did his utmost to avoid giving his assent to the petition, but at last, under pressure from the majority in both Houses, he gave in; the Commons promptly completed a bill granting him five subsidies. They had hitherto held back from attacking Buckingham, but now did so, in debates of escalating fury and emotion.[64] When the House drew up a remonstrance denouncing Buckingham's misdeeds, the king prorogued Parliament, to protect his favourite.[65] Soon after, Buckingham was stabbed to death by John Felton, a disgruntled (and probably deranged) army officer, who had a copy of the remonstrance in his pocket. When he heard the news Charles, prostrated by grief, took to his bed; Londoners danced for joy in the streets.[66]

Buckingham's murder added a further strand to Charles's hostility to Parliament; he held the Commons morally responsible for his friend's death. It also freed him from a decade of psychological subordination and enabled him to emerge as a person in his own right. One positive result of this was that he fell in love with his queen. Another was that he was now prepared to listen to advisers other than Buckingham. The second La Rochelle expedition was abandoned and so, in practice, were the wars against France and Spain, although peace was not made until 1630. Charles was even persuaded to allow Parliament to reconvene in 1629, but the session merely confirmed his prejudices. The complaints and criticism continued and Charles decided to dissolve Parliament. When Black Rod arrived with the king's summons, instead of the Commons trooping up to the Lords, the speaker was held down in his chair while the House passed resolutions condemning Arminianism and the collection of tonnage and poundage without Parliament's consent.

This expression of rage and frustration offered Charles a rare public relations advantage, which he seized. He issued a declaration, justifying his decision to dissolve Parliament and highlighting the deplorable scenes at the end of the session. The Commons, he said, had tried 'to erect a universal, overswaying power to themselves, which belongs only to us and not to them'. He wished to give emotions a chance to calm down and to give his people time to see his government as it really was, rather than accepting the views of his more malevolent critics.[67]

Charles had become disillusioned with Parliament by the end of 1626. He had recalled it partly because some of his advisers urged him to, partly because it seemed one of the better ways of securing money for war. He had asked a French envoy how the French kings had got rid of the Estates General; the envoy replied that they had not done so in the middle of a war.[68] Now, in 1629, with hostilities at an end, the well-informed Venetian resident believed that Charles intended never to call Parliament again.[69]

This seemed plausible enough. Financially, Charles could get by on what he had and his advisers were to find other sources of revenue. His income was now sufficient for his needs, provided there was no war. He was able to finish the Queen's House at Greenwich and embellish the Banqueting House in Whitehall, adding Rubens's painted ceiling of James I being received into heaven. War was unlikely. As England was an island, its rulers could opt out of European power politics. Admittedly, the Stuarts' peripheral involvement in the Thirty Years War had not been popular with the English public in the 1620s, as Catholic forces carried all before them in Germany. In the 1630s the picture improved. Gustavus Adolphus of Sweden won spectacular victories against the Catholics and in 1635 Catholic France reluctantly entered the war on the 'Protestant' side. The English still complained of Charles's failure to support continental Protestantism, but Charles (unlike his puritan subjects) felt little sense of solidarity with foreign Reformed churches. After four turbulent years he felt that he, and his subjects, needed a little peace.

If most of the next decade was quiet compared to the 1620s, this was due primarily to the absence of Parliament. In addition, some of the divisive issues of the late 1620s had disappeared: Buckingham, the mismanagement of the war, the threat of a military coup. But others remained, notably non-parliamentary taxation and Arminianism; new fiscal devices added to the sense of resentment. But without Parliament, criticism of the crown had no obvious voice. The press was censored and the authors of a few anti-episcopal pamphlets were brutally punished by Star Chamber. There were occasional riots in the forests and fens, but these did little to disturb the general tranquillity. A few hardy souls refused to pay ship money, but the verdict in Hampden's case showed that resistance was useless. Others tried to obstruct the tax by arguing about their rating, but these disputes were settled and ship money became one of the most successful of early modern taxes, collected far more quickly than the subsidy – and almost in full. Until 1639 at least 90 per cent was collected each year, although a little more slowly each time. In 1639 the king asked for a much reduced sum: 80 per cent had been collected by the following spring. Only in 1640, when the king again asked for a larger sum, did collection collapse, with nearly 75 per cent remaining uncollected.[70]

Diaries and correspondence show that there was considerable discontent, about ship money and Arminianism especially.[71] But there were few riots and no rebellions. England was no longer a militarised society and the English had become used to dealing with their kings through Parliament or the law courts. As the courts would not give them redress, they had to wait until the king called a Parliament.[72] The only alternative (which many puritans took) was emigration, which had the effect of removing the most discontented people from England. As Clarendon later wrote, the English now seemed to enjoy 'the greatest calm and the fullest measure of felicity that any people in any age for so long time together have been blessed with'.[73]

The lack of reaction to Charles's 'personal rule' showed how docile the English had become. As far as England was concerned, it seemed that Charles was right to ignore opposition and to pay no heed to public opinion. Without the distraction of Parliament, he was able to retreat into an artificial world where all was order and peace. His court became more formal and more remote. Access was restricted, and the nobility and gentry were urged to leave London and live on their estates. The culture of the court was refined but also removed from reality. Court masques celebrated the love of the king and queen, which was shown calming storms and bringing order out of chaos.[74] Policy debates were carried on with little reference to the wider public. The king assumed that he could command his people as easily as he commanded the elements in a masque. In 1640, as disobedience mounted on all sides, the privy council responded to complaints that people were not paying ship money by saying blithely that people would pay, 'there having been a public judgment passed for the king'.[75]

By the summer of 1640 such confidence seemed sadly misplaced. The cancer of disaffection had spread to England, but its source lay in Scotland. The Covenant was a resounding expression of national resentment, but it was not a standard of rebellion. The Scots wanted to negotiate, not to embark on a war against their richer neighbour. Indeed, they were at pains to stress that their dispute was not with the English people but with a small 'Canterburian faction'. Charles, however, was not disposed to negotiate with 'rebels'. As always, he was convinced that he was right, so there was nothing to discuss. In 1639 he began to gather an army to teach the Scots a lesson; it was the first time since 1323 that a king had prepared for war without summoning a Parliament. He looked everywhere for money, organising a collection among the English Catholics, who had most to fear from the combined puritan forces of England and Scotland. News of the collection soon leaked out.[76] Great efforts were made to mobilise the county militias and to raise the money needed to pay them – but then, after some inconclusive skirmishing, the king changed his mind and came to terms with the Scots in the Pacification of Berwick. Both sides saw this as little more than a truce and it soon transpired that the king understood its terms very differently from the Scots. Painfully aware that Charles's word could not be relied on, the Scots became more defiant. In 1640 both the Scottish Parliament and the general assembly met without a summons from the king, and the Parliament appointed a committee to act on its behalf when it was not in session – in effect an alternative government.[77] The king now had no effective authority in Scotland.

Charles's response was to gather another army and to call an English Parliament, for the first time since 1629. The so-called Short Parliament was willing to vote money, but only in return for substantial concessions, including the abolition of ship money. Charles refused, and resumed his attempts to recruit forces, but with less success than the previous year. Lords lieutenant and militia officers, who in 1639 had made great efforts, only to see them go to waste, were less enthusiastic a second time.[78] Disaffection was spreading. The City, outraged by its recent treatment, rebuffed a request for a loan.[79] Scottish propaganda won

considerable sympathy among English people resentful of religious innovation. The increasingly independent stance taken by the Scots made
the English more confident that they could defy the king with impunity.
Tax refusal spread, ship money yields plummeted. There was also widespread refusal to pay coat and conduct money, yet another medieval
device resurrected in the hope of paying for the army.

In a similarly medieval gesture, Charles summoned the English peers
to attend him in person and to bring armed men. A few refused to
come, many sent excuses (illness would appear to have been rife among
the peers at this time), and those who did come brought few soldiers
and advised the king to come to terms with the Scots.[80] As always,
Charles ignored unpalatable advice. He cobbled together a ramshackle
army of reluctant militiamen; some units mutinied or lynched their
officers.[81] This force marched uncertainly northwards, where it faced a
Scottish army, fired up by the sermons of the Presbyterian clergy and
commanded by the experienced David Leslie. It was no contest. The
Scots swept the English aside at Newburn, their first major victory since
Bannockburn in 1314. They marched into England, occupied Northumberland and Durham, and demanded to be paid £850 a day in cash for
their subsistence. They also demanded negotiations, with both the king
and the English Parliament.

For Charles this was a humiliating defeat. He summoned Parliament
reluctantly, but he had no choice. The elections, like those in the spring,
were fiercely contested, with political and religious issues playing a
significant part in the electors' decisions. The Houses assembled on
3 November 1640 with long lists of grievances; the king's exceptional
position of weakness gave them a bargaining strength that they intended
to exploit to the full. They were in no hurry to reach agreement with
the Scots, whose presence in the north east offered a guarantee of
Parliament's continued existence. The Scots insisted that any settlement
had to involve Parliament as well as the king, and that they should
also have a say in any settlement between the king and his English
subjects. Experience of dealing with Charles had taught them that he
would keep an agreement only if he lacked the power to break it. They
demanded that in future neither England nor Scotland should make
war without the consent of their respective Parliaments. And they
demanded that episcopacy be abolished in England; their church could

be truly secure only if the English church were brought into line with that of Scotland.[82]

There was considerable sympathy in the English Parliament for both these demands. While some believed that Charles was a basically good king led astray by evil counsellors, others believed that his power had to be curbed to prevent a recurrence of rule without Parliament. Similarly, a significant proportion of MPs believed that the only way to root Laudianism out of the church was to get rid of bishops. But many disagreed, not because they had any affection for Laud and Laudianism, but because they feared that abolishing the church hierarchy would seriously weaken hierarchy, subordination and order in society at large: 'if we make a parity in the church we must come to a parity in the commonwealth'.[83] They were also concerned at the activities of the Presbyterian clergy, a number of whom accompanied the Scottish delegation to London and worked with militant English puritans to whip up popular support for the abolition of episcopacy 'root and branch'. Resentment grew at Scottish attempts to dictate to the English and there were complaints against their troops in the north east. As the months passed, hostility towards the Scots mounted and in May 1641 their delegation asked permission to return home, with most of their demands still unmet. Negotiations continued desultorily for some months and the Scots army finally left England on 25 September.[84]

Meanwhile, progress towards the redress of grievances was painfully slow. Almost the first action of the Commons was to impeach Wentworth, recently raised to the peerage as earl of Strafford. When Charles was trying to gather an army in 1639, he had summoned Wentworth from Ireland to command it, because he could rely on Wentworth to fight to the utmost – too many peers urged compromise. The earl gave his king robust advice: Charles was, he told him, 'loose and absolved from all rules of government'. With the safety of his kingdom at stake, he should do whatever he judged necessary – exhilarating counsel to a fundamentally weak king with an exaggerated sense of his own authority.[85] Strafford also advised the king to bring over a predominantly Catholic army from Ireland – he saw the Catholics as more reliable than the New English – to bring 'this kingdom' to heel. He presumably meant Scotland, but 'this kingdom' could easily be construed as applying to England.[86] Although the 'Irish popish army' remained in Ireland in 1641, Charles refused to disband it while the Scots army remained in England, keeping alive fears that it might be used against his English subjects.[87]

Strafford's uncompromising stance made him many enemies. The Scots saw him as their most dangerous foe, as did those English politicians who were clandestinely in touch with the Scots. These were playing a dangerous game – comforting and abetting the king's enemies was treason – but they saw the Scots as offering the only hope of salvation. They also believed that Strafford, alone among the king's advisers, was capable of urging him to use violence against his opponents in England. (Laud, who was even more hated, was also impeached in 1641, but not brought to trial until 1644.) Strafford knew that some English politicians (including the most active figure in the Commons, John Pym) had been in contact with the Scots, and there were rumours that he planned to accuse them of inciting the Scots to invade.[88]

For both the Scots and their English allies, it was essential to destroy Strafford before he destroyed them. They had a procedure ready to hand in impeachment, but securing a conviction proved difficult. They wanted the earl dead, so had to prosecute him on a charge that carried the death penalty – treason. But the law defined treason as an act against the king's person. The prosecutors argued that to give advice that alienated the people from the king in effect put his person in danger. The Lords, who acted as judges in impeachment cases, were not impressed by this argument. The proceedings petered out, so the Commons tried another tactic, a bill of attainder. Such bills were often passed after unsuccessful rebellions and declared that certain named rebels were guilty of treason; their lives and property were forfeit and, in the case of peers, their blood was tainted and they were stripped of their peerages. In such cases, the guilt of those condemned was normally obvious, as they had been taken in arms. This time it was not. A significant minority in the Commons and a majority in the Lords regarded the bill as no better than legislative murder. The bill passed the Commons but stuck in the Lords – until large and threatening crowds around Westminster persuaded them to pass it. The crowds moved to Whitehall. The queen and her Catholic ladies rushed to their confessors, convinced that the people would break in and massacre them. The king, fearing for his family, gave his assent to the bill and signed Strafford's death warrant.[89]

On 12 May 1641 a crowd estimated at two hundred thousand watched the earl's execution on Tower Hill.

Strafford's death marked a watershed in Charles's relationship with Parliament. He had made every effort to save the earl and had even agreed to take several of his leading critics onto the privy council – Pym and the earls of Bedford, Warwick and Essex. But Essex was not prepared to spare Strafford's life – 'Stone dead hath no fellow', he declared – and the deal was off.[90] Charles felt deeply responsible for Strafford's death. His remark, as he signed the death warrant, that Strafford's condition was happier than his own, might savour of self-pity, but there can be no doubt that he felt deeply ashamed – and very angry.[91] An element of blood feud was added to his contest with the leaders of the two Houses; he wanted them dead and they knew it.

To save themselves they had to reduce his power to a point where he would no longer be able to harm them. Before Strafford's execution only two significant measures had been passed to limit the king's powers. The Triennial Act (following a similar measure in Scotland) decreed that the king had to call Parliament at least once every three years, and that it had to sit for at least fifty days; there were to be no more eleven-year periods without Parliament and no more Short Parliaments. The Act also made provision for elections if the king failed to summon Parliament. A second Act made it illegal for the king to dissolve the present Parliament without its own consent – the king could not save Strafford by a snap dissolution. In the weeks after Strafford's death Parliament swept away most of the fiscal apparatus of the 1630s: ship money, impositions, knighthood fines, monopolies and the like. It was now illegal to collect tonnage and poundage without Parliament's consent. Little remained of the king's personal and prerogative revenues, so he was now almost totally dependent on parliamentary grants. Some of the judicial apparatus of the personal rule was abolished too, including Star Chamber and the church courts. In a few short weeks, with little disagreement, the Houses remedied many of the grievances that had concerned MPs in 1640.

But there was no reconciliation, no return to normal. On one hand, the king did not want it. He regarded the concessions that he had been forced to make as unjust and dishonourable, and he made his dislike of some of them very clear. He longed for revenge, for his own humiliation and for the death of Strafford, and revenge could come only through military force. Again and again, in 1641–42, he (and the queen) plotted to use force against his opponents. Again and again, he was found out; it got to the point where, even if he was not implicated in violence, his subjects suspected that he was. He raised a thousand soldiers, ostensibly to serve as volunteers for Portugal against Spain, but really to spring Strafford from the Tower. Unfortunately, he had not told this story to the Portuguese ambassador; so, when asked about the troops, the latter knew nothing about it. The plan had to be abandoned.[92] Charles also twice planned to make use of the English forces, who were disconsolately watching the Scots in the north, first to secure Portsmouth, where he hoped to bring in a French army, and then to march on Parliament to demand their pay. Neither plot succeeded and the officers implicated in the first rushed to testify to Parliament.[93]

Much of the impetus for an appeal to force came from the queen, who could not understand why her husband allowed his subjects to disobey him. There was much talk in the queen's circle of raising troops to teach Parliament a lesson. Details were passed to Pym by Lady Carlisle, a lady in waiting and confidante of the queen since the 1620s.[94] This information, which he could not divulge without revealing the source, reinforced Pym's conviction that compromise with Charles was impossible and that his power had to be reduced to prevent him from harming his critics and his people.

Pym identified two key prerogatives: the king's power to command the armed forces; and his right to choose his advisers. He urged that the king be made to share both with Parliament. The former was crucial because of the king's obvious eagerness to suppress his enemies by force. The latter went to the heart of decision-making. It was conventional to assume that the king could do no wrong and that any royal misdeeds were due to bad advice from his ministers. If the king were properly 'counselled', good measures should emerge. But Charles was unwilling to appoint ministers whom he disliked or distrusted. He believed that he should employ only those who had done something to deserve it.[95] Only the hope of saving Strafford's life had led him to agree to appoint Bedford and the others. So Pym persuaded the Commons first to ask

Charles to appoint acceptable counsellors and then to demand that he
should do so. There was also the danger that ministers who initially
seemed acceptable to Parliament might be misled or corrupted. Something had to be done to ensure that they remained accountable to
Parliament. By June 1642 Parliament was demanding that all important
policy decisions should be reached in the privy council, and that all
councillors who approved those decisions should sign their names. As
one MP remarked, evil counsels tended to be whispered in corners.
Parliament wanted to bring counsel into the open.[96]

In June 1641 Pym persuaded both Houses to petition the king to
remove evil counsellors and appoint such 'as the Parliament may have
cause to confide in'.[97] When Charles rebuffed this proposal, saying he
knew of no evil counsellors, the Houses showed no inclination to press
the matter, especially as he had agreed to disband the English army.
Strafford was dead, Laud and some of the judges were in the Tower, and
most of the other advisers of the 1630s had scattered. The king retained
most of the traditional powers that he needed to run the government,
but MPs were happy with that – that was his job. They had secured
regular Parliaments and had made the king so dependent on Parliament
for money that he would have to heed its wishes in the future. But that
assumed that he would not use force to renege on his concessions. Pym
and others were quite convinced that he intended to do just that.

For the moment, they could not carry the majority of the Commons
with them. The withdrawal of the Scots army and the disbanding of the
English and Irish Catholic armies removed the immediate threat of
military force, but there was anxiety when Charles went to Scotland in
August. He offered the Scots extensive concessions, including a say for
the Scottish Parliament in the choice of ministers in Scotland. (The
English must have wondered why the king had not granted this in
England as well.) In return he hoped for Scottish military assistance
against the English, or to detach the Scottish parliamentary leadership
from their brethren in England; he may also have hoped for evidence
of English politicians' dealings with the Scots.[98] His credibility was
reduced by the 'Incident', a mysterious attempt to kidnap or assassinate
leading Covenanters. There was much evidence suggesting that Charles
was implicated and no clear evidence that he was not.[99] His English
critics feared the worst. The English Parliament had sent a committee

to Scotland to keep an eye on the king and had also appointed a committee to act on Parliament's behalf during the summer recess. This followed another Scottish precedent, but it was also a response to the king's failure to make any reasonable provision for government in his absence, which almost invited the Houses to take the first steps towards an active role in government.

While the king was in Scotland, the situation was transformed by rebellion in Ireland. Wentworth had achieved the near-impossible feat of driving Catholics (even Gaelic Catholics) to join with Protestants in appealing to the English Parliament. The Catholics soon realised that this had been a mistake. Appealing to Westminster implied that the English Parliament could legislate for Ireland and indeed almost invited it to do so. Catholics and Protestants agreed on the need to get rid of Strafford and agreed in deploring his methods of government. But some of the case against Strafford rested on his alleged partiality towards Catholics. The Irish Catholics became anxious about the fierce anti-Catholicism of both English and Scots. They felt isolated and threatened, and turned to the king. Charles was willing to reopen the question of the Graces yet again. The Catholics of Ireland constituted the one major group among his subjects who had an interest in maintaining his power, because they needed his protection against the Protestant majorities in England and Scotland. But, for all his kind words, Charles could not deliver without provoking a furious outcry from the Protestants of all three kingdoms.

The Catholics returned to Ireland, convinced that the king's power was crumbling and that an Anglo-Scottish crusade against Irish Catholicism was only a matter of time. As this news spread, some in Ulster decided on a pre-emptive strike. Catholics rose up and attacked their Protestant landlords and neighbours. Deeds and rent-rolls were burned, houses were looted and many Protestants were slaughtered, although not nearly as many as English press reports made out. As the revolt spread into Leinster, some of the Old English joined in, either because they were coerced by Irish tenants or because they saw it as a less bad option than waiting for the English and Scots to come.[100] Despite the fears of Ireland's governors, there was no attempt to take Dublin Castle,[101] but the revolt spread throughout Ireland and in October 1642 a provisional government, the Confederation of Kilkenny, was set up at the behest of the Catholic clergy.

Back in England, the Houses reconvened on 21 October 1641, after their summer recess. News of the rebellion arrived on 1 November. For Charles it was an unmitigated disaster. It wrecked his attempts to drive a wedge between the English and Scottish Parliaments, which now agreed on joint action to help their beleaguered co-religionists in Ireland. It also raised, in an acute and urgent form, the question of the king's prerogatives. Hitherto, English MPs and peers had been able to avoid confronting the issues raised by Pym – the king's choice of advisers and control of the armed forces. Now that an army had to be raised to put down the Irish, they had to decide whether the king, with his present advisers, could be trusted not to use it against Parliament and people. Pym argued that he could not and laid details of the second army plot before the Commons. News of the Incident did not make MPs inclined to trust the king either. After an emotional debate, the Commons resolved on 8 November that, unless the king appointed councillors whom they could trust, they would provide for Ireland without him.[102] The wisdom of this move seemed to be confirmed when news came, on 3 December, that one of the rebels, Sir Phelim O'Neill, claimed to have a commission from the king to take up arms against Parliament. The story was apparently untrue, but (as atrocity stories continued to come out of Ireland) it did Charles great political harm.

The Commons now passed a bill to vest control of the militia, army and navy in Parliament. The committee appointed to sit during the recess had deployed the militia while Charles was in Scotland, but the bill was still the most fundamental assault yet on the king's prerogative; the Lords received it coolly, as they had several measures from the Commons. When the Lords had opposed Strafford's attainder bill, the Commons' leaders had put pressure on them by mobilising popular support; angry crowds had overborne the resistance of the Lords and the king to Strafford's execution. Now the Commons' leaders used similar tactics. On 8 November, the day the Commons resolved to provide for Ireland without the king, Pym and his allies put before the House the Grand Remonstrance, a long denunciation of the king's misdeeds since 1625. These were blamed on courtiers, Arminians (the 'corrupt part of the clergy') and papists. Among the proposed remedies were that the king should employ councillors acceptable to Parliament (without which the Commons would feel unable to vote him any money), and that a programme of church reform should be drawn up by 'a general synod of the most grave, pious, learned and judicious divines of this island' – that is to say, Scots as well as English – 'assisted with some from foreign parts, professing the same religion with us'.103 In other words, the king was to be stripped of his powers and the Church of England was to be brought into line with the Calvinist international.

The Grand Remonstrance was an extraordinary document. Unlike most addresses, it was endorsed by the Commons alone; it stated that no good could be expected from the Lords while the bishops and Catholic peers sat there. And it was addressed not to the king but to the people. On 22 November the Commons debated whether to print it. Feelings ran high, swords were drawn and the motion was carried by only eleven votes – 159 to 148. This was much the closest division on a major issue so far, in a full House, and it demonstrated that the king now had a 'party' in the Commons. When Charles summoned Parliament in the autumn of 1640 he was isolated. He had too little support to fight off a Scots invasion and certainly not enough to fight a civil war. In the first half of 1641 there had been significant opposition in the Commons to the attainder bill and a bill to abolish episcopacy, and considerable hostility to the Scots, but the reform programme of the summer had been carried through with virtual unanimity.

It was only after Parliament reconvened in October that a substantial Royalist party emerged. This owed little to anything that the king did. At the start of the winter session he was still in Scotland (throughout the 1640s Charles tended to garner most support when he did least). It owed something to the continued assault on the bishops and the existing liturgy of the church. In December 1641 a crowd smashed the altar, organ and several tombs in Westminster Abbey. The Commons had failed to censure clergy who did not use Common Prayer: indeed, the Grand Remonstrance initially included a condemnation of 'errors and superstitions' in the prayer book.104 There was also anxiety at the multiplication of separatist congregations, especially in London. The emergence of a 'Royalist Party' owed much to the fact that the Commons had moved from condemning abuses of the king's authority to challenging his central prerogatives. A king who could not command the army or choose his own advisers was hardly a king at all. The reforms of the summer could be seen as restoring the constitution to its proper state; the Commons' new demands threatened to change it radically, which many, probably most, MPs did not want. Most seriously of all, these threats of radical religious and constitutional change seemed to fit ominously into a larger picture of the subversion of the whole of the religious, political and social order.

The assembly of the Long Parliament had aroused a wide variety of expectations. Eleven years and more of grievances would be redressed, wrongs of all sorts would be righted. Parliament was seen as the embodiment of justice. As press censorship collapsed, the English were presented with an unprecedented deluge of news and opinion. Those who presented petitions to Parliament – and there were around one thousand dealing with religious issues alone – sought additional publicity by having them printed.[105] Many were not prepared to wait for Parliament and took matters into their own hands. Enclosures were pulled down, deer parks were plundered, manorial records were burned. In many churches altar rails were ripped out and stained-glass windows broken.

Far from condemning this self-help, the Commons seemed to encourage it. In May 1641, as the proceedings against Strafford approached their climax, the Commons drew up a 'Protestation', which Protestants were invited to subscribe. This was essentially a promise to defend the 'true reformed Protestant religion' as expressed in the 'doctrine' (not the liturgy) of the Church of England, together with the power and privileges of Parliament and the rights of the subject, against 'popery and popish innovation'. The only reference to the king was the promise that subscribers should also defend 'his majesty's royal person, honour and estate' – there was no reference to his powers or prerogatives.

Many took the Protestation voluntarily. In the more polarised circumstances of 1642 Parliament ordered that it should be taken by all adult male Protestants. More than any other parliamentary statement before the Grand Remonstrance, the Protestation identified popery and papists as the enemies of the Protestant nation.[106] It authorised action, even violent action, against those identified by Parliament as the enemies of the people. Even before the Irish rebellion raised fears of popish violence to fever pitch, there was extensive violence against papists, Laudian clerics and the most active and vociferous supporters of the king. At times, as on the Essex-Suffolk border in August 1642, attacks on Catholics' houses degenerated into something approaching general plunder.[107]

Many conservative gentlemen, inside and outside Parliament, regarded these developments with alarm. The country seemed to be sliding into anarchy; but, instead of seeking to restore order, the Commons' leaders encouraged riot and plunder. As their impatience with the Lords mounted, the Commons passed (and printed) resolutions that could only inflame popular opinion against the upper House: for example, that anyone who opposed the militia bill was an enemy to the safety of the kingdom.[108] Pym and his 'junto' were equally intolerant of opposition within the Commons. It was natural to use the language of anti-popery when attacking innovations in the church and the perceived threat of royal absolutism. Anti-popery was a defining part of English Protestant identity; it was as natural for good Protestants to be against popery as it was for good Christians to be against sin.

Anti-popery was a powerful but not a precise weapon. In Protestant eyes, 'popery' embraced phenomena which were identified with Catholicism, but could also be identified with non-Catholics – for example seeking to make the monarchy absolute. It was all too easy to label Protestant opponents as 'popishly inclined' or 'favourers of popery' – and those who were so labelled deeply resented it.[109] This was a way of browbeating and intimidating those who did not share Pym's analysis of what was wrong and what needed to be done. He described the measures he promoted as essential for the Protestant interest, which suggested that those who opposed them were not good Protestants. He was also eager to decide issues by votes, which flouted the Commons' traditional preference for consensus.[110] There was much resentment of his methods in the Commons and some MPs stayed away in protest. In December 1641 the king, aware that the tide of opinion was running in his favour, issued a proclamation for all MPs to return to the House after Christmas; he now saw a full House as being in his interests.[111]

It made sound political sense for the king to encourage the Royalist backlash in the Commons and to encourage the Lords' opposition to the militia bill and other measures. The more he could pose as the

defender of the traditional order in church and state, the more support
he would attract. But Charles still harboured dreams of reasserting his
authority by force. The cycle of distrust accelerated and the threat of
violence grew after he returned from Scotland to London on 25 November. He re-entered the capital with a large escort of ruffianly soldiers,
who threatened to teach the citizens to respect the king.

On 21 December, in the annual London common council elections,
supporters of Pym's 'junto' gained a large majority. The king responded
by appointing Colonel Lunsford, a soldier with a thuggish reputation,
lieutenant of the Tower. Fearing that he might shell the city, people
took to the streets in their thousands; after three days the king removed
Lunsford, but the crowds remained active. The Grand Remonstrance
had blamed the Lords' obstructionism on the Catholic peers and the
bishops. The former no longer attended, but on 28 December a large
crowd prevented most of the bishops – easily identifiable by their dress
– from taking their seats. The Lords protested, but Pym replied 'God
forbid the House of Commons should proceed in any way to dishearten
people to obtain their just desires in such a way'.[112] The next few days
saw repeated affrays in the streets between soldiers and citizens. The
French ambassador remarked that in any other country the city would
have been consumed by fire and bloodshed.[113] On 4 January 1642 Charles
counter-attacked. With 400 armed men he marched from Whitehall,
into the Commons, demanding that they hand over Pym and four other
MPs, whom he had 'impeached' on charges of seeking to deprive him
of his rightful powers, alienating his people and making war against
him. But Pym had been tipped off by Lady Carlisle (and others),[114] and
the five were nowhere to be seen. The king did his best to beat a dignified
retreat, with cries of 'privilege of Parliament' ringing in his ears.

Even by Charles I's standards, the attempt to arrest the Five Members
was incredibly foolish; it may have been triggered by rumours of a
plan to impeach the queen.[115] His strategy of fostering the Royalist
backlash in the Commons fell apart as MPs united in condemning this
invasion of their chamber and their privileges. To make matters worse,
Charles also tried to arrest a peer, Lord Mandeville, which enraged the
Lords. The attempt led to a revolution in the government of London.
Although supporters of Pym's junto now dominated the annually
elected common council, the day-to-day running of the City was in

the hands of the lord mayor and aldermen, who served for life. On 4 January the common council met and, on the orders of the Commons, set up a 'committee of safety'. That night there was panic in the City, with rumours that the Cavaliers would fire the City and the papists would massacre the citizens.[116]

Next day the king came to the City to demand the persons of the five MPs, who had taken refuge there; he was met with great cries of 'privilege of Parliament' as he passed through the streets. On the 6th the trained bands assembled without a summons from the lord mayor, and the committee of safety, ignoring the protests of the aldermen, took over the government of the city. One of its first acts was to change the membership of the lieutenancy, which commanded the city militia.[117] Thousands of Londoners armed to defend themselves. The king saw this as a direct threat to his person and safety.[118] On 10 January, he and his family left London for Hampton Court. He was not to see his capital again until he was brought there for trial. His loss of control of London, before hostilities had even started, was a potentially crippling blow.

As far as Charles was concerned, civil war had already started: his final charge against the Five Members was 'that they have traitorously conspired to levy, and actually have levied, war against the king'.[119] In leaving London he left Parliament in control of the normal machinery of government. Once the bishops and Royalist peers had left, the Lords passed the militia bill and the resultant 'ordinance' was declared to have the full force of statute. As Parliament removed unreliable commanders from the militia, the king (like a medieval rebel baron) appealed to peers and gentry to join him. Who, one might ask, was rebelling against whom?[120] Charles tried to gain admission to Hull, which possessed the largest arsenal outside London, but the gates were shut against him. As weeks turned to months, each side used the press to blame the other for the breakdown. Parliament continued to extend its demands. It called for a say in the education and marriage of the royal children, and for the king to create an international Protestant alliance against 'the pope and his adherents'. While Parliament continued to stress the threat from the papists, the king played heavily on the threat of revolution from below. In appealing to the people, he said, Parliament had unleashed a force that would eventually destroy it, leading to a 'dark equal chaos of confusion'.[121]

In June the king sent commissions to those he regarded as his supporters; Parliament responded by resolving to raise an army. The king
formally raised his standard at Nottingham on 22 August. It was promptly
blown down, which was not seen as a good omen. Meanwhile around
the country zealous supporters of king or Parliament seized key towns,
castles and bridges.[122] Although many in the provinces expressed horror
and bewilderment at the political breakdown in London and tried to
avoid taking sides, inexorably the rival demands on the allegiance of the
gentry forced them to choose. Gradually the war spread, with few areas
of the country outside the extreme south east untouched by fighting.

It has been estimated that one adult male in three was in arms at
some time during the years 1642–46 and that (if one allows for 'indirect'
deaths, from disease and the like) the percentage of the English population losing their lives was larger than in the First World War and
many times larger than in the Second World War.[123] Although there
were large field armies on both sides, much of the fighting was on a
smaller scale, as garrisons tried to raise supplies and money and to
maintain control of their immediate area. As 1642 turned into 1643, the
propaganda battle escalated even further and knowledge (or at least
some dim grasp) of the issues percolated into the remotest areas of
England and Wales and into the consciousness of many who normally
played no part in the political process.

Initially the advantage seemed to lie with the Royalists. Although
Parliament controlled the south east, much of the north, the midlands,
the south west and Wales declared for the king. He had the more experienced officers, including his nephew Prince Rupert, son of Elizabeth
and Frederick. Although only twenty-three in 1642, Rupert had years of
military experience; parliamentarian writers claimed his skills as a cavalry
commander depended on sorcery. Parliament boasted few experienced
soldiers; men like Oliver Cromwell learned soldiering from scratch.
Although the initial battle at Edgehill was inconclusive, Royalist forces
pushed towards London, deciding to withdraw only at Turnham Green,
near Chiswick. The king set up his headquarters at Oxford, the spiritual
home of Laudianism.

It became apparent that, despite controlling much the greater part of
the country, the Royalists suffered serious disadvantages. In every area
where they were strong there were parliamentarian enclaves, from which

Royalists could be attacked if they removed their troops for another push on London. They never controlled all the towns in the Severn valley and so were unable to move men and goods along the main transport artery in the Royalist heartlands of the west midlands and Welsh border. Nor did they control the sea, because the bulk of the navy had sided with Parliament. And, above all, Parliament had London, with 10 per cent of the nation's population but 70 per cent of its trade. Landowners (on both sides) brought cash and jewels, Oxbridge colleges melted down their plate, but these were assets that soon ran out. London's trading wealth continued to produce cash for loans to Parliament. If wars are won by superior resources, Parliament was in the stronger position.

But wars are also won by determination. Many, probably most, Parliamentarians went to war reluctantly, hoping that it would not last long. Their aim was to avoid defeat and negotiate a settlement with the king. Only gradually did it become apparent that the king was not interested in compromise; he wanted a victory that would enable him to impose terms on Parliament. In the course of 1643 Parliament made two major decisions that upped the stakes and made major contributions to its ultimate victory. First, it devised new taxes to pay for the war effort. It had swept away the ragbag of feudal and customary royal revenues in 1641, but had put nothing in their place. Indeed, it had raised no new taxes in 1642 because it had been unsure whether it could legally do so without the king. Now Parliament introduced the assessment – a property tax modelled on ship money, but levied at about twelve times the rate. It also introduced a series of excises. Following the example of the Dutch, Parliament imposed taxes on a variety of items of everyday consumption, including meat and salt, but above all alcoholic drinks – beer, ale and cider. The excise hit the poor proportionately harder than the rich and there was considerable resistance, some of it violent. Parliament learned from experience that it was unwise to collect the meat excise from butchers in the market or the beer excise in the alehouse. But the taxes remained and, by and large, they were paid. It has been estimated that between 1643 and 1650 the English paid ten times as much in taxation (or even more) as they had paid in the 1630s. It was a sign of their respect for law, and for Parliament, that they paid up with so little fuss.[124]

Parliament's other major decision was to enter into an alliance with the Scots, who had watched events in England with interest but without wishing to take sides. In the Solemn League and Covenant, the Scots agreed to give military assistance to Parliament. Parliament in turn agreed to embrace the Covenant and to reform the Church of England 'according to the word of God and the example of the best Reformed churches', and then to 'bring the churches of God in the three kingdoms to the nearest conjunction and uniformity in religion'.[125] Quite how the English understood this was not clear, but it certainly implied the ending of episcopacy, which was abolished in 1646.[126] This commitment made it harder to come to terms with the king, who had made it clear that he would never agree to radical changes in the church. Against this should be set the military benefits brought by the Scots. The alliance meant that the Royalist army in the north could not be deployed elsewhere. The Scots also played a significant role in the first of Parliament's two decisive military victories, at Marston Moor in 1644. In time the Scots came to be seen as a liability. Their soldiers were ill-disciplined and their clergy sought to meddle in the religious reforms which were being discussed in the Westminster Assembly of Divines, set up in 1642. But they helped tip the military balance towards Parliament.

Charles was not a good war leader. He showed plenty of physical courage, but lacked experience of warfare and found it hard to control strong-minded and wilful military commanders, some of whom went their own way regardless of his orders. His indecision led to a lack of direction, which was compounded by a fatalistic conviction that he was in the hands of God. He worried that God might punish him for sacrificing Strafford: 'either I will be a glorious king or a patient martyr'.[127] Talk of martyrdom was not designed to inspire the troops and Charles was also hampered by his commitment to behave constitutionally, while Parliament became increasingly ruthless. The estates of alleged 'delinquents' (Royalists) were confiscated without due legal process and managed for the benefit of Parliament. Members of the committees appointed to run the war effort, in Parliament and the localities, rode roughshod over individual rights as they mobilised the men and money, horses, carts and provisions that they needed to win the war.[128] In the winter of 1644–45, weary of the lacklustre performance of regional armies with mediocre aristocratic generals, Parliament created the New Model Army, which proved well disciplined and highly motivated.

Charles, meanwhile, took his stand on the 'ancient constitution'. He tried to follow traditional procedures and respect the rule of law, and he sought consent wherever possible. This was not always easy in wartime, but Rupert and other commanders often did seek consent to taxation from grand juries, JPs or others with a claim to represent local opinion. Charles also called a Parliament, at Oxford, which voted him taxes similar to those being collected by the Westminster Parliament. After Marston Moor, the Royalists were very much on the defensive; after the second crucial defeat, at Naseby in 1645, their position was desperate. Royalist commanders became increasingly ruthless and brutal as they tried to extract more and more from a shrinking territorial base. They encountered increasing civilian resistance; even in ultra-loyal south Wales a 'peaceable army' sprang up to resist the military.[129]

Charles's defeat cannot be explained solely in terms of resources or losing the vital battles. Civil wars are also battles for hearts and minds, and Charles did himself great harm by handing propaganda coups to his opponents. Given the prominence that Parliament gave to anti-popery, and the allegation that many or most Royalists were papists, it was unfortunate that Charles had a habit of becoming embroiled in ill-considered negotiations with Catholics and getting found out.[130] Most damaging of all were his approaches to Irish Catholics. Although the Confederate Catholics had an instinctive loyalty to the king, it made little practical sense to remain loyal to a king who was incapable of protecting his people. Irish Catholics had to look to themselves and, as the king's fortunes waned in England, the Catholics' safety seemed to depend on throwing off English rule. This view owed less to Irish nationalism than to pragmatism, together with the clergy's insistence on putting religion first. They looked to Rome for guidance and the pope sent a nuncio, Rinuccini, to act as his agent and to ensure that the Confederates made no compromises that could damage the faith.

Charles's hopes of securing military help from Ireland were limited. The commander of the Royalists, Ormond, was a staunch Protestant, who opposed any substantial concessions to Catholics. He did agree to a year's truce with the Catholics in 1643, which freed some Protestant regiments to go to England; the parliamentarian press claimed that they were Catholics. In 1645, becoming desperate, Charles went behind Or-mond's back, sending over the earl of Glamorgan, a Catholic, to negotiate with the Confederates. In a complex set of negotiations, which also involved the queen, now in Paris, and the pope, Charles agreed to extensive concessions, but Rome moved agonisingly slowly. By the time Glamorgan was ready to bring Catholic troops over, in the spring of 1646, the Royalist cause was all but dead.[131] In the meantime, papers relating to the king's earlier negotiations with Irish Catholics, and many others, were found in the Royalist baggage train, captured at Naseby. They were published under the title *The King's Cabinet Opened*, and did him great political harm.[132]

After Naseby the Royalists' defeat was only a matter of time; one by one, Royalist towns and fortresses were taken. Charles had already sent the queen away; early in 1646 his eldest son, Charles, followed. The king's only cause for optimism was that his enemies were deeply divided. In Parliament two parties, known as Presbyterians and Independents, were at each other's throats. There was also severe friction between the English and the Scots. MPs complained bitterly of the Scots' indiscipline and brutality, and belittled their contribution to the war effort. The promise in 1643 to involve the Scots in the conquest and settlement of Ireland was quietly repudiated. There were even proposals to use the New Model to drive the Scots out of England.[133] It was thus with a view to making mischief that Charles decided, in June 1646, to surrender to the Scots.

Throughout the first civil war, Parliament's war aims had remained constant. They insisted that the king should share with Parliament his control of the armed forces and his choice of advisers. They demanded further reform of the church, which from 1643 included the abolition of bishops. And they wanted punitive measures against the most active 'delinquents', or Royalists. Initially they had hoped that Charles would concede these terms without fighting to a finish. When it became clear that he would not, they geared up the war effort, determined on total victory, after which Charles would have to make concessions. Those who lost wars always did; but Charles did not. He was prepared to give up the contested powers (and even bishops) for a period of years, even perhaps for his lifetime, but he was not prepared to give them up forever, because they were not his to give. The powers belonged to the monarchy and bishops were God's designated means of running the church.

Charles believed that his powers came from God – and that in the final reckoning he would have to answer to God for his stewardship. In the years after his defeat, Charles talked often of honour and conscience. Given his record, it would be easy to be cynical about this, but his letters to the queen in 1646 suggest that he was sincere. As a Catholic, who saw little difference between one variety of Protestantism and another, she urged him to abandon bishops and agree to the introduction of Presbyterianism, but he was quite adamant that his conscience would not allow this.[134] Being Charles, there was also an element of calculation. He expected his enemies to fall out amongst themselves and believed that they needed him more than he needed them, because there could be no settlement without him.

And he was right. In 1646 hardly anyone could conceive of a settlement without the king. Parliament's demands clearly envisaged that the king would continue to rule, albeit with reduced powers. Parliament was under strong pressure to settle with the king from a populace weary of high taxes and sectarian radicalism. By 1644 there were strident complaints of 'parliamentary tyranny' and not only from Parliament's more radical followers. Parliament and its agents could plausibly be accused of behaving more arbitrarily than the king ever had, confiscating property and imprisoning without due process of law.[135] Even the best-disciplined soldiers were driven to rely on free quarter – taking food and lodging without payment – if they were not paid; and many units were far from well disciplined. Mass protests against the military and against Parliament's agents, similar to the 'peaceable army' in South Wales, were found in many counties in the south and west.

As memories of the Personal Rule were eclipsed by more recent resentments, there were calls to settle with the king on terms much more lenient than those laid down by Parliament. The king was well aware of this. His refusal to make meaningful concessions created a seemingly insoluble dilemma for the Houses. Either they could settle on his terms, or they could settle without him. Both seemed unthinkable, so Parliament could see little option but to continue negotiating with the king, hoping that sooner or later he would see sense. But he did not and Parliament became increasingly desperate. By late 1648 it seemed that, if anyone was going to weaken, it would be Parliament.

The dilemma was to be resolved in a totally unexpected way. A body emerged that was prepared to think the unthinkable, and that body was the New Model Army. Regarded from the outset as more committed (and more radical in religion) that the other parliamentarian armies, it showed no signs of autonomous political action until the spring of 1647 when Parliament tried to disband it without proper provision for the soldiers' arrears of pay and other professional concerns. In a matter of weeks, the army created its own organisation, the general council, and, in a ferment of discussion, placed its professional grievances in the wider context of Parliament's failure to reach a settlement with the king. On 14 June it issued its own manifesto, which stated that it was not a 'mere mercenary army', but had been called into being to secure the liberties of the people – and that was what it intended to do.[136]

This was not necessarily bad news for the king. The army's quarrel was with the Presbyterian majority in Parliament, not with him. On 3 June a junior officer invited Charles, then under house arrest in Northamptonshire, to accompany him to headquarters. The king agreed and in July the army leaders offered him perhaps the most generous terms he ever received, the Heads of the Proposals. As the army favoured religious toleration, it had no wish to introduce Presbyterianism and was prepared to allow him to keep his bishops, so long as they had no power over those who wished to worship outside the church. Charles was tempted, but rejected the offer, confident he could get something better from Parliament. But Parliament was no longer a free agent. Early in August the army marched into London and demanded the removal of eleven leading Presbyterians from the Commons. The House complied and, although it resumed outwardly cordial relations with the army leaders (or grandees), there was no doubt on either side that the army possessed the power, and the will, to make Parliament do its bidding.

The army's disillusionment with the king began with his rejection of the Heads of the Proposals. It was greatly increased when he negotiated the so-called Engagement with a section of the Scots nobility in December. Since their withdrawal from England the Scots had become deeply divided. Both factions deplored what was happening in England, especially the emergence of the New Model and the spread of religious separatism. One faction argued that the best way to keep the kirk pure and to safeguard Scottish interests was to keep out of England altogether, but the 'Engagers' argued that only the king could halt the slide towards religious anarchy in England, which might sooner or later infect Scotland as well. Watering down the Solemn League and Covenant's commitment to Presbyterianism in England was a price worth paying. Charles was ready to ally with anyone and agreed to establish Presbyterianism in England, for three years only, in return for Scottish military help – even though he believed that at bottom Presbyterianism was incompatible with monarchy.[137] He was encouraged by his growing popularity among his English subjects, who were weary of the burdens of war and the military. Both Parliament and army were well aware of this surge of popular Royalism. The army's response to the Engagement was to force the Houses to pass a vote that they would make no further overtures to the king. In the spring and summer of 1648 the army put down a series of local revolts – in south Wales, Kent and Essex – which constituted the 'second civil war'. When the Scots eventually arrived, delayed by bad weather and divisions at home, Cromwell crushed them at Preston on 19 August.

As the army rushed from one local conflagration to another, its sense of isolation and anger grew. There were pro-Royalist demonstrations in London. A considerable military presence was needed to keep the City quiet.[138] Parliament was less than zealous for the war effort. The Commons were slow to vote money and the Lords refused to declare that the Scots were enemies. As soon as the Scots had been defeated, the Commons went out of their way to snub the army. They recalled the eleven MPs expelled in 1647, passed a bill establishing a Presbyterian church system and reopened negotiations with the king. The army was livid. A story which originated a decade later tells of an army prayer meeting at Windsor in May 1648 in which it was resolved to bring 'Charles Stuart, that man of blood, to an account for the blood that he has shed'.[139] Whether or not this meeting took place, such sentiments already existed in the army in late 1647 and became much more widespread in 1648.

Charles had not only reopened old wounds and brought more bloodshed upon his people, he had also refused to accept God's verdict against him in the first civil war. Many seventeenth-century people, including Charles I, saw events as the working out of God's providence; repeated military success had convinced many in the New Model that it was God's chosen instrument. This gave it the confidence, in the face of general civilian hostility, to go on doing what it believed was right, because rightness came not from majorities, or compliance with the whims of the world, but from following the will of God. A good Christian should submit to God's judgments and be guided by them, but the king would not. He was incorrigible and had to be prevented from harming his people further. And he deserved to be punished. As Cromwell wrote after the battle of Preston, the Commons should ponder the significance of the victory and do God's work 'and not hate His people who are as the apple of His eye and for whom even kings shall be reproved'.[140]

After Preston, army and Parliament were on a collision course. On 5 December, despite intense army pressure, the Commons resolved to continue negotiating with the king. The following day Colonel Thomas Pride came to the doors of the Commons with a file of musketeers. He arrested about forty MPs and kept out another sixty; many others stayed away in protest. The minority who remained after Pride's Purge were soon nicknamed the 'Rump'. Urged on by the army, the Rump brought the king to Windsor and, having declared sovereignty to lie in the people, prepared to try the king in the people's name, setting up a 'high court of justice'. Frenetic negotiations followed, involving (among others) Scots and Royalists. The Scots reminded the English that Charles was their king too, while some Royalists hoped to revive their cause by replacing the king (whom they saw as a political liability) with one of his sons.

Although those who promoted the king's trial had a variety of motives, few wanted or expected it to lead to his execution. Some expected him to be deposed, others hoped that the prospect of conviction and punishment would lead Charles (at last) to make sensible concessions and so open the way to a broadly acceptable settlement.[141] But Charles refused to recognise the court, saying that it was illegal, having been set up by a fraction of one House of Parliament, and so it could not try anyone, especially a king. He also refused to plead, despite being asked to do so forty-three times. The court proceeded to hear evidence to support the charge that he had made war against his people. Some hoped that he would be found guilty of specimen charges and given a nominal punishment, but his refusal to plead forced the court to take a tougher line, if only to vindicate its authority and that of the Parliament that had created it. Charles defended himself resolutely and articulately – it was said that his habitual stammer disappeared – but his stubbornness ensured that there could be only one outcome. He was sentenced to death. On 30 January 1649, he was brought to the Banqueting House in Whitehall. Above him, on the ceiling, was Rubens's apotheosis of James I, a work full of monarchical symbolism. On this day his son put on two shirts: it was cold and he did not want to seem afraid. When he was led out onto the scaffold, he made a short speech. He declared that he was going from a corruptible to an incorruptible crown and that 'a subject and a sovereign are clear different things'. A single blow of the axe severed his head from his body. When the executioner held up his head, the cheers of the soldiers were drowned by a great collective groan.

4

The Interregnum

With the execution of Charles I, the crown (in the eyes of Royalists) passed to his son, who was quickly proclaimed in Edinburgh as Charles II, but it was far from clear that he would be able to wield effective authority in any of his three kingdoms. The picture seemed bleakest in England, where on 17 March 1649 the Rump passed an ordinance abolishing the monarchy as useless and dangerous. Two months later it declared England 'a commonwealth or free state' – in other words, a republic.[1] The Rump also abolished the House of Lords. So few peers had continued to sit that to treat it as a House of Parliament had become a farce.

Charles was in France when he heard the news of his father's death, but if he harboured hopes of French aid in securing his kingdoms he was doomed to disappointment. Even though the Thirty Years War had ended in 1648, the war between France and Spain continued. In addition, France was experiencing its own civil war, the Fronde, in which the boy king, Louis XIV, had to flee from Paris and dissident nobles controlled entire regions. Although Henrietta Maria enjoyed some favour at the French court, and secured money to support the Stuart court in exile, she sought to use her control of that money to impose her will on her sons. She tried in vain to persuade Charles to convert to Catholicism, in order to win the support of Catholic princes and the pope and to secure acceptance from the majority in Ireland. Ironically, in view of his later conversion, her second son, James, also resisted her pressure, so she concentrated on trying to convert the youngest, Henry, duke of Gloucester, who was carried off to a country retreat and forced to receive instruction from Jesuits. Charles, furious, ordered his brother's release. He understood, if his mother did not, that the conversion of any of the three brothers would seriously harm his prospects of becoming king of England in anything but name.

Those prospects were not good. The exiled court was impoverished and full of spies and faction. The French were reluctant hosts, who saw the Stuarts' presence as hindering a rapprochement with the new regime in England. Both the French and the Spaniards were eager to secure English support in their war against each other. In 1654, after Cromwell had expelled the Rump and been proclaimed lord protector, Louis XIV's mother, Anne of Austria, and her chief minister, Cardinal Mazarin, agreed to expel Charles and his brothers in return for English support against Spain. After reluctantly leaving France, the princes might have hoped to join their sister Mary, who had married William II, prince of Orange, the most powerful man in the newly independent Dutch Republic. William, however, had died in 1650, at the height of a bitter political conflict with the rulers of the great cities of the province of Holland, who believed that William wished to destroy the republican constitution and establish an absolute monarchy. His opponents took advantage of his death to exclude his widow and their young son, also called William, from any position of power.

The Dutch Republic's leaders had no wish to provoke Cromwell and made it clear that Charles and his brothers would not be welcome in their territories. The princes eventually found a haven of sorts at Brussels, in the Spanish Netherlands, where they served in the Spanish forces fighting the French (with whom James had recently served). But the Spaniards had no intention of helping Charles to recover his kingdoms. They made numerous promises, which they did not keep. When Spain and France finally made peace in 1659, the interests of the Stuarts were ignored, even though Charles travelled to Spain in an effort to influence the terms of the treaty.

If the international situation was far from favourable to the Stuarts, the position within the British Isles was little better. In England, there was strong evidence of popular Royalism in 1647–48, and the execution of the king provoked widespread dismay and revulsion, but there was little prospect of a revolt in favour of the new king. The Royalists had been comprehensively defeated in the first civil war. Many had lost their lands, or were in the process of buying them back, and they had no wish to risk all by an ill-advised rising. The second civil war of 1648 had shown how the New Model could put down uncoordinated local risings with ease and ferocity. Royalist conspiracies continued through the 1650s, but their planning and security were poor and the two risings that actually started, in 1655 and 1659, were quickly suppressed.[2] No hastily gathered force of volunteers could be any match for the professionals of the New Model.

If the new regimes were widely regarded in England as illegitimate, they were not entirely unacceptable. First and foremost, they provided effective government. The law courts continued to function and order was maintained. Although the regimes ultimately depended on the army, they were by no means exclusively military, at least in England. After the horror of the regicide, and the abolition of the monarchy and the Lords, the Rump carefully refrained from further provoking conservative opinion by carrying through unnecessary changes. Aware of its many enemies, and its narrow basis of civilian support, the Rump resisted pressure from the army for radical law reform and the abolition of tithes. The former would alienate the legal profession (and so possibly jeopardise the operation of the law courts), while the latter would destroy the parish system, which continued to function despite the abolition of the old Church of England.

Even Cromwell eventually became impatient with the Rump's reluctance to embrace reform and to provide for the election of the sort of Parliament that the army demanded, consisting exclusively of those the army regarded as godly and morally upright. Like many in the army, and Charles I, Cromwell believed that divine providence governed everything that happened. Charles had believed that his defeat in the civil war was God's punishment for his sacrificing Strafford. Cromwell believed that his victory in the civil war showed God's favour to His chosen people – the small minority who were truly godly and especially those in the army. God had given them strength out of all proportion to their numbers and earthly worth, and it was He who empowered them to conquer and to rule. Cromwell was sufficiently humble to accept that his mere human reasoning was incapable of reading the mind of God; but when he believed he saw God's will manifest in events he acted decisively. In addition, as he pondered his rise from Huntingdonshire squire to supreme authority in the British Isles, he became convinced that God had great things for him to do.

When (as Cromwell saw it) the Rump's sloth and duplicity forced him to dismiss it, his initial instinct was to seek divine aid in constitution-making. He called a nominated Parliament of godly men, known variously as the Parliament of Saints or the Barebones Parliament, after one of its members, Praise-God Barbon (or Barebones). The Parliament was constructed on impeccable Old Testament lines, and Cromwell was confident that a godly new constitution would soon emerge. When it did not, he decided that he had been too ready to anticipate God's will and responded to a scheme of his second-in-command, John Lambert, for England's first written constitution. The Instrument of Government was far removed from a modern model of 'military government'. It was based on a careful separation of powers between a single-person executive, the lord protector, an advisory council and an elected Parliament.

The lord protector was to command the armed forces and had overall responsibility for foreign policy, law enforcement and the conduct of government. His position resembled that of a king – a constitutional rather than an absolute monarch, but a king nonetheless. His status was emphasised by the quasi-regal state in which he lived in former royal palaces, notably Hampton Court. He also travelled with an entourage almost as large and dignified as that of a king. When most of the late king's art collection was sold off, Cromwell insisted that Mantegna's 'Triumphs of Caesar' remained at Hampton Court. Although Cromwell was in many ways a modest man, those around him saw political (or public relations) advantages in emphasising his authority and dignity. This was an age that respected pomp and pageantry, and it was appropriate to highlight England's new-found status as a major international power, in Europe and beyond. If Cromwell himself did not claim to be an emperor, there were those in the administration who believed that England was destined to become a major imperial power, bringing the benefits of English civilisation not only to Scotland and Ireland but also to the native peoples of the Americas.

As protector, Cromwell embarked on a process of 'healing and settling'. He sought to entice members of the old ruling elite back into local government and the political process. Above all, he aimed to attract the support of moderate parliamentarians, or Presbyterians. These had been repelled by Pride's Purge and the regicide, believed in a single national church, and were appalled at the excesses of the radical sects, and especially by the aggressive and confrontational missionary tactics of the Quakers, at this stage far from being pacifists. The Presbyterians were prepared to be enticed, but ultimately their aims were incompatible with Cromwell's. He saw the main gain from the civil wars as religious liberty, particularly for the godly. This depended on the continuance of the republic and the army. If the monarchy were restored, especially the Stuart monarchy, there would again be a uniform national church, which would be very acceptable to the Presbyterians but would almost certainly persecute the sects.

The Presbyterians were prepared to go along with Cromwell's regime in the hope of converting it into something more congenial. After his first elected Parliament had failed to rewrite the Instrument of Government, his second, early in 1657, offered a complete alternative package, of which the keystone was to make Cromwell king. The proponents of the offer of the crown argued that the re-establishment of a monarchy would make the regime legitimate in the eyes of the people. Centuries of tradition ensured that a king would be able to command acceptance in a way that no new-fangled constitution could. The powers of, and limitations on, the monarchy were clearly defined by existing law and were understood and accepted by the people. There was also a less public argument for making Cromwell king. His health was not good and there were fears that when he died he might be succeeded as protector by Lambert, or some other army officer, who would be much less acceptable to civilian opinion than Oliver had been.

Cromwell agonised over whether to accept the crown. When eventually he decided to turn it down, he gave as his reasons the dislike of many godly people (especially in the army) for the title of king and his belief that the monarchy had been abolished because God had shown that He disapproved of it. 'I will not seek to set up that that providence hath destroyed and laid in the dust', he declared, 'and I would not build Jericho again.'[3] Although Oliver rejected the crown itself, he agreed to the rest of the package. He was now able to nominate a successor, presumably within the Cromwell family, making the protectorate hereditary. He would also take on another royal power, that of creating 'lords', who would sit in a second chamber in Parliament (the 'Other House'). He also agreed to a variety of other provisions acceptable to the Presbyterians. All this did not lead to peace and harmony. Cromwell had been able to work with his elected Parliaments only after removing about a hundred unacceptable members from each.[4] When these were restored, in February 1658, his Parliament became unmanageable and he dismissed it angrily. He died, on 3 September 1658, a disappointed man.

Nevertheless, Oliver's efforts to heal and settle and to find a civilian basis for his regime help explain why he secured broader popular acquiescence than the Rump, if not enthusiastic support. In addition, after the regicide, the successive regimes enjoyed spectacular military success. The army comprehensively conquered both Scotland and Ireland. In 1652–54, after a massive programme of naval shipbuilding, England was able to take on Europe's greatest maritime power, the Dutch Republic, in the First Dutch War. If the Western Design, an expedition to the Caribbean in 1655, was widely seen as a failure, England did acquire Jamaica, adding to its Caribbean empire. Later, the army fought against the Spanish in the Low Countries and in 1658 took Dunkirk, England's first territory on the Continent since the loss of Calais a century before. In stark contrast to the abysmal record of Charles I and Buckingham in the 1620s, here was good reason for national pride.

The regimes of the 1650s could not command an acceptance founded on unquestioned legitimacy, as the monarchy had been able to do. On the other hand, the resistance that they faced, in England, was little more threatening than that faced by Charles I in the 1630s. Only in the last months of 1659, as the regime began to unravel and the army became divided, did it face widespread civilian opposition. Until then, to the English habit of obeying authority (and paying taxes which had been voted by a Parliament) was added the fact that day to day government was not that much different from before. The nearest Cromwell came to establishing direct military rule, under the Major Generals in 1655–56, made only a limited difference to people's lives, with the exception of the Royalists, who came under oppressively close surveillance.[5]

Charles II faced a dilemma. To turn vague disaffection into serious rebellion, he needed effective aid from abroad. To secure that aid he needed a strong rebellion within England. Neither seemed likely in the 1650s, but at first the prospects of help from his other kingdoms seemed brighter. At the beginning of 1649 there was still a Royalist army in Ireland, under Ormond, and there was some hope that the Confederate Catholics might rally to the new king, especially after the nuncio

Rinuccini returned to Rome. The response of the Rump was to send over a large army, commanded by Cromwell, who set out to secure the eastern and southern coasts before turning his attention inland. The brief sieges of Drogheda and Wexford were followed by the system-atic slaughter of the garrisons, Catholic clergy and many ordinary inhabitants.

Cromwell made it clear that these massacres – for that was what they were – were in retaliation for the killings in 1641. But Drogheda had never sided with the Confederates and much of the garrison, though Catholic, was English, including the commander, Sir Arthur Aston, who was allegedly beaten to death with his own wooden leg. Cromwell claimed that, under the rules of war, a garrison that had failed to surrender when a breach was forced in the walls could be put to the sword. But this rarely happened in practice – hardly at all in the English civil war – and it could be argued that Wexford *had* surrendered before the crucial moment. Cromwell also claimed that the severity he showed at Drogheda and Wexford would save casualties in the long run, because garrisons would surrender rather than risk sack and massacre.[6] Some did, but elsewhere the brutality had the opposite effect, with towns such as Clonmel and Limerick determined to hold out to the last.[7]

The New Model had to undertake one siege after another and suffered heavily from rain, cold and dysentery. As the army moved away from the coast, it faced serious problems of supply; there was no food to be had, the roads were bad, and small parties of soldiers were always at risk from Irish irregulars or brigands. Cromwell's original force of 10,000 increased to 33,000 and lost thousands of men.[8] The conquest of Ireland, which added further to the sufferings of an exhausted country, was not effectively completed until April 1652, and even then guerrilla warfare continued.

By the end of 1649 it was clear to Charles II that he now had little hope of using Ireland as a base from which to recover England, so he turned his attention to Scotland. There the Royalists had never been strong and the dominant Presbyterians were still divided. The failure of the Engagement discredited those responsible. Their eclipse was com-pleted when Cromwell entered Scotland after Preston and installed the hardline Presbyterians, or 'Kirk Party', in power. Rather to his surprise, they proclaimed Charles II as their king as soon as they heard of the regicide. They believed firmly in monarchy and were not pleased that the English had executed their king without consulting them. Both the Kirk Party and its opponents disliked the new regime in England, because it was republican and because it allowed toleration to sectarian radicals; there were fears that their influence could seep into Scotland.

The Kirk Party's leaders hoped to exploit Charles II's weakness and convert him into a model Presbyterian ruler. They had an ally in Henrietta Maria, who still saw no difference between different types of Protestantism and advised her son to make concessions (notably a promise to establish Presbyterianism in all three kingdoms if he were restored). After all, she argued, he could always renege on his promises later. Charles did not share his mother's enthusiasm for this strategy. Although his religious preferences were unclear, he was a pleasure-loving young man who found the kirk's rigorous moral discipline and unbending sabbatarianism distasteful. He deeply resented having to listen to long sermons denouncing the sins of his father, and he was conscious that to become a Scottish-style Presbyterian would do him almost as much political damage in England as turning Catholic. As his senior adviser, Sir Edward Hyde, later earl of Clarendon, never tired of reminding him, his staunchest supporters in England were Royalist in politics and Church of England in religion; if he alienated them, he would never recover his throne.

But Charles was a desperate man. After lengthy negotiations characterised by bad faith on both sides, he agreed to impose Presbyterianism on Scotland and England. He made this agreement with great reluctance and he was determined to abandon the commitment about England at the earliest opportunity. News that he was in Scotland created the likelihood of yet another Scottish invasion of England. Faced with this, the Rump decided to attack first. Cromwell was recalled from Ireland and sent north with an army of 16,000 men. He was faced by a determined army, commanded by David Leslie, and driven by religious zeal. Leslie adopted what seemed a sound defensive position, which Cromwell was unable to break. As his army was weakened by hunger and sickness, Leslie's larger army surrounded it at Dunbar, only to be taken by surprise by a dawn attack, on 3 September 1650, and routed. It was Cromwell's greatest victory. It gave him control of Edinburgh and by the spring of 1651 the New Model controlled all of Scotland south of Stirling.

Ironically Dunbar, by seriously damaging the credibility of the Kirk Party, strengthened the position of the king. The pastors had insisted on commissioning only officers of impeccable Presbyterian rectitude, which had not made for military efficiency. Charles and his Scottish allies began to readmit hardened professionals to the officer corps. They realised that if they wished to march into England they would have to do so quickly; one more campaigning season and Cromwell would conquer the rest of Scotland. Charles's army slipped past Cromwell's and began an exhausting march through the north west of England, down into the west midlands. Their hopes of success depended on their being joined by large numbers of English Royalists, but the Royalists were cowed and demoralised; the English authorities arrested many and kept others under surveillance. Meanwhile, Cromwell left part of his army in Scotland and followed Charles as fast as he could with the rest. He caught up with the Royalists at Worcester on 3 September 1651 and won another crushing victory. It signalled, or rather confirmed, the end of Royalism as an effective force in any of the three kingdoms.

Charles made his way back to France, undergoing a series of picaresque adventures on the way. At one point he hid in an oak tree, which has given its name to inns and pubs from that day to this. Despite a large price on his head, he was helped and concealed by Royalist sympathisers, including a number of Catholics. Meanwhile, Cromwell returned to Scotland, sacking Dundee as a warning to other towns to surrender when attacked. By May 1652 all resistance had ended and Cromwell was master of Scotland. Charles's hopes of regaining his kingdoms seemed to have vanished and he and his brothers spent the remainder of the 1650s enjoying themselves as best they could – they were, after all, young – and lurching from one dashed hope to another.

It is difficult to overstate the achievement of the Rump and the army in conquering Scotland and Ireland. No English king, even Edward I, had conquered Scotland, and Cromwell's conquest of Ireland was far more complete that the medieval conquest or that of 1603. The conquests made it possible for the English, if they chose, to impose a whole new order. In Scotland, the military government showed little inclination to do so. There were no projects for colonies or plantations. Although Cromwell disliked the intolerance and dogmatism of the Presbyterian clergy, they were at least Protestants who spoke a similar language: 'I beseech you in the bowels of Christ', Cromwell pleaded with them, 'think it possible that you may be mistaken.'[9]

In Scotland, the lands of Royalists and others seen as enemies of the regime were confiscated, but the confiscations were far less extensive than in Ireland, partly because the government preferred to impose fines, but more because the Scots were seen as far less culpable than the Irish; there had been nothing in Scotland like the Irish rising of 1641. The English authorities also abolished heritable jurisdictions, which they saw as giving the nobles despotic power over the peasantry. This reduced the landowners' ability to keep order as well as plunging many of them into debt and the reform was later abandoned.[10] But in general the main aim of the London government and its agents in Edinburgh was containment through military occupation and the control of key castles, especially in the Highlands. There was no attempt to refashion Scottish society and in time General George Monk, the military commander in Scotland, and his leading civilian counterpart, the Anglo-Irish Lord Broghill, found it more practical to work with the natural leaders of Scottish society, especially in maintaining law and order.[11]

Ireland was a very different matter. It had always been seen by the English as a subordinate kingdom and the gulf of understanding between English and Irish was far greater than that between English and Scots. At Wexford priests tried in vain to protect themselves from Cromwell's soldiers by brandishing crucifixes.[12] Cromwell apparently believed that the Irish were too stupid or ignorant to be responsible for their actions, proclaiming that all peasants and common soldiers who surrendered would be pardoned. He reserved his venom for their military leaders, and above all their priests and bishops, who 'saddled and bridled' the people:

> Your covenant is with death and hell ... You are a part of Antichrist, whose kingdom the Scripture so expressly speaks should be laid in blood, yea in the blood of the saints. You have shed great store of it already and ere it be long you must all have blood to drink, even the dregs of the fury of the wrath of God, which will be poured out unto you.[13]

He accused the Confederation of Kilkenny of rebellion, of unlawfully seizing the property of English settlers and massacring thousands. He even claimed, with a wilful ignorance of history, that the Catholic religion had never legally been established in Ireland.[14] For all this the leaders of Irish Catholicism, and all those involved in the 'rebellion' against Parliament, deserved condign punishment.

The rising and the conquest offered an opportunity to resume and greatly to extend the policy of plantation. Opposition had been utterly crushed, there was a large army of occupation, and the country was devastated and exhausted. Crops, homes and towns had been burned, cattle slaughtered; killing, starvation and disease had reduced the population by as much as one third. English motives in the massive transfer of land that followed were mixed. To the element of punishment was added a determination that the Irish should never rebel again. They were also economic considerations. The perception remained that Ireland was fundamentally fruitful and would prosper under English management. And the Rump had debts to pay. In 1642 Parliament had passed an ordinance inviting 'undertakers' to advance money for the reconquest of Ireland, to be reimbursed out of the estates of the rebels. From the start Parliament was determined that the cost of the English reconquest would be met by the Irish, so the soldiers who fought in Ireland and Scotland were paid in 'debentures', redeemable against Irish land.[15]

The ordinance of August 1652, which authorised the confiscations in Ireland, was complicated. It laid down a variety of different degrees of 'guilt' for involvement in the 1641 rising, the Confederation of Kilkenny and the Royalist armies in Ireland. Interpreted strictly, 80,000 men – not much less than half the adult male population – would have forfeited life and estates. These included some Protestant Royalists, headed by Ormond. In fact, relatively few were executed, although these included Sir Phelim O'Neill, who sealed his fate by denying that he had received a commission from Charles I in 1641. Some 34,000 men were allowed to leave Ireland, the majority to serve in the French or Spanish armies, but as many as 12,000 were sent to virtual servitude in the Caribbean and the American colonies.

Others were to lose part or all of their estates. Ireland was to be divided into three zones. In the south east, in the area (which included Dublin) east of a line from the mouth of the River Boyne to the mouth of the River Barrow, *all* Catholics – landowners, farmers and labourers

– were to be removed. In Ulster, Munster and the rest of Leinster, those Catholics who were entitled to retain some or all of their land were to give up their existing estates and to be compensated with land west of the Shannon, in Connacht and County Clare. Catholic farmers and labourers were to remain, but it was hoped that many Protestant soldiers would settle as tenants and so create a denser, militarily experienced Protestant population. Finally, in Connacht and Clare Catholics were not to receive land, or settle, in towns, near the sea coast or along the banks of the Shannon.[16]

This was an immensely ambitious programme of land transfer and (particularly in the south east) what would now be called ethnic cleansing. Some advocates of the programme used language reminiscent of apartheid, arguing that a crucial weakness of earlier 'mixed' plantations, like that of Munster, had been the tendency of English settlers to 'go native'. But they were also concerned to attract settlers to areas that would still contain Catholics, which would not be easy if the Catholics were officially depicted as irredeemably bent on driving out or slaughtering the Protestants. Moreover, Cromwell and others placed the blame for the rebellion and atrocities on the leaders and the priests. The ordinance of 1652 offered pardon to ordinary Catholics who submitted to the new government; in Ireland, as in Scotland, the English regimes of the 1650s at least went through the motions of liberating the peasantry from oppressive landlords.[17]

Pragmatism and even occasional hints of benevolence tempered the worst excesses of ethnic hatred and religious revenge, but the scale of the planned confiscation was still enormous; there had been no comparable transfer of land in England since 1066. If carried through, it would have removed the threat from Catholics to Dublin as well as securing the coast that offered easiest access to England. The remaining Catholic landowners would be separated from their tenants, rupturing traditional loyalties and family connections. They would be cordoned off beyond the Shannon. Denied access to the sea, they would be unable to receive foreign assistance. The area to the east of the Shannon would be policed by soldier settlers. Although the elements of punishment and expropriation were obvious, so too was the concern for security.

In the event, the programme proved too ambitious. At the time it was laid down, there had been no national survey of Ireland and nobody knew whether there was enough land to go round. Parts of Connacht were later appropriated for Protestant settlers. It proved impossible to clear the south east of Catholics, because the Protestant landowners needed tenants and labourers. Far fewer soldiers than had been hoped settled in Ireland. Many had sold their debentures to their officers for a fraction of their face value, so officers acquired claims to large tracts of land – for which they needed Catholic tenants and labourers. And some Catholic landowners managed to avoid being transplanted to Connacht. Even so, there was a massive shift in the balance of landholding. According to informed estimates, in 1640 Catholics held about 60 per cent of the land; by 1660 they held as little as 10 per cent.

The land settlement was the keystone of English policy towards Ireland in the 1650s. There was also the first serious attempt to prohibit Catholic worship. Hitherto, the laws against Catholics had been limited in scope, but now their archbishops and bishops were ordered to leave the country. The order was not fully enforced and there was little attempt to convert the peasantry. Army commanders encouraged Baptist and Quaker missionaries and little congregations formed, but these were very much garrison churches and made little impact on Irish society as a whole. Protestant parish worship had never been vigorous and had lost its coherence with the abolition of bishops and the banning of the Prayer Book. Like the missions of the Baptists and Quakers, it used only English and made no effort to communicate with the Irish in their own language. The aim of the authorities was to root out Catholicism. They showed little interest in the spiritual lives or salvation of the Irish – it was as if they did not matter.[18] Meanwhile, the New English landed elite consolidated their estates and their hold on power.

For much of the 1650s military rule in England and English military rule over Scotland and Ireland seemed solid, indeed impregnable; it was difficult to see where any serious challenge could come from. In the end, it collapsed from within. When Oliver Cromwell died on 3 September 1658, the anniversary of Dunbar and Worcester, it became apparent how much the regime had depended on him. He alone commanded the loyalty of the army, while retaining the acquiescence, and sometimes more, of the English political elite. The army still wanted godly reform, the civilian population wanted a return to the old order; Oliver had managed to retain the trust of both.

He was succeeded as protector by his older son, Richard. Popular among civilians, Richard was unable to secure the loyalty of the army and fell from power in May 1659. The army needed a civilian 'front', some sort of Parliament, to vote taxes for the soldiers' pay, but without interfering in the running of the army. Unwilling to face the electorate, the army leaders recalled the Rump, which was still smarting from its expulsion six years before. The Rump and the army detested but needed each other; they could at least agree on the need to prevent the return of the Stuarts, but their relationship soon broke down. When the Rump demanded control over military appointments and dismissals, the generals expelled it again.

By now, for the first time, the army was divided. From Scotland Monk denounced the expulsion of the Rump and demanded its recall, taking his stand on the principle (consistently rejected by the army) of civilian control over the military. When the English high command refused, Monk prepared to use the army of occupation in Scotland to intervene in England. News of his preparations emboldened civilian opposition in England. For the first time, government seemed in serious danger of collapse. The judges refused to hear cases, taxpayers stopped paying. The soldiers were confused and demoralised. Frequent purges of the officer corps had eroded the men's loyalty to their officers and they were increasingly unsure who or what they were fighting for. They found themselves jeered wherever they went, especially in London. In late December, with part of the fleet blockading the Thames and the garrisons of Dublin and Portsmouth declaring for the Rump, the generals gave in. The Rump was recalled and General Fleetwood declared that God had spat in his face.

The recall of the Rump did not stop Monk's march into England. On 1 January 1660 he crossed the Tweed at Coldstream; his regiment was later renamed the Coldstream Guards. Nobody – perhaps not even Monk himself – knew what his intentions were. As a military man he valued order in both state and church, but he was a taciturn man who kept his thoughts to himself and people found it impossible to read his mind. He could hold his liquor as well as his tongue and had earned the trust and loyalty of his men. It quickly became apparent that the

English army was unwilling to oppose him, especially after the old New Model commander, Fairfax, came to meet him in Yorkshire. As he came south he was bombarded with advice and petitions for a free Parliament, which (although nobody admitted it) would be likely to restore the monarchy. Monk continued to proclaim his commitment to the Rump and to government without a king or House of Lords, but he was quietly assessing the mood of the public and the English army. Suddenly, in February, he demanded that the Rump readmit the MPs expelled in Pride's Purge, restoring the Long Parliament as it had been in 1648 – with a majority who had wished to continue negotiations with Charles I. The Rump had no choice but to comply, on which Monk demanded that the Parliament should prepare for fresh elections and then dissolve itself.

The majority of members of the restored Long Parliament were monarchists, but the overwhelming majority had been Parliamentarians. They tried to debar Royalists from standing or voting in elections, but many Royalists – and sons of Royalists – stood or voted. Meanwhile, Monk purged the army's officer corps of those likely to oppose the restoration of monarchy. The new Parliament (or Convention, because it had not been called by a king), which met in April, was evenly divided between men of Royalist and of Parliamentarian antecedents. Almost all agreed that the king should be invited to return. They disagreed on whether to insist on preconditions. The Royalists called for his unconditional recall, the Parliamentarians called for restrictions on his prerogative, like those demanded by Parliament in the 1640s, notably sharing with Parliament his choice of advisers and control of the armed forces.

Charles II watched these momentous events with joy tinged by incredulity. He had done nothing to bring about his return (but equally nothing to hinder it). Now he issued his Declaration of Breda, which addressed the issues likely to make Parliamentarians fearful of restoring the monarchy. For those who feared punishment for fighting against his father, he promised a general indemnity, with a few exceptions (notably the regicides) to be selected by Parliament. For those who feared a return to persecuting Anglicanism, he referred the settlement of the church to Parliament and declared his preference for liberty to tender consciences, provided they did not disturb the peace. He even offered to take the New Model into his service.

Faced with these assurances, and the stubborn opposition of the Royalists, moves to impose restrictions on his power collapsed. Charles was proclaimed king in early May, amid scenes of wild rejoicing, and returned, without preconditions. He entered London in triumph on 29 May, his thirtieth birthday.[19] The scene in London was memorably described by the diarist, John Evelyn. The king entered his capital accompanied by 200,000 men, on horseback or on foot. The roads were strewn with flowers, the church bells rang, the fountains ran with wine. Everybody wore their finest clothes, the houses were hung with tapestries and everywhere there was music. The road from Rochester (about thirty miles from London) was lined with people, and it took the cavalcade seven hours to pass through the City, such was the press of people in the streets. 'I stood in the Strand', wrote Evelyn 'and beheld it and blessed God. And all this without one drop of blood.'[20]

Those who had lived through the civil wars were in no doubt that they had changed England profoundly. The phrase 'before the civil wars' runs like a mantra through the anecdotes and potted biographies of John Aubrey's *Brief Lives*. Sir Edward Hyde expressed the hope, in September 1660, that England could return to 'its old good manners, its old good humour and its old good nature', but he was clearly not optimistic.[21] The civil wars had been 'unnatural', setting brother against brother, neighbour against neighbour; such wounds could not easily heal. Faced with apparently universal rejoicing at his return, Charles II remarked cynically that it must be his own fault he had been away for so long, but euphoria soon turned to recrimination.

The king insisted that there should be a very broad indemnity and pardon, as promised at Breda. The two Houses in the Convention accepted this, but when they considered who should be excluded from pardon the debates became distinctly unpleasant. There was general agreement that the surviving regicides should be punished, at least those who had not managed to flee the country. Three of them – Oliver Cromwell, his son-in-law Henry Ireton and John Bradshaw, president of the court that had condemned the king – were pursued beyond the grave. On 30 January 1661 – the anniversary of the king's execution – their bodies were dug up and hanged at Tyburn; they were then de-capitated and their skulls set on spikes on Westminster Hall.[22] But the real argument in the Convention centred on those who had not signed the king's death warrant. MPs and peers schemed to save their friends and condemn their enemies. On the king's insistence, the indemnity bill went through with relatively few exceptions. The much more Royalist 'Cavalier' House of Commons elected in 1661 tried repeatedly to reopen the question, but the king was adamant that the indemnity must remain inviolate.

In theory those who had fought against the king were not to suffer for it and the past was to be forgotten. The Act of Indemnity and Oblivion laid down that the victims of recrimination could seek damages – but only for a period of three years and only modest sums (£10 for a gentleman, £2 for a commoner).[23] But it was impossible to forget. Parliament decreed that the anniversary of the king's execution should be solemnly remembered in every parish church each year and the Church of England drew up a special form of service; Parliament also decreed that 29 May, the king's birthday and the anniversary of his return to London, should be celebrated. Clerical ordinands and members of municipal corporations were required to swear that they did not believe themselves to be bound by the Covenant (which all office holders had been required to subscribe in the 1640s).

In alehouses and law courts, former enemies frequently reminded one another about the wars. In 1670 the duke of Ormond went hunting in Staffordshire with three hundred gentlemen – 'and not one Roundhead'.[24] Taunton, Gloucester and Lyme Regis commemorated the lifting of Royalist sieges into the 1680s.[25] The tendency to dwell on the past was intensified by Charles II's habit of favouring his father's former enemies at the expense of his friends. Ex-Parliamentarians were prominent on his privy council and garnered many of the most lucrative offices at court and in the administration, while the old Cavaliers were given unpaid posts in the localities, as JPs and deputy lieutenants. Moreover, while crown and church lands confiscated during and after the wars were restored, lands sold by Royalists, to pay debts or to recover forfeited estates, were not. Those who had suffered financially, whose houses had been destroyed and estates plundered, watched in impotent fury as their former enemies continued to prosper. Within days of the king's return, old Cavaliers were claiming that the king's policy was one of indemnity for his enemies and oblivion for his friends.[26]

Memories of civil war continued to play a part in politics for at least a century after 1660. The party divisions, of Tory and Whig, which emerged in the early 1680s, in many ways replicated those of Royalist and Parliamentarian. The Tories called their opponents Roundheads and regicides, the Whigs accused the Tories of favouring popery, arbitrary government and a 'Laudian' regime in the church. Few Whigs were prepared to defend the regicide, but many no doubt privately believed that Charles I had deserved his fate – and that his sons were not much better. Against this, Clarendon's *History of the Rebellion*, the first volume of which was published in 1702, depicted Charles I as well-meaning but poorly advised, and blamed the civil wars on a small group of ambitious men, who had cynically exploited the gullibility and animal instincts of the mob. In anonymous introductions Clarendon's son, the earl of Rochester, emphasised the lessons that his father's work offered for contemporary politics.[27]

So did the divisions of the civil wars dominate political and social life into the eighteenth century? And did the legacy of the civil war seriously weaken the monarchy? The answers to these questions are complex and ambivalent. Historians of England have often argued that Charles I's defeat and execution fatally weakened the crown and that the monarchy of Charles II was a pale shadow of that of his father. By contrast, historians of France traditionally argue that the Fronde provoked a backlash against disorder and a willingness to accept strong, indeed absolute monarchy. Assessing the 'strength' of a monarchy is always subjective. Charles I seemed 'strong' in the 1630s: he ruled without Parliament, imposed his will on the church and punished those few of his critics who dared raise their heads above the parapet. But he was unable to embark on a foreign war and was humiliated by the Scots in 1640. Conversely, Charles II suffered some resounding defeats at the hands of Parliament. He was forced to make peace with the Dutch in 1674 and to make war on France in 1678; he also faced a political crisis in 1679–81 that many compared to that of 1640–42. Yet he survived to crush his enemies and to break the independence of the corporate towns. He even destroyed the autonomy of London, something that the Tudors would never have dared to attempt.[28] But, like his father in the 1630s, he could not risk a foreign war.

There can be no doubting that the first civil war rent English society from top to bottom. As a Welshman commented in 1644: 'the deep stains these wars will leave behind I fear all the water of the Severn, Trent or Thames cannot wash away'.[29] The divisions were perhaps at their sharpest in 1642–44. During the next two years, they were overlain by a resentment of the burdens of war – heavy taxation, free quarter, military indiscipline and high-handed county committees. In many counties 'clubmen', peasants and craftsmen, often encouraged by gentry and clergy, armed to defend themselves against the soldiers and negotiated with military commanders.[30] Resentment of 'parliamentary tyranny' was a key factor in the surge of support for the king after 1646. Meanwhile, the divisions among the victors, and the army's emergence into politics and eventual purge of Parliament, created new resentments and blurred political boundaries. People became increasingly unsure where they and others stood and, in the words of one historian, politics resembled a poker game in which the red cards were wild.[31]

Many – indeed most – former Parliamentarians were deeply perturbed by the rise of the army and the regicide. Although military rule became blatant only under the Major Generals and in 1659, no regime could survive against the wishes of the army. If former Parliamentarians participated in government in the 1650s, they did so because they hoped to transform Cromwell's regime into something more traditional – and monarchical. To some extent they succeeded, only for the army to slam the door on change when it removed Richard Cromwell in 1659. These 'Presbyterians' shared with the Royalists a dislike of military rule and a belief that the civil wars had turned the world upside down, dislocating social hierarchy and order. They were especially resentful of the Quakers, who were aggressive and subversive, disrupting church services and flouting the authority of magistrates. Bitterly unpopular among ordinary people as well as ministers and magistrates, Quakers were beaten, stoned and even killed.[32]

Common enemies – the army and the religious radicals – brought together old Cavaliers and old Roundheads in the 1650s.[33] The divisions caused by one civil war, while not forgotten, were outweighed by a common visceral fear of anarchy; one reason why Oliver's regime was tolerable was that it maintained order. From the point of view of former Parliamentarians, *the* problem had been Charles I. His son was an unknown quantity, who could reasonably be given the benefit of the doubt. In time, many came to believe that this had been a mistake. Charles II seemed set to repeat the errors of his father, provoking criticisms and divisions reminiscent of 1640–42. But memories of what had happened later in the 1640s helped ensure that there would not be another civil war.

The legacy of the civil war period was equally ambivalent in terms of political ideas. At the beginning of the seventeenth century, royal power (like everything else) was seen as created by God. England's 'ancient constitution' was seen as having evolved over the centuries. Monarchy, Parliament and the law had developed together, mutually supportive and mutually dependent. This concept made sense in a political and administrative system that depended heavily on the participation and cooperation of the people, but it offered little guidance when things went badly wrong, as they had done by 1642. The king *ought* to rule in his people's best interests, but what if he did not? The traditional teaching of the church was that, if a king misused his power, the people's only remedies were prayers and tears; rebellion was both a crime and a sin. Besides, it was argued, a king who abused his power a little was a lesser evil than the anarchy that could ensue if the people had the right to resist him.

In several countries in the sixteenth century – France, Scotland, the Netherlands – Calvinist writers had argued for a right to resist a 'tyrant', defined as a king who repressed their religion. Such ideas were slow to develop in England, but when war started in 1642 Parliamentarians had to justify taking up arms against the king. They could reasonably claim that the king had started the war and that they were fighting only in self-defence; some argued that natural law gave all creatures a right of self-preservation. Others argued that the king was so deluded by evil counsellors that he was 'deranged', not responsible for his own actions. Parliament was therefore not really fighting the king at all. Indeed, as the king had brought Parliament into being, they were taking up arms by the king's authority against his person.[34]

For many Parliamentarians, such arguments were not convincing. They argued instead that the safety of the people, their liberty and property, took precedence over the rights of the king and royal family. Although the logical implication of the charges against Strafford was that he had advised Charles to rule tyrannically, the terms 'tyrant' and 'tyranny' were rarely used in the early 1640s.[35] Instead, lawyers and pamphleteers developed an essentially legal view of the limitations on the king, expressed in terms of 'fundamental laws', basic principles that were held to underlie the ancient constitution.[36] It seemed logical that if the king broke these fundamental laws, and threatened his people's liberty and property, his people had a right to resist him – or rather Parliament did, on their behalf. Calvinist political theorists had countered the claim that a right of resistance would lead to anarchy by saying that the right lay in 'inferior magistrates', already invested with authority, not in the people as a whole. Parliamentarian writers claimed that Parliament derived its right to resist the king from the fact that it represented the people, while insisting that 'the people' had no right to tell Parliament what to do. They were neither as wise nor as well-informed as MPs, who were the best judges of what was good for the nation.[37]

Not all Parliament's supporters were convinced by this argument. As early as the winter of 1642–43, with the war going badly, there were claims that, if Parliament failed to fight the war vigorously enough, the people could rise against Parliament.[38] Later Parliament's own radical supporters (as well as Royalists) accused Parliament of behaving as tyrannously as the king. It claimed to be fighting for the liberties of the people, but the methods it used to win the war were denounced as oppressive. MPs were accused of perpetuating their hold on power; this was much the longest continuous Parliament in English history and there was no sign of its coming to an end. The two Houses imposed high taxes, overrode individual legal rights and dealt harshly with dissidents.

The army, and its most active civilian associates, the Levellers, turned Parliament's rhetoric against itself.[39] While accepting that the Commons should act as a check on the king, they argued that checks should be imposed on the Commons, through regular elections in a more equit-able electoral system and by laying down certain 'fundamentals' that Parliament could not alter. They claimed that government's only pur-pose was to serve the people and to protect the people's natural rights. If it failed to do so, it could be resisted or changed. No form of government was sacrosanct; neither God nor centuries of tradition could confer legitimacy.

Such arguments are commonplaces of modern liberal democracies.

To Royalists, and most Parliamentarians, they were novel and shocking. The monarchy and the whole existing order derived its legitimacy from long usage; it was held to embody the collective wisdom of countless generations, its evolution guided by God. The authority of a king or magistrate was as natural as that of the head over the body or the father over the child. 'Democracy' was a pejorative term: giving the people power over their destiny was a recipe for anarchy. This was a fundamentally conservative society. Most English people lived in villages and worked at least some of the time in agriculture; and, as Karl Marx complained two centuries later, peasants were deplorably conservative. The more the army threatened the existing order, the louder grew the cries to reinstate the king. Rioting crowds in London drove Charles I out in 1642. In 1648 many Londoners celebrated the anniversary of his coronation. In 1659–60 London crowds demoralised the army, smashed Baptist meeting houses and called for Charles II's return

The arguments of the Parliamentarians and the Levellers may seem the most interesting, and the most original, of the 1640s and 1650s, but theirs was not the dominant ideological legacy of the period. Under Charles II the Levellers were scarcely mentioned, even as bugbears.[40] Instead contemporaries emphasised the divine right of kings and more specifically non-resistance. The clergy hammered away at the traditional principle that resistance could never be justified, adding to the horrors of past revolts the ultimate horror of the regicide.[41] To emphasise divine right might seem backward-looking, even medieval, but it struck a strong emotional chord in the minds of people conditioned for centuries to see kings as in some sense sacred. Charles II touched tens of thousands of people for scrofula in the course of his reign.

The mental world of the people had little room for the concept of progress. The church taught that humankind was hopelessly corrupted by original sin and that true happiness could be found only in the after-life. *Pilgrim's Progress*, one of the finest expositions of the traditional depiction of life in this world as a hard and painful journey, was published in 1678. For most people life really was 'nasty, brutish and short', while the experience of civil war did nothing to instil confidence in the possibility of earthly progress. Even when, later in the century, there was a growing confidence, fuelled by scientific knowledge and commercial expansion, that progress really was possible, it coexisted with very widespread belief in magic and witchcraft, even among highly educated members of the Royal Society.[42]

In England, as in France, subjects responded to upheaval by emphasising authority, and especially kingly authority. Two further developments also strengthened the restored monarchy: the fragmentation of puritanism and the growth of the state. Whether or not one sees the civil wars as 'wars of religion', puritanism gave Parliament and the New Model much of the moral force they needed to fight the king. They believed that they were acting out God's plan for the world, as prophesied in the books of Daniel and Revelation. Initially the 'godly' had been confident that God would not only cast down the bishops but bring about a new godly order in church and state. Instead their views increasingly diverged.[43] Most ministers wished to establish the sort of puritan national church that their forebears had longed for under Elizabeth, with parish discipline and the power of bishops either much reduced or eradicated. But a minority believed that a true church should include only 'visible saints', and that the godly should dissociate themselves from the ungodly by forming separate churches. Many of these were led by laymen rather than trained ministers and increasingly they splintered into sects: Congregationalists, Baptists, Quakers. The Quakers shared the puritan commitment to strict personal morality, but abandoned most of the other attributes of traditional puritanism. They valued the spirit, the inner light, more than the Bible. They had no set services, no sacraments and, initially, no leaders; anyone could speak in Quaker meetings, even women. They were accused of denying the divinity of Christ when they said that His spirit was within themselves. Their reliance on the inner light created a risk of total religious anarchy as everyone followed different beliefs in their own way.

In the 1640s the Westminster Assembly of Divines had laboured long and hard to bring forth a limited Presbyterian system, in which deacons and elders assisted the parish clergy, but Parliament decided that any association above the parish level should be voluntary, so pastors and elders could call on no higher authority to make parish discipline work.[44] Parliament passed an ordinance in 1648 to establish this system, but the army prevented its implementation and in practice all except Catholics and those who wished to use the old prayer book enjoyed freedom of worship.[45] In the 1650s godly parish ministers became frustrated by their lack of power over their flocks and were worried by the proliferation of sects. Their long-held hopes of a godly national church withered away. Most of the sects became equally gloomy, as the Quakers seemed to jeopardise and discredit all that they stood for.[46]

Their disillusionment was completed by the Restoration. Those who believed in providence saw Charles II's return as God's punishment for their sins. With few exceptions, they had avoided political activism, relying on God to bring about change in His own good time. Now they subsided into fatalism and quietism. Even the Quakers reinvented themselves as pacifists, who eschewed 'carnal' weapons in their fight to win converts. All the major groups, from Presbyterians to Quakers, assured Charles II that they were peaceable and harmless – and so they were. But many were not convinced by their assurances. The 1660s saw several 'plots' – one or two of them genuine – and many rumours of plots. Moreover, ex-Royalists who had suffered at the hands of the godly in the 1640s and 1650s were not inclined to trust them – and wished to enjoy a little revenge.

It can be seen with hindsight that the nonconformists (or dissenters) of Charles II's reign were divided, demoralised and defensive – a far cry from the powerful and confident puritans of the early 1640s. They posed much less of a threat to the Restored monarchy than Charles and many others believed. The other development that strengthened the monarchy was the growth of the state. Having swept away the crown's ragbag of traditional revenues, Parliament in 1643 introduced the excise and the assessment, which (together with the customs) constituted a rational and efficient system of taxation. The state was now tapping national wealth far more effectively than ever before. When the Commons chose, they could vote much larger sums than under previous monarchs, confident that the money would be collected more or less in full and on time. In December 1664 the Commons voted £2,500,000 for war against the Dutch – about eight times the largest parliamentary grant of the 1620s. These taxes also provided solid security for loans and government borrowing increased – eventually to dangerous levels – in the 1650s.

In addition, this period – especially the years 1648–52 – saw a major expansion of the navy, which had three times as many ships in 1662 as in 1642. In the First Dutch War England showed itself at least the equal

of the greatest naval power in Europe. Experience of running wars –
mobilising men, money and ships – helped create an administration
more efficient and professional than had existed before 1640.[47] Last but
not least, in the New Model England had an army that was respected
throughout Europe. It was not inevitable that Charles II would inherit
these advantages – that was up to Parliament – but at least they existed.
If Charles could work with Parliament he might become one of the
most powerful kings that England had ever seen.

Charles II's entry into the City of London, 1660.

5

Charles II

Charles II arrived in his kingdom in 1660 amid enormous public rejoicing, buoyed up by a surge of public goodwill. As his own cynical comments recognised, this goodwill was unlikely to last, because past animosities would reappear as soon as the details of a political and religious settlement were hammered out. Unlike his father and grandfather, Charles had no experience of kingship and only a limited knowledge of his kingdoms and his peoples. He was also, despite the joy expressed on his return, in a weak bargaining position. He had no money or revenues and the powers of the monarchy had been trimmed in 1641 and then swept away in 1649. His return owed little or nothing to his own efforts and so he was entirely dependent on what his Parliaments chose to give him.

The Restoration settlement in England was shaped by two very different bodies: the Convention of 1660, balanced between men of Royalist and of Parliamentarian extraction, and the much more Royalist Cavalier House of Commons elected in 1661. The Convention passed the Act of Indemnity and disbanded most of the New Model, which Charles had offered to take into his pay. It addressed, but failed to resolve, the questions of the church, the militia and the king's constitutional position. It also did something that no previous Parliament had attempted. It calculated how much money the king would need to run the government (£1,200,000 a year) and agreed in principle to vote taxes, for his lifetime or forever, sufficient to raise that amount. This meant that the king would be able once more to 'live of his own', to rule as well as reign, and to carry on the government without having to come continually to Parliament for money. Given that Charles II was in many ways an unknown quantity, and was in no position to demand such financial provision, this was a remarkable leap of faith. Time was to show that it had been unwise.[1]

The Cavalier Parliament quickly resolved the question of the constitution. The previous twenty years had seen a wide range of legislation
passed by a variety of Parliaments. The Houses decided that any Act that
had not received the royal assent was null and void. This swept away
the ordinances abolishing episcopacy and the monarchy, but left in place
the reforming legislation of 1641. Some of this was repealed – church
courts were re-established, for example, and the bishops were restored
to the House of Lords – but ship money and Star Chamber were not
revived. Parliament passed an Act declaring that the monarch had, and
had always had, the right to command the militia and the armed forces,
remarking that challenges to that right had contributed greatly to the
recent troubles.[2] Thus one of the key issues of the 1640s, control of the
armed forces, was settled resoundingly in favour of the king. The two
Parliaments conceded the other by default. Nothing was said, after the
king's return, about his right to choose his advisers and to direct the
government. Charles did so from the outset and there was no protest.

The Cavalier Parliament also in some ways went out of its way to
increase the king's powers, at least in relation to the perceived threat of
revolution from below. Remembering the threat posed to Parliament's
freedom of debate by large crowds that assembled on the pretext of
presenting petitions, the Act against Tumultuous Petitioning limited the
number of people who could accompany a petition, to Parliament or
to the king. The accusation that Charles I was influenced by Catholics
led to a clause imposing penalties for calling the king a papist. Most
remarkably, Parliament passed the Licensing Act, the first to give the
king power to censor the press, by laying down punishments for the
authors, printers and publishers of works that had not been licensed by
designated officials and clergymen. This Act was temporary, but was
extended and expired only in 1679.

The fact that Parliament endorsed press censorship, which under
Charles I had rested on the royal prerogative, shows how fearful it was
of revolution from below. The fact that the Act was temporary showed
that the Commons were not prepared to trust the king too far; the
power of censorship would last only as long as Parliament thought fit.
The Cavalier House of Commons was Royalist, but was not prepared
to enhance the king's power any more than MPs judged strictly necessary. Many Royalists had supported the king out of duty and with

reservations. Most had strongly opposed the Personal Rule of the 1630s and supported the reforming legislation of 1641. Indeed, one reason for supporting the king in 1642 had been that he seemed more likely than Parliament to respect the ancient constitution.

One can see the limits to the Cavaliers' loyalism very clearly in the corporation bill of 1661. Since 1642 many Royalists had been ousted from town governments and replaced by Parliamentarians and puritans. The Commons passed a bill to purge the newcomers by forcing them to swear the oaths of allegiance and supremacy and to make declarations renouncing the right of resistance and the Covenant; they were also required to take communion in an Anglican church. The Lords, presumably encouraged by the king's ministers, amended the bill by adding that the king should have powers to approve those chosen as mayors and other officers, and requiring corporations to bring in their charters for renewal, which would give the king the chance to add new requirements. The Commons protested angrily that the amendments would enable the king to intervene widely in the towns' affairs and influence elections. The Lords backed down. The king appointed commissioners, mostly Royalists, who visited the towns and removed those they judged to be 'disaffected', even if they had taken all the oaths and declarations required by law.[3]

In other ways, too, the Commons showed that they were not prepared to trust the king too far. The Convention had insisted on disbanding the New Model Army. In the Cavalier House of Commons, suggestions that the king needed a standing army fell on deaf ears. Charles was able to keep up some regiments, known euphemistically as 'guards and garrisons', which eventually totalled 10,000 men, but Parliament never recognised the army's existence. It voted no money specifically for the army (in peacetime), nor did it pass legislation making it possible to punish mutiny and desertion in the common law courts; it continued to regard courts martial and martial law with deep suspicion. More important still, although the Commons made good the Convention's undertaking to vote the king revenues expected to bring in £1,200,000, they were careful not to vote too much. They were prepared to make one-off or temporary grants, but not to add to the king's permanent revenue.

Only in the 1670s, as trade boomed, did yields match the Convention's initial estimate and by that time Charles had accumulated substantial debts. As he was in constant need of money, he called Parliament more regularly than his predecessors, so that between 1660 and 1681 there were only two years without a session of Parliament. This made the Triennial Act of 1641 somewhat redundant; it was replaced in 1664 by a weaker Act, with no minimum duration of sessions or mechanism for summoning Parliament if the king failed to do so. This meant that Charles could dismiss Parliaments after as little as a week and get away with not calling Parliament in the last four years of the reign. By that time, the revenues voted at the Restoration were bringing in far more than expected. He had no financial need to call Parliament and was even able to afford to build a new palace, at Winchester, which was almost complete when he died. But until 1679 Charles was sufficiently short of money to need to call Parliament frequently and pay at least some heed to its wishes.[4]

The key to kingship lay in managing Parliament and, more generally, ruling in ways acceptable to the wider political nation. Paradoxically, a king was strongest when he ruled as his people wished, but Charles II was reluctant to do so. He was a complex character. Quick-witted and intelligent, he resembled his grandfathers (James I and Henry IV of France) far more than his father. And yet, despite his intelligence, certain misconceptions and flaws of character led him into exactly the sort of political crises that he tried to avoid. For a start, he believed that the English were a disaffected and capricious people, and that there was a real danger of another 'great rebellion'. Acting on the premise that he faced more danger from his enemies than from his friends, he tried to appease the former. The old Cavaliers found him so far from being a partisan king that he seemed totally unwilling to reciprocate their loyalty to him.

Charles, however, was unwilling to trust in something as nebulous as 'loyalty'. In his early teens he had had to contend, in councils of war, with grown men who tried to engage and use him against one another. In exile those close to him (notably his mother) had tried to use and bully him. The French had expelled the royal brothers as part of a deal with Cromwell. It was thus small wonder that Charles had become cynical about human nature and reluctant to trust anyone. This meant that his ministers could not rely on him to back them up in time of crisis. In 1667 he not only dismissed his oldest and most trusted adviser, Clarendon, but urged the House of Lords to condemn him to death.[5] In the marquis of Halifax's words, Charles 'lived with his ministers as he did with his mistresses: he used them but he was not in love with them'.[6] Halifax played down the consequences of this lack of mutual loyalty. Ministers had always to keep in mind that the king might abandon them if Parliament became too critical and so avoided advising measures that they might find it hard to justify to the Houses. As the earl of Essex put it, he needed both to give the king the best advice he could and to keep himself 'Parliament proof'.[7]

Charles accepted that he would have to work with Parliament, but not all the advice that he received was acceptable to Parliament. His policy of 'divide and rule' towards his ministers prevented them from ganging up on him, but also ensured that he received conflicting advice, some of it self-interested, some not. Much advice came from those who did not have the responsibilities of high office – body servants, mistresses, companions of pleasure. Clarendon complained that these 'little people' distracted the king from the business of government and undermined his ministers, through mimicry, mockery and sly insinuation.

Clarendon wrote from bitter experience. At the Restoration he was much the most experienced and important of the king's English ministers. A lawyer by training, in 1640–41 he had bitterly condemned Charles I's misuse of the law and the legal system. By the end of 1641, however, he had become convinced that the innovations demanded by Pym and his allies posed an even greater threat to the traditional constitutional and social order. He became a leading adviser to the king, urging him to take his stand on the ancient constitution and denouncing those who pressed the king to act more forcefully and arbitrarily. In exile with Charles II, he continually opposed the arguments of the queen mother and her allies that Charles could be restored only with the assistance of Catholics or Presbyterians. He understood instinctively the mentality of most of the Royalist party and indeed a significant proportion of the Parliamentarians – conservative, constitutionalist and Anglican. He repeatedly told the king that, if he did not betray these Royalist principles, he would sooner or later be restored. And, as the king acknowledged, he was proved right.

Although Charles saw Clarendon as the architect of the Restoration, his ascendancy in the English government was not unchallenged. Hyde was a generation older than the king, bossy, solemn and not a little boring. He continually told his master to devote more time to the business of government and was deeply distrustful of innovation. Charles, however, was determined to enjoy himself and was open to the possibility of change and progress. Clarendon was also politically vulnerable. He was denounced by partisans of the queen mother for allegedly failing to take the opportunity to make the monarchy absolute at the Restoration. He was accused of dynastic ambition after his pregnant daughter, Anne, secretly married the king's brother, James, duke of York. (Clarendon had known nothing of the pregnancy or the marriage.) To make matters worse, Catherine of Braganza, the Portuguese princess whom Charles married in 1662, proved unable to have children, although she was pregnant at least twice and once miscarried when a pet fox jumped suddenly onto her bed. Clarendon was accused of knowingly having selected a 'barren queen' so that his grandchildren could inherit the throne – as indeed they did. Meanwhile, the queen's failure to produce an heir led to proposals that Charles should divorce her or else send her away, perhaps to a nunnery. Others advanced the claims of the king's eldest illegitimate son, James, duke of Monmouth. There were repeated rumours that Charles had married Monmouth's mother, Lucy Walter, in exile, but Charles, although tempted by the idea of remarriage and fond of his son, refused either to divorce the queen or to declare Monmouth legitimate. Lacking legitimate children, Charles's heir presumptive was his brother James. (His youngest brother, Henry, died in 1660, as did his sister Mary.)

The king's habit of 'hearing everybody against anybody' might have worked better had he taken the trouble to investigate matters in detail, but he did not.[8] He hated routine and paperwork. Although he prided himself on his cynicism and his ability to make up his own mind, he was easily led by those close to him and found it difficult to say no to those who pressed for favours; in this he was very like James I. He was most likely to be influenced by whoever had spoken to him last. Those who had secured a promise of action knew that they had to procure the necessary written order then and there, or someone might persuade the king to change his mind. Even then, the king might 'allow' Clarendon, as lord chancellor, to stop the order or grant, knowing then that the odium would fall on the chancellor, not on himself. Similarly, those outside the king's sight needed to guard against being undermined by their enemies. When Ormond was lord lieutenant of Ireland, he always kept at least one of his sons (and other allies) at the royal court, to counter misinformation.

Charles was not encumbered with either ambitions or clear principles: his overriding concern was that he should not have to go on his travels again. His approach to all three of his kingdoms was pragmatic – to work with the dominant elements and avoid trouble. His strategy did not always work, partly because he sometimes could not tell which the dominant elements were. But he was in no danger of making his father's easy assumptions about authority and obedience. He trusted no one; past loyalty counted for far less than present usefulness. He placed his trust in those who could maintain order and deliver help if needed. If that meant collaborating with his and his father's former enemies, and abandoning their former friends, so be it. It was a hard world, and there were always winners and losers in civil wars. Charles's main concern was to look after himself.

In England, as in the other two kingdoms, Charles's approach was dominated by pragmatism and a wish to avoid trouble. Perhaps the most likely source of trouble was religion. In 1660 it was taken for granted that there would be some form of English national church, governed by bishops of some kind. But should it be the comparatively broad and flexible church of James I, or the narrower, more rigid church of his son? Or perhaps one closer to the ideals of Elizabethan puritans? A second question was what to do about those who did not want to belong to any national church. Should Congregationalists, Baptists, Quakers and the rest be allowed to worship freely, or should the law be used to force them to attend their parish churches?

Charles's position on these questions owed little or nothing to religious principle. He probably believed in some kind of God, one who was suitably indulgent to the frailties of kings, which in his case meant an insatiable appetite for women. He had some moral principles, saying that he believed that God hated those who deliberately did harm. He had an interest in theology, born of intellectual curiosity rather than conviction. He gave little evidence of piety or devotion. He converted to Catholicism on his deathbed and would probably have done so earlier, had he judged it feasible, which, for most of the time, he did not. He certainly had no emotional attachment to the Church of England, which revered his father as a martyr.

His attitude towards the various types of Protestant was shaped by politics. Recent experience suggested (wrongly) that the church puritans (or Presbyterians) and the sects were very numerous and that supporters of the prayer book and the old Church of England were not. Indeed, he seems at times to have believed that Anglicans formed only a minority of the population. Aware of this, Gilbert Sheldon, archbishop of Canterbury from 1663 to 1677, gathered statistics on the numbers of conformists and nonconformists, which showed that the latter comprised only a small percentage of the population. After the religious census of 1676 Charles showed less inclination to appease Protestant dissenters, but in the 1660s he was considerably more anxious. So he set out to remove any possible threat from the Presbyterians and the sects.[9]

His promise in the Declaration of Breda had been carefully worded. He wished to give liberty to tender consciences – but with the consent of Parliament and provided the nonconformists did not disturb the peace. The Cavalier Parliament had no intention of giving its consent, because, in the eyes of a majority of MPs, the sects posed a very definite threat to the peace and to the government. MPs had been bewildered by the king's conduct in 1660. He quickly started to appoint bishops, but entered into negotiations with leading Presbyterian ministers, offering bishoprics to three of them. In October he issued the Worcester House Declaration, which addressed puritan complaints going back to Elizabeth's reign. It made optional the wearing of the surplice, the use of the sign of the cross in baptism and other ceremonies, and stated that bishops were to be assisted by lesser clergy in the management of their dioceses.

A significant number of MPs in the Cavalier House of Commons had a strong emotional and spiritual commitment to the old church and were horrified to see the king sacrificing it in this way. They were determined to restore the church in its old form and to drive out as many as possible of the puritan clergy intruded into parishes in the 1640s at the expense of those denounced as 'scandalous' by the Long Parliament. The Act of Uniformity of 1662 showed strong elements of

9. Charles II, studio of John Michael Wright, *c.* 1665. (*National Portrait Gallery*)

10. Catherine of Braganza, wife of Charles II, studio of Jacob Huysmans, *c.* 1670. (*National Portrait Gallery*)

11. Louise de Kéroualle, duchess of Portsmouth, by Pierre Mignard, 1682. (*National Portrait Gallery*)

12. Nell Gwynn, studio of Sir Peter Lely, *c.* 1675. (*National Portrait Gallery*)

13. James, duke of York, and Anne Hyde, duchess of York, by Sir Peter Lely, *c.* 1665. (*National Portrait Gallery*)

14. James II, by unknown artist, 1690. (*National Portrait Gallery*)

15. Mary Beatrice of Modena, second wife of James II, by William Wissing, *c.* 1685. (*National Portrait Gallery*)

16. William III, after Sir Peter Lely, 1677. (*National Portrait Gallery*)

17. Mary II, by unknown artist. (*National Portrait Gallery*)

18. Anne, by John Closterman, 1702. (*National Portrait Gallery*)

revenge and spite. It reflected anger at the king's refusal to reopen the question of indemnity; if they could not be revenged on the Parliamentarian laity, they could strike at their clerical allies – especially those appointed against the wishes of Royalist patrons of livings. The Act laid down that all parish clergy and schoolmasters had to declare their 'unfeigned assent and consent' to everything in the prayer book and to renounce the Covenant (which all ministers had been required to take in the 1640s). They had to do so by 24 August, shortly before Michaelmas, traditionally the day on which the clergy received their tithes for the year. Whereas the Royalist clergy ejected in the 1640s were supposed to receive one fifth of their former income from their successors (many never did), the Commons were adamant that these ejected clergy should receive nothing.[10]

The Act of Uniformity completed a process of ejection in which some 1800, or one fifth, of the parish clergy were removed. This is depicted in nonconformist histories as a disaster for the church, as well as a personal tragedy for those ejected. The chance to recover the breadth of the church of Elizabeth and James I had been lost. Without its evangelical wing, it is alleged, the church became concerned with formal observance, a religion of works. In a way this is true, but it is a great exaggeration and is in some ways misleading.[11] Of those who had served in the 1650s, in a church without bishops or prayer book, four fifths remained after 1662 and the church continued to include a wide range of views and practices. If ceremonies and works came to play a more central role in Anglicanism, this was due to changes after 1662, as new generations of young clergymen passed through the universities and into the parishes. They helped to create a distinctively 'Anglican' spirituality, appealing to the senses as well as the intellect, a spirituality embracing visual elegance and church music, but also a vigorous commitment to traditional Christian morality and practical philanthropy. Archbishop Laud would not have disapproved.

How far this was intended by the Cavalier House of Commons is uncertain. What cannot be doubted is that MPs wanted the Presbyterian clergy out and to re-establish the control over church appointments and revenues that the laity had enjoyed before the civil wars. They were slower to pass measures against the sects. The first Act passed against conventicles (meetings 'on pretence of religion' of more than four people besides the immediate family) applied mainly to Quakers. Not until 1664, following a pathetic attempt at rebellion in the north west, did an Act pass against conventicles of all kinds. As with the Licensing Act, it was temporary. A permanent Conventicle Act was passed in 1670. This laid down small fines for those attending meetings, many of whom were poor and could not afford to pay much. It imposed much larger fines on those on whom nonconformist worship depended – preachers and those who allowed meetings to be held in their houses. In an effort to improve enforcement, the Act encouraged informers to give evidence against nonconformists by allocating them a share of any fines imposed. Constables and JPs who failed to act against conventicles could be fined heavily; a share of these fines was also to go to informers.[12]

Andrew Marvell described the 1670 Act as 'the quintessence of arbitrary malice'.[13] It empowered informers to profit from the sufferings of others and to dictate to magistrates and constables. At times the laws were enforced severely, but usually they were not.[14] Neighbours were reluctant to harass those whose religious views differed from their own; constables and JPs showed little eagerness to enforce the laws. Informers were often bitterly unpopular and some were beaten up or even killed. Among the nonconformists, Quakers, who met publicly and defiantly, suffered most. But in many places, and for long periods, even the Quakers were left unmolested. The Conventicle Acts, like so many laws, were left in force but not enforced, to be used if nonconformists became too defiant or disruptive, but normally held in reserve. It should be stressed that the initiative for this legislation came from the House of Commons, not the king. Charles II fought the uniformity bill every step of the way and dropped his opposition only when the Commons threatened not to complete the settling of his revenue. Even after it had passed, he tried to curb its rigour. Both the Act of Uniformity and the 1670 Conventicle Act can be seen as 'the price of money'.[15] They show the irritation of the Cavalier Commons at Charles II's repeated failures to stand up for the church for which they believed his father had died.[16]

Charles took it for granted that England was much the most important of his three kingdoms. The impact of the Scots and Irish on English affairs between 1637 and 1651 led him to view his two outlying kingdoms as potential sources of instability that needed to be kept quiet. He did not share his father's obsession with uniformity and was not going to repeat his mistake of trying to bring Scotland and Ireland into line with England; each was to be governed on its own terms. Charles II could see only one positive use for either kingdom – as a reservoir of armed force in case of another civil war in England. By the 1680s he had a sizeable army in Ireland. The Scottish army was small (but highly professional and ruthless), but an Act of 1663 created a substantial Scottish militia and explicitly allowed it to be used outside Scotland.[17]

In Scotland the civil wars had been the swansong of noble military power. Nobles marched at the head of their tenants, clan feuds and banditry revived. The disorder and destruction were never on the scale seen in Ireland, but the economic damage was severe. Cromwell's army of occupation restored a semblance of order, and the temporary abolition of heritable jurisdictions weakened the nobility further. The forces in society which valued order emerged more opposed than ever to the misuse of noble military power.

To some extent the Scottish nobles re-established their position after 1660. Heritable jurisdictions were restored and a few magnate families (such as the Campbell earls of Argyll) established effective control over large tracts of territory. As part of this process, the nobles (like so many continental nobilities) ceased to struggle against the state and instead colonised it.[18] When a militia of 20,000 foot, but only 2000 horse, was established in 1663, magnates installed their kinsmen in it, as they did in local government. The militia became the main means of coercing dissidents, nonconformists and recalcitrant taxpayers, but it could also be used by those in power to pursue their feuds and harass their enemies.[19] Magnates also began to mobilise voters in parliamentary elections – Scotland's electorate was tiny compared with England's – and built up blocs of supporters in Parliament. But above all they sought high government office and positions at court and on the privy council.[20] The nobles remained fiercely competitive, but their competition was expressed less through violence than through politics and the law. The first coherent digest of Scottish law appeared in 1681 and most clan disputes were now settled in the courts.[21] Violence and feuding continued, especially in the Highlands, but on a smaller scale. Evidence of a more orderly society can be found in the growing habit of building unfortified country houses and a great increase in the number of public markets.[22]

The greatest threat to the royal government was not noble violence but religious disaffection. For many, perhaps most, Scots the civil wars had been wars of religion and the kirk had become the most powerful expression of Scottish identity. Charles II believed that hardline Presbyterianism was incompatible with monarchy – as his grandfather had said, 'no bishop, no king' – and saw episcopacy, not as an essential attribute of a true church, but as a necessary means of controlling the clergy. He did not repeat his father's mistake of introducing an English prayer book into Scotland, and he would probably have been prepared to revert to the limited episcopacy established by James VI. This was restored when the Scots Parliament passed the Act Recissory, which declared null and void all Scottish legislation passed since 1633, including that abolishing the lords of the articles and bishops. Charles was then persuaded by a small group of Scottish nobles and clergy to establish a more thoroughgoing episcopacy. He hoped that leading Presbyterian clerics would accept bishoprics, but few did. Clergy who refused to accept the authority of the bishops – at least a quarter of the total – were removed from their livings.

The decision to strengthen episcopacy created serious problems for the king's government in Scotland. Charles himself soon decided that he had given the bishops too much power and the Scottish Act of Supremacy of 1669 was designed to bring the bishops and the church under tighter royal control.[23] The majority of the population disliked or despised bishops; indeed their removal had been the *raison d'être* of the national Covenant. Many moderate Presbyterians were prepared to suffer episcopal government so long as the services and parish discipline remained unchanged, which they did.[24] But for a substantial minority episcopacy was intolerable; one group, the Cameronians of the south west, refused to recognise the restored monarchy at all, because for them there was no king but Jesus. Charles therefore faced a problem of religious dissent that at times exploded into rebellion.

For much of Charles's reign, his viceroy in Scotland was John Maitland, earl (later duke) of Lauderdale, who had never been a Royalist and had a record of firm Presbyterianism. Lauderdale was tough and brutal even by Scottish standards, and for almost twenty years he oscillated between limited toleration and targeted repression, as he sought the best way of dealing with religious dissent.[25] Generally he ignored small nonconformist meetings ('house conventicles'), while trying to crack down on larger meetings in barns or fields. In 1678 he quartered a 'host' of 8000 militiamen, mostly Highlanders, on the extreme Covenanters of the south west, much as Louis XIV's intendants were to use dragoons to 'convert' the Protestants of southern and western France a few years later. Sustained lobbying by many of the other nobles, who argued that Lauderdale's brutality provoked more trouble than it prevented, finally persuaded the king to dismiss him in 1679.

Although there was talk of a political union between England and Scotland under Charles II, and serious negotiations in the late 1660s, Charles in general accepted that Scotland had to be governed as a separate kingdom, using a privy council made up of Scottish nobles. The Scottish Parliament, thanks to the lords of the articles, passed the bills put before it and made few complaints. Although the military resources of the Scottish government were insufficient to cope with a Covenanting rebellion in 1679 – an army had to be sent from England – the decline of noble power and the creation of the militia meant that normally the government was able to maintain order. After the collapse of the 1640s, the economy revived and parts of Scotland began to enjoy a modest prosperity, which in itself was a force for order. Although religious dissent continued, in time the episcopal church began to win acceptance and even a degree of affection, especially in the north east. Charles II's ambitions in Scotland were limited and he achieved them, despite the handicap of committing himself to full-blooded episcopalianism.

As Charles's first priority was England, and as English opinion was strongly anti-Catholic, he realised that in Ireland he would have to work exclusively with Protestants. Protestant Royalists (as in Scotland) were in relatively short supply and New English Protestants were firmly entrenched in power at the time of Charles's return. They had extended their landholdings and increased in numbers as a result of the confiscations of the 1650s. They had also played a key role in the Restoration. A group of moderate Cromwellians, led by Lord Broghill, had seized Dublin Castle at the end of 1659 and had called a Convention, which met before that of England. Charles was proclaimed king on 14 May 1660, a few days after he was proclaimed in England.[26]

The Dublin Convention asked the king to appoint Broghill and one or two other New English to head the Irish executive, but Charles decided to appoint a lord lieutenant and chose Ormond. He was a Protestant, but came of an Old English Catholic family, and so had a wider knowledge and range of contacts than most Protestants in Ireland; he had also been a staunch Royalist. Unlike the New English, he was inclined to see the divisions of Ireland in terms of nationality rather than religion. He regarded the Old English as more loyal than the Irish, and tried to divide the Catholic clergy by devising a loyalty oath, the Remonstrance, which many of the ordinary priests were prepared to take, but the Jesuits and other religious orders were not.[27] Ormond's policy of divide and rule was based on a pragmatic awareness that the Dublin government lacked the military resources to expel all the priests from Ireland,[28] but it was condemned by the New English, who claimed that all Catholics were potential or actual rebels. They feared that, under Ormond, the land settlement of the 1650s might be tampered with or even reversed. Dispossessed Catholics lobbied vigorously at the English court to get their lands back, claiming unblemished loyalty to the House of Stuart and emphasising the Cromwellian past of many of the new proprietors. Charles was sympathetic to the Catholics' claims, as in some cases was Ormond, but (as the latter sagely remarked) if Charles wished to satisfy both the old and the new proprietors he would need a second Ireland.[29]

When Charles summoned a new Irish Parliament, it passed the Act of Settlement in 1662 (followed by the Act of Explanation in 1665), which tried to create a framework for resolving these conflicting demands. It empowered the king to set up a court of claims to hear the cases of Catholics who claimed to be 'innocent' of complicity in the rising and the Confederation of Kilkenny. It would decide how much land, if any, they should get back, and how far the new Protestant proprietors should be compensated. Aware that the Catholics stood little chance of a fair hearing from the New English, Charles appointed Englishmen to the court, which also heard claims from dispossessed Protestant Royalists, such as Ormond and the duke of York. The members of the court were subjected to all kinds of pressure and importunity. Protestant Royalists and Catholics with good connections secured part or all of what they claimed, to the rage and fury of the new proprietors, who claimed that many of the allegedly 'innocent' Catholics had in fact been rebels. Led by the former Lord Broghill (now earl of Orrery), the New English raised the issue in the English Parliament and intrigued at the English court, and succeeded in having Ormond removed from the lord lieutenancy in 1669. At the end of the whole sordid process, the Catholics' share of the land had increased from as little as 10 per cent to 20 or 25 per cent. The majority of the land transfers were confirmed.[30]

Although the New English felt aggrieved and insecure, the 1660s ended with Ireland firmly under Protestant control. Not only had many Catholics lost land, but the transplantation to Connacht had weakened the ties between lord and peasant. Nevertheless, the influence of the Irish landlords continued. In 1691 William King, later archbishop of Dublin, wrote that formerly the power of Irish landlords over their tenants had been absolute. Even after they had lost their estates, landlords continued to regard the estates and tenants as theirs:

And by their pretended title and gentility, they have such an influence on the poor tenants of their own nation and religion … that these tenants look on them still … as a kind of landlords [and] maintain them after a fashion in idleness … [They support themselves] by stealing and torying [banditry], or oppressing the poor farmers and exacting some kind of maintenance, either from the clans or septs or from those that lived on the estates to which they pretended.[31]

King was writing with a polemical purpose, at the end of the Jacobite wars of 1689–91, trying to show that the Catholics remained dangerous. But banditry remained a serious problem – Charles II's reign has been described as the golden age of torying. Although many tories were thugs who preyed indiscriminately on English and Irish, Catholic and Protestant, some were seen by the Catholic peasantry as heroes.[32] Other observers, notably the statistician Sir William Petty, claimed that the greatest influence over the peasants was that of the Catholic priests and bishops, who constituted the 'internal and mystical' (as opposed to the 'external and apparent') government of Ireland. It was the priests, he claimed, who collected the money to support the gentlemen who lobbied at the English court.[33] The access that these Old English Catholics enjoyed at the court of Charles II, along with the continued power of the Irish former landowners, alarmed the New English. In addition, although Catholics were excluded from public office, they were allowed to practise law, giving rise to fears that they might find legal flaws in the Protestants' titles to land.[34]

There can be little doubt that Charles sympathised with the dispossessed Catholics, but normally he did nothing that might disturb Protestant opinion in England. In 1672, when he briefly allowed Catholics partial freedom of worship in England, he relaxed the restrictions on Catholics living and holding office in Irish corporate towns and commissioned two Catholic officers in the Irish army. He abandoned these policies after an outcry from the English Parliament in 1673.[35] At the very end of the reign, in late 1684, he again began to commission Catholic officers; this reflected the growing influence of his now Catholic brother, James.

There was little real attempt to suppress Catholic worship in Ireland and the ordinary clergy were rarely persecuted, although there were occasional orders to expel Catholic bishops and those clergy who refused to take the Remonstrance. Neither the earl of Essex (lord lieutenant from 1672–77) nor Ormond, who returned to the lieutenancy in 1677, could be described as bigoted against Catholics.[36] Petty thought that most Irish Catholics were too wretchedly poor to rebel. Three quarters of them, he wrote, lived in cabins, without chimney, door, stairs or windows; they 'feed chiefly on milk and potatoes, whereby their spirits are not disposed to war'.[37] The New English were much more anxious about the danger from the Catholic majority, not least because they had no forum within Ireland in which to state their case or seek remedies for their problems. The Dublin Parliament was dissolved in 1666, after voting the crown generous revenues in perpetuity. The revenue was showing a comfortable surplus by the 1680s and no Parliament met again in Ireland until 1689. The New English found some reassurance in the militia, numbering 10,000 horse and 14,000 foot, which became the settlers' primary mode of self-defence; Charles and Ormond regarded it with some suspicion. The army, which numbered between five and seven thousand, was wholly Protestant, but was seen as an instrument of the crown rather than of the Protestants of Ireland, especially when dissenters were excluded in the latter part of Charles's reign.[38] Together the army and the militia proved more than sufficient to maintain English control over Ireland. Ormond remarked in 1679 that he had little to fear from the Irish, except torying. He saw the Ulster Scots and English-born dissenters as a greater threat to the Dublin government.[39] Apart from a plot to seize Dublin Castle in 1663, however, Ireland remained quiet throughout Charles II's reign.

The clashes between Charles and the English House of Commons about religion showed that the Cavalier Parliament was far from being the lapdog of resurgent monarchy. MPs had definite expectations and tried to ensure that Charles lived up to them. Nevertheless, considered in the longer term, it is striking how much was restored at the Restoration, especially as the king was in no condition to make stipulations or demands. Charles II no longer had the pretext to raise taxes without Parliament, but he had little need to. His revenues were voted by Parliament and undoubtedly legal. Taxpayers paid up, although sometimes reluctantly. Yields increased substantially in the second half of Charles's reign and his ministers developed a highly professional and efficient revenue administration.[40] Star Chamber and the other prerogative courts were not revived, but the king still appointed the judges. The common law courts could deal ruthlessly with critics of the regime and there were many more political executions under Charles II than under Charles I.[41] Charles II had a modest standing army, a large navy and a revamped militia. He appointed ministers and councillors, generals and bishops, JPs, lords lieutenant and a wide range of other officials. He had ultimate control over the machinery of justice, the armed forces, the administration and the church. In most respects he exercised the same powers as his father, if not more. And he had the advantage of a substantial, growing, permanent and uncontested revenue. Perhaps most important of all, criticism and opposition were inhibited by fear of another civil war.

It is therefore possible to make a case for seeing the restored monarchy as robust and strong. It is also possible to argue that serious weaknesses remained and that major problems were not addressed at the Restoration. The state's means of coercion remained weak. Charles's army was not insignificant but it was widely scattered, with units as far afield as Barbados and Tangier.[42] The militia coped well enough with unarmed rioters but was little use against trained soldiers, and the fact that militiamen were ordinary citizens reduced their reliability in times of crisis. Although the revenue was collected by salaried professionals, much of the rest of the administration at a local level was carried on by unpaid amateurs, which meant that it was still necessary to maintain their goodwill. As long as effective government depended on cooperation, as long as the king needed additional revenues from Parliament – which he always would for war – the question remained: what would happen if that cooperation broke down?

The ancient constitution rested on the cosy assumption that the interests of king and people were congruent, or at least compatible. Usually they were, but in 1640–42 they were not and people had been forced to ask themselves which took priority. This question was not addressed at the Restoration, because it did not seem relevant. The breakdown of trust in 1640–42 had been the exception, not the norm, and could be blamed on Charles I (or his evil counsellors); the system was sound, but it had been badly used. At the Restoration, the main priority was to return to normal – to get government working again and to take steps to ensure that there could be no recurrence of civil war. To dwell on the exceptional circumstances of 1640–42 was not helpful; to ask what would happen if the system failed again might be seen as tempting providence.

It was far from inevitable that Charles II would lose the confidence of his Parliament and his people. In the 1660s criticism of the king's government owed much to the perception of the court as corrupt and incompetent, as well as flagrantly immoral. Charles was not helped by events outside his control, such as the Plague of 1665 and the Great Fire of 1666, both of which badly damaged public morale. On the other hand, it was the decision of the king and his ministers not to put out a battle fleet in 1667 that opened the way for the Dutch to sail up the Medway, burn the pride of the king's fleet and carry off his flagship, the *Royal Charles.* As panic reigned in London, the king (according to Pepys) was with his mistress, Lady Castlemaine, chasing a moth.[43] After Parliament had voted so much money for the Dutch War, Londoners complained bitterly that the government had left the capital defenceless and exposed to the enemy.

Charles's problems also owed much to his inability to take seriously the concerns of the Cavalier House of Commons. This was seen most clearly in 1667–72, after the fall of Clarendon. In these years there was no dominant minister, but a motley group, who were rivals as much as colleagues, and whose initials happened to spell out the word 'Cabal'. Lauderdale's main concerns lay in Scotland, but like every chief minister of Scotland or Ireland he needed to exercise influence in the English court as well and so was at times drawn into English affairs. Sir Thomas Clifford was a relatively obscure Devon gentleman who rose to become lord treasurer, and a peer, in 1672. He was an efficient man of business, utterly devoted to the crown and more than willing to contemplate the creation of a more absolute monarchy. He owed his rise to the patronage of Henry Bennet, earl of Arlington, whose influence with the king dated back to the 1650s. Arlington was the model courtier, polished, urbane and deferential. He was also an experienced diplomat, whose linguistic skills far outstripped those of the more insular Clarendon. If he had views of his own, Arlington normally subordinated them to those of the king, his master, and he was, of all the king's ministers, the one Charles most liked and trusted.

The other two members of the Cabal were very different. Anthony Ashley Cooper, Lord Ashley, had started as a Royalist in the civil wars, but had changed sides and had served under the republic and Cromwell. He was one of the former Parliamentarians taken into office by Charles II, who gave him the then relatively minor office of chancellor of the exchequer. He was promoted to the much more prestigious post of lord chancellor in 1672 and created earl of Shaftesbury. Ashley was a complex character. Often denounced by contemporaries as a turncoat and a republican, he was certainly committed to limited monarchy and opposed to absolutism, but he saw no difficulty in serving the crown, judging that it was vital for the king to receive responsible counsel. He was also deeply committed to colonial expansion and founded the colony of South Carolina, where the city of Charleston was built at the confluence of the Ashley and Cooper rivers. Ashley was also deeply and consistently committed to securing liberty for Protestant dissenters.[44]

The final, and strangest, member of the Cabal was the second duke of Buckingham. The son of the favourite of James I and Charles I, Buckingham had been brought up with the royal children and had a familiarity with Charles that nobody else could match. Buckingham inherited much of his father's verve and charisma, but his energies were even more undirected than his father's had been. The poet John Dryden famously described him as 'fiddler, chemist, statesman and buffoon', 'everything by starts and nothing long'. For the historian Gilbert Burnet, who usually found some good even in the worst of people, Buckingham had 'a perpetual unsteadiness about him. He is revengeful to all degrees and is, I think, one of the worst men alive, both as to his personal deportment and as to the public.' [45]

When the duke was prepared to focus on the business of government – and often he was not – he urged the king to abandon the old Cavaliers and the church and to win the support of the dissenters by removing the laws against them. Although Buckingham does seem to have been committed in principle to toleration, at least for all Protestants, there was a large element of personal hatred in his campaign against Clarendon and Ormond; Buckingham was good at hating. In urging the king to remove the remaining 'Clarendonians' (or Cavaliers) from office, Buckingham and his political allies wished to secure places for their own clients. He pursued a vendetta against the Anglican clergy and especially the bishops; he told the king he could solve his financial problems by selling off the lands of the cathedrals. The king, for his part, made it clear to most of the bishops after Clarendon's fall that, because of their support for the former chancellor, they would not be welcome at court. Apart from playing on the king's concern to defuse opposition, Buckingham encouraged his belief that dissenters constituted a substantial majority of the population and claimed that they included most of the leading manufacturers and merchants, on whom the nation's wealth (and much of the king's revenue) depended. Advocates of toleration argued that the spectacular economic success of the Dutch owed much to their willingness to allow freedom to those of all religions, or none.[46] Persecution, on the other hand, would drive dissenting craftsmen abroad and severely weaken the economy.

In the late 1660s Buckingham and Ashley tried to persuade the king that the toleration of Protestant Dissent would be popular in the nation and that if he called a new Parliament it would be very sympathetic to Dissent. Charles was only half convinced. He still saw religious dissent as evidence of political disaffection and was reluctant to put himself fully into the hands of those he distrusted. The Cavalier House of Commons, although truculent, was fundamentally loyal. Buckingham convinced himself and the king that he could manage even the Cavalier Parliament, provided the 'Clarendonians' were removed from office, but the king's attempts to propose a measure of toleration were brusquely rebuffed.

When the king changed tack and agreed to the 1670 Conventicle Act, the response of the Commons was euphoric. MPs walked two by two to Whitehall Palace and the Speaker gave the king the House's formal thanks. They were then invited down into the royal cellars, where they spent the rest of the day drinking the king's health on their knees. The sessions of 1670–71 were the most harmonious of the reign. It seemed as if Charles had at last learned the lesson that he should rule as the Commons wished. Such joyful moments as the 'going into the cellar' were, alas, rare and had to be treasured.[47] MPs remembered them fondly as relations between king and Commons deteriorated.

In the long history of the Cavalier House of Commons – it last sat in December 1678 – the years 1672–73 marked a watershed. Until then MPs had been perturbed by the king's insistence on favouring former Parliamentarians and his plans to broaden the church and alleviate the burden on dissenters. They had been irritated by incompetence, dismayed by corruption and repelled by the immorality – or amorality – of the royal court. The Commons had been alarmed by the Act of the Scottish Parliament allowing the king to use the militia abroad – presumably in England; why should the king want this? Convinced that huge amounts of public money had been embezzled or wasted in the Second Dutch War, the House had set up a committee to examine accounts and interrogate officials. But they had still been able to persuade themselves that this was all due to poor advice and that the king was basically well-intentioned. After 1673 they were not so sure. Many came to suspect that the king and his brother were plotting to bring in popery and arbitrary government.

The origins of this sea change lay in the king's foreign policy. By the 1660s, with Spanish military power on the wane, the three leading powers in western Europe were France, the Dutch Republic and England. France was much the largest of the three, but had hitherto failed to convert its large population and resources into military might. That soon changed under the young and ambitious Louis XIV, who in 1667 invaded the Southern Netherlands, contemptuously sweeping aside Spanish military resistance. This French success alarmed the Dutch and English, as did

France's extensive naval shipbuilding programme. In 1660 the Dutch and English fleets were both much larger than that of France, but the balance of naval power was shifting rapidly towards France. In addition, France was emerging as a serious commercial and colonial competitor to the Dutch and English, its spheres of interest coinciding with England's – North America, the Caribbean and India. In 1665 many still regarded the Dutch as England's main commercial and naval rivals, which was why the Commons voted £2,500,000 for a war against them. By 1672 informed Englishmen regarded the French as both a serious rival and a threat to Protestantism and liberty. Indeed, Louis XIV was seen as aspiring to a 'universal monarchy', spreading Catholicism and absolutism throughout western Europe.[48]

In these circumstances, many came to believe that it would be in England's best interest to ally with the Dutch against the French. The Dutch were Protestants and their constitution guaranteed the liberties of the people, as well as allowing a degree of religious freedom. With hindsight, this seemed even clearer. For the next century and a half hostility to France was to be the keystone of English and British foreign policy, as well as a central feature of British national identity. This did not seem so clear in the 1660s, at least to Charles II. From the outset he had tried to secure an alliance with his cousin, Louis XIV. To Charles, he and Louis seemed natural allies. France was a monarchy whose society was permeated by aristocratic values. The Dutch Republic was dominated by the merchants of the great cities of Holland, grubby bourgeois, who denied Charles's young nephew, William of Orange, his rightful place in the great offices of the Republic. The Dutch also gave shelter to English radicals and regicides, their tolerance extending to political as well as religious dissidents. Charles suspected that disaffection in England was encouraged and perhaps masterminded from Holland.

Charles also had plausible geopolitical reasons to favour a French alliance. In 1665 Philip IV of Spain died and was succeeded by Carlos II. Carlos was mentally retarded, the product of too much inbreeding within the Habsburg family. In his case the jutting Habsburg lower jaw, already prominent in the person of Philip II, stuck out so far that his teeth did not meet and he could not chew his food. Although he married, he had no children and his health was so poor that his death was imminently (and in some quarters eagerly) expected for the next thirty-five years. When he died, the great Spanish empire was likely to break up. The Austrian emperor and the French king were the most likely to grab the lion's share (especially as Louis had cannily married a Spanish wife), but Charles had his hopes too. He calculated (correctly) that Louis's most immediate concern was to seize as much as possible of the Spanish Netherlands, to secure his northern frontier and put an end to the encirclement of France by Habsburg territories. Charles had no objection to this. Unlike many of his subjects, he did not see Louis as posing a military threat to England. He hoped that, in return for his assistance in Europe, Louis would allow the English a free hand to seize as much Spanish territory as they could in the Americas. Far from embracing the principle of the balance of power, Charles calculated that England would gain most from joining with a stronger power against a weaker one.

Charles's relationship with Louis got off to a poor start. There were arguments about money, particularly in relation to the sale of Dunkirk to the French. There were also arguments about protocol and precedence. Charles insisted that French ships should salute English naval vessels in the Narrow Seas. Louis was irritated by the patronising attitude of his older cousin, remarking that losing one's kingdom was not an ideal qualification to rule. Above all, in 1662, Louis signed a defensive treaty with the Dutch, leaving Charles out in the cold. Louis saw the Dutch as a possible threat to his designs on the Spanish Netherlands – and England as no threat at all. In 1666 Louis reluctantly fulfilled his treaty obligations, coming in on the Dutch side against England in the Second Dutch War, but his main concern was the Spanish Netherlands. In 1668 the Dutch and English threatened to make war on France if Louis did not accept the (very extensive) concessions offered by the Spanish. Louis was annoyed, but Charles had at least shown that he could hurt him. After Louis's armies had withdrawn from the Netherlands, the two kings resumed negotiations about an alliance. Charles proposed a joint war against the Dutch; Louis was wary. And then, suddenly, Charles introduced a new element into the negotiations.

On 25 January 1669 (the feast of the conversion of St Paul) Charles convened a small meeting. His brother James, a recent but still secret convert to Catholicism, was present, as was Clifford, who was to convert some time later, and the ever-present Arlington, who was to follow his master's example by converting on his deathbed. Charles declared, with tears in his eyes, that he was convinced of the truth of Catholicism and wanted the advice of the meeting as to how best to advance the Catholic interest. After some debate, it was decided that the best step would be an alliance with France. Charles sent a Catholic peer, Lord Arundell of Wardour, to inform Louis. He also wrote, in cipher, to his only surviving sister, Henriette, who was married to Louis's effeminate and spiteful brother, the duc d'Orléans. (He bore the courtesy title 'Monsieur', so she was know as 'Madame'.) The contacts were very secret; neither of the accredited ambassadors was informed. Charles told Louis that he was desperate to declare himself a Catholic, but feared his people might revolt if he did, so he asked for military help or (preferably) money to raise troops. He also suggested that he should declare his conversion before beginning the war with the Dutch.

Opinions have varied about Charles's motives. Some suggest he was seeking extra money, others that he wished to control the timing of the war against the Dutch. Another possibility was that giving Louis inform-ation that could ruin him was a gesture of trust on Charles's part – or perhaps that he wished to create a religious reason why Louis should choose the English rather than the Dutch. All assume that Charles was a consummate liar and lacked religious commitment. After all, his grandfather, Henry IV, had converted back to Catholicism in order to secure the loyalty of Paris. It is also possible that, for once, Charles was sincere. It seems likely that, if he had been free to choose his religion, he would have been a Catholic. He also appreciated the loyalty of many Catholics to the king's cause in the civil wars and to himself during the famous journey from Worcester. James had just converted; so, more importantly, had the great Huguenot general, Turenne, with whom James had served in the French army and for whom the two royal brothers had the greatest respect. One should not be too swayed by the talk of tears in his eyes – Charles could summon them as well as the most accomplished thespian – but it is possible that, for once, they were real. The mood did not last, and by 1670 he was finding pretexts for delaying his declaration of conversion. He also, in May 1670, allowed his sister to talk him into agreeing that the Dutch war should come first. She had come over, bringing a treaty of alliance, signed at Dover, which committed the two kings to attack the Dutch. There were also several secret clauses, relating to Charles's conversion, that in the end were never acted upon and remained secret long after Charles's death.

By the time the treaty of Dover was signed, Charles's war aims had shifted. The English negotiators had initially had great hopes of the alliance: 'if we must presently enter into the war on the death of the king of Spain', wrote Clifford excitedly, 'the charge will be defrayed and America his Majesty's'.[49] But Louis had no intention of allowing the English a free hand in the New World. In 1668 he had signed a secret treaty with the Emperor Leopold, partitioning the Spanish empire between them, under which Spain's American possessions would go to the emperor. Louis did not disabuse Charles of his hopes, but did nothing to encourage them; seeing this, Charles's attention turned elsewhere. In the Dover treaty Louis agreed that Charles's reward for defeating the Dutch would be a group of towns and territories at the mouth of the Rhine and Maas rivers, notably Walcheren. These would enable him to harass the Dutch economically and militarily, with a view to overthrowing the republican regime and establishing William of Orange as a puppet ruler. Thwarted in his hopes of enlarging his American empire, Charles planned to establish a bridgehead on the Continent and to elevate his nephew to his rightful offices.

The Third Dutch War offered the prospect of considerable gains, but carried great risks. Charles was under no illusion that it would be popular in England, but hoped that military conquest would bring the public round. Like his father in 1639, he went to war in 1672 without calling Parliament. He gave several other hostages to fortune. He had secured a grant of money from Parliament in 1671 by warning of the alleged threat posed to England by France. To raise ready cash for the war, he suspended the repayment of his debts, which naturally harmed his credit. Anxious that dissenters might rebel once England was at war against the Calvinist Dutch, he issued a declaration of indulgence. Although Buckingham, Ashley and perhaps Lauderdale favoured the toleration of Dissent in principle, Charles's main concern was to regulate and control it. Arlington probably spoke for the king when he wrote that the aim of the indulgence was to 'keep all quiet at home whilst we are busy abroad'.[50] Meeting houses and preachers had to be licensed by the crown. They had to meet with the doors unlocked, showing that there was still the suspicion that they might be plotting instead of praying. Catholics were to be allowed to worship in their homes, which in practice they already did. The addition of the clause about Catholics no doubt reflected the influence of James and Clifford, but perhaps the king wanted it too. When asking Parliament in 1662 to allow him to soften the rigour of the Act of Uniformity, Charles had asked the Houses also to do something for the Catholics, in recognition of their loyalty in the civil wars.

In preparing to launch the Dutch War, Charles showed damning signs of political and financial bad faith. The indulgence overturned the Conventicle Act, passed barely two years before, and the liberty granted to Catholics was highly controversial. The fact that Catholics did not have to seek licences led some to argue that they were granted more liberty than Protestants. The declaration was also constitutionally questionable. Charles's advisers assured him that he had the power to grant the indulgence, but were very vague about its nature. The declaration referred to 'that supreme power in ecclesiastical matters which is not only inherent in us but hath been declared and recognised to be so by several statutes and Acts of Parliament'.[51] But the fact that Charles had asked the Houses in 1662 to enable him to allow a few Presbyterian ministers to avoid full conformity did not suggest that he had believed then that he possessed the power to dispense individuals from the penalties of the law, let alone suspend whole categories of statutes.

The normal and proper way of annulling an Act of Parliament was by another Act of Parliament. If the king could do this on his own authority, even if only in ecclesiastical matters, where might it end? Might he not suspend the legislation of the 1530s and carry England back to Rome? Suspicions that the declaration was part of a design to impose popery and arbitrary government were strengthened by the alliance with France. Louis was the self-conscious epitome of absolute monarchy and his war demands on the Dutch included complete freedom and civil equality for Catholics within the Republic. To make matter worse, Louis's armies crossed the Rhine and swept towards Amsterdam, until the Dutch halted them by cutting the dykes and flooding the land. Meanwhile, Charles was unable to seize his share of the spoils because he could not establish supremacy at sea. The expeditionary force he had raised to seize Walcheren remained in England, grumpy and ill-disciplined. Rumours abounded that the real purpose of the army was to enable the king to impose absolutism at home.

It was also noted that James did not take Anglican communion at Easter 1672. There had long been complaints about Catholics at court, including those in the household of the queen, although Catherine of Braganza, unlike Henrietta Maria, showed no inclination to meddle in politics. James was far more politically active and had the reputation of being tough and authoritarian. Also, as Charles had no legitimate children, although he was to father seventeen acknowledged bastards, James was heir presumptive to the throne. The English faced the possibility of their first Catholic monarch since Mary Tudor.

The naval and military failure of 1672 forced Charles to recall Parliament early in 1673, as the war could not continue without money. The Commons were prepared to grant money, but at the price of annulling the declaration of indulgence. Most of his ministers urged Charles to maintain the indulgence and find money elsewhere, but the French ambassador (and Arlington) urged him to give in and he did. News of the cancelling of the declaration was greeted with bonfires and rejoicing in many places. Now thoroughly alarmed about popery, the Commons complained loudly of the favour recently shown to Catholics in Ireland and passed the first Test Act. This required all office holders to take communion according to the Anglican rite and make a declaration against several key aspects of Catholic belief, notably that the bread and wine in the eucharist turned into the body and blood of Christ. There were few Catholics in civilian and military offices, but the test was designed to flush them out. Its victims included James, whose resignation as lord admiral confirmed what many already suspected, and Clifford, who laid down the post of lord treasurer and died (probably committing suicide) soon after.

Charles had got his money for the war, but at heavy political cost. His regime was more identified with popery than ever. James, whose first wife Anne had converted to Catholicism shortly before her death, was seeking a new, Catholic wife. An increasingly frantic search around the courts of Catholic Europe ended when James married, by proxy, the fifteen-year-old Mary Beatrice, princess of Modena. As she made her way to England, Charles reconvened Parliament. The Commons passed a resolution to ask the king that the marriage should not be consummated, an extraordinary interference in the private life of a member of the royal family. James had two daughters by his first wife, both educated as Protestants. If his new wife bore him a son, he would take precedence in the succession over his Protestant half-sisters, which opened up the prospect that the Stuarts would become a Catholic dynasty. As the princess and her mother arrived in London, effigies of the pope were burned on bonfires, a forceful indication of what the public thought of the marriage.

Meanwhile, the war had gone no better in 1673 than in 1672. The English fleet was still unable to defeat the Dutch at sea, so the army remained in England. In the Dutch Republic, where the leaders of the republican regime had been lynched soon after the French invaded, William III, still not quite twenty-two, had become the political and military leader of the republic. He gained allies, notably Spain and the emperor; the latter's involvement opened up a new theatre of hostilities in Germany. The French gradually ceded ground in the Republic and sought conquests instead in the Spanish Netherlands, to consolidate their northern frontier. Charles pleaded with Louis to help him secure Walcheren and the other promised places, but Louis, despite fair words, had no intention of doing so. He did not want the English to become even a minor continental power and Charles had served his purpose by keeping the Dutch fleet engaged while Louis advanced by land.

As the focus of the war shifted, Charles became irrelevant. When he was forced by lack of money and pressure from Parliament to make peace with the Dutch, Louis was gracious. Charles could be of little use to him as an ally in what was now essentially a land war. All he now asked was that Charles should remain benevolently neutral, which Charles was happy to do. His shattered credit and depleted finances left him unable to consider war without substantial help from Parliament, and he had no intention of allowing Parliament to push him into making war against France. He feared, as James I had, that, once Parliament had embroiled him in a war, it would exploit his need for money in order to strip him of his powers and take over the direction of government. Other reasons for avoiding war against France included the fear that Louis might publish details of the Secret Treaty of Dover and the hope that Louis might send military aid in the event of a renewed civil war in England. It was not a very realistic hope: Louis had shown no evidence of altruism in his dealings with Charles and it was probable that bringing over French troops would make any civil war worse. Nonetheless, it was a hope to which Charles clung at a time when everything seemed to be falling apart.

The events of 1672–73 were widely seen as a watershed in England and Europe. Burnet wrote later that 1672 marked the beginning of the fifth, and greatest, crisis of the Protestant religion.[52] The belief that the king was basically well-intentioned could not survive so much evidence of his bad faith. There seemed all too many indications that Charles, his brother and Louis had joined in a great plot to impose popery and arbitrary government on England and Europe – and perhaps Scotland and Ireland as well. These fears were highly exaggerated, but there had been some at court who talked of making the monarchy stronger, and several ministers (including Lauderdale) urged the king to use force rather than abandon the indulgence. Charles was not normally a man of great ambitions and plans, his instinct being to avoid trouble. But the French alliance and the proposal to link it to the announcement of his conversion were both his ideas. They originated in grandiose and implausible dreams of empire and conquest. By the beginning of 1674 these had collapsed in ignominy and Charles faced the problem of making good the damage.

He chose as his chief minister a man untainted by association with the Third Dutch War. The ministerial Cabal of the past few years dispersed. Clifford was dead and Arlington ceased to be involved in policy-making. Lauderdale remained in charge of Scotland, but the English House of Commons was sufficiently concerned by his conduct there, and his influence on the king, to impeach him in 1674. The charges included claiming that the king's edicts had the force of law. Buckingham, too, was impeached. He survived, but the king deprived him of his offices and he retreated into surly, but ineffectual, opposition. Shaftesbury lost his post of lord chancellor and became the most effective critic of the government.

The new chief minister, the lord treasurer, Thomas Osborne, earl of Danby, was a former client of Buckingham. A tough, blunt Yorkshireman, he explained the king's financial predicament to him with brutal simplicity, telling Charles that, as he could not manage without money from Parliament, he would have to rule as Parliament expected.[53] This would include enforcing the laws against both Catholics and dissenters and dissociating himself from France. This was not palatable advice, but Charles was gradually persuaded to comply with it. In 1675 he ordered that the penal laws against all types of nonconformity should be enforced. As Louis conquered more and more of the Spanish Netherlands, Charles tried to persuade him to moderate his demands. When Louis refused, Charles (encouraged by William III) presented him with an ultimatum. When this was rejected early in 1678, Charles prepared for war, sending a large expeditionary force to Ostend. Louis was furious, threatened and blustered, but eventually made peace at Nijmegen in 1679.

Although Charles followed Danby's advice, his relationship with Parliament did not improve. Trust had been the greatest casualty of the Dutch war and many could not believe that Charles would ever really turn against France. The Commons called on him to declare war, but would not promise to provide the necessary money. In 1678 they refused to vote money until they were satisfied that steps were being taken to prevent the growth of popery at home. Many feared that the army raised against France in 1678 would be used to establish absolutism in England. Wits said that the Commons wanted a war without an army and the court wanted an army without a war.

Fears of arbitrary government were intensified by Danby's methods of political management. He insisted that Charles should give offices only to reliable supporters of the government and organised a 'court party' in the Commons. His opponents, the 'country party', claimed that he was corrupt, giving jobs and money in return for votes, and that he was setting up absolutism by stealth, eroding the independence of Parliament so that it was no longer an effective check on the king.[54] Meanwhile Charles still had no legitimate heir and his brother was a Catholic. James's unpopularity was temporarily reduced when his elder daughter, Mary, married William III in 1677, but fears for the future of Protestantism grew in 1678, especially after the raising of the army. Might the king, James and Danby use it to impose popery?

Into this highly charged atmosphere came Titus Oates with stories of a popish plot to kill the king on a variety of occasions and using a variety of improbable means. Although he had an unsavoury past, Oates told his story confidently, reeling off names, places and dates. Many who heard his story believed him; the few who did not kept their doubts to themselves. Both history and the current mood predisposed the general public to believe the story and it seemed to be devastatingly and independently confirmed.[55] First, Sir Edmund Berry Godfrey, the magistrate who took Oates's original sworn statement, was found murdered in mysterious circumstances. Then the papers of Edward Coleman, James's former secretary and a very active Catholic, were seized and were found to contain talk of the reconversion of England and the eradication of Protestantism (that 'pestilent northern heresy'). Although the letters contained no mention of a plot against the king, the language was alarming enough and it was clear from their contents that James had known of Coleman's dealings with Louis XIV's confessor and others. James denied this point blank; Coleman was quickly tried for treason and executed before he could do any more harm.[56]

Even without Coleman's letters, the story of the plot raised the question of what would have happened had it succeeded. Although Oates had declared that James had no knowledge of the plot, he was its obvious beneficiary, as he would have succeeded to the throne if his brother had been killed. The many informers who were inspired by Oates's fame and financial rewards to add to his story had no such inhibitions; some also accused the queen. Their testimony and the evidence in Coleman's letters convinced most Protestants that James must have had something to do with the plot and forced them to consider the prospect of a popish successor. Meanwhile, Danby's tarnished and increasingly shaky ministry came to an end. Ralph Montagu, recently ambassador in Paris, had been recalled for seducing one of the king's illegitimate daughters. Eager for revenge, he produced in the Commons a letter from Danby (countersigned by Charles) ordering Montagu to ask Louis for money in return for making peace, at a time when Danby was asking Parliament for money to make war on France. The revelations destroyed Danby's remaining credibility and did little for the king's. After almost eighteen years Charles decided to bring the Cavalier Parliament to an end.

The period between February 1679 and March 1681 is often called the 'Exclusion Crisis'.[57] It saw three general elections (the first since 1661) and three attempts to pass bills to exclude James from the succession.

The thinking behind the bills was that, as a Catholic, James would be bound to seek to establish popery and arbitrary government. Even if he did not wish to do so, his priests would force him to. One of the bills was rejected by the Lords, the others were aborted when the king dissolved Parliament. There were numerous petitions asking the king to summon Parliament and agree to exclusion and counter-petitions, 'abhorring' such attempts to dictate to the king. There were also massive demonstrations, particularly associated with ritual burnings of the pope. After the lapsing of the Licensing Act, political issues were debated vigorously in the press. There were great complaints about 'corruption' and bitter denunciations of Danby's methods of government. Danby was impeached, raising echoes of the trial of Strafford. By the end of 1680, indeed, impeachments were flying thick and fast. As the Anglican clergy defended James's right to the throne, they were attacked as 'papists in masquerade' and 'favourers of popery'. Some claimed that Charles's words did not represent his true wishes, because he had been so misled by evil counsellors that he did not know what he was doing. It was said that he was morally obliged to do whatever the Commons advised him to do. It was all horribly reminiscent of the crisis of 1640–42.

Many feared civil war, yet none ensued. Charles II handled the crisis far better than his father had done. Charles I had made substantive concessions that he had no intention of observing. Charles II made cosmetic concessions. Where his father had refused to take his opponents onto the privy council, Charles II appointed a new council, consisting of his opponents, with Shaftesbury as its president. He offered to agree to limitations on a future Catholic king, which he and the Commons knew would be ineffective. He agreed to the investigation of the plot, rewarding Oates and his imitators and ordering the execution of those convicted on their evidence, although he believed there was little truth in it. He maintained informal contacts with opposition politicians, leading them to hope that he would eventually allow himself to be 'forced' to abandon his brother. His basic approach was conciliatory, because he was deeply afraid of rebellion and civil war; he read widely on the events of 1640–42. But he refused to make any substantive concessions. He granted Danby a comprehensive pardon and made it clear that this chief minister would not be sacrificed. He ignored or evaded suggestions from his new privy council that he should change the officers of the army, navy and militia. In 1678 he vetoed a bill to allow the militia to remain in arms longer than usual, which few other than himself saw as a threat to his prerogative. He responded to petitions to allow Parliament to meet by delaying it for many months. And, above all, he refused to agree to his brother's exclusion from the throne.

Charles's mixture of insubstantial concessions and steely determination was in stark contrast to his father's extensive concessions and dreams of resorting to force. In the spring of 1679 Charles II agreed, with some trepidation, to disband the forces raised for the war against France. He sought to maintain the moral high ground by eschewing any recourse to violence. He also kept a tight control on the reins of government, refusing to cede his right to make appointments in the magistracy and the armed forces and exploiting his control over the machinery of the law. After the initial panic generated by the plot, and the execution of the first batch of those convicted for their alleged part in it, the courts began to acquit the accused, starting with a case in which the informers also accused the queen. The judges, who had steered the proceedings in order to secure convictions in the cases of Coleman and others, now pointed out flaws in the evidence. They also did what they could to limit the new found freedom of the press.

Unlike his father, Charles had enough military units in and around the capital to deal with disorders.[58] He also kept a firm grip on London, where the militia was in loyal hands and the lord mayor and aldermen maintained order.[59] Other circumstances favoured him too. Apart from the Covenanting rising in Scotland in 1679, which was quickly suppressed by Monmouth at Bothwell Brig, there was no disorder in either of the outlying kingdoms. Ireland's main contribution to the Popish Plot was a group of informers, all Catholics, recruited by Shaftesbury as witnesses when the supply ran out in England. Ormond remarked that he suspected that they were motivated less by zeal for the Protestant religion than by the prospect of money and of exchanging their rags for fine clothes. They were not ideal witnesses. Their thick brogue made it difficult for the English to understand them, and when the political tide turned they were quick to testify against their Whig patrons. Most important of all, despite the superficial similarities with 1640–42 (which both the supporters and opponents of exclusion exaggerated for their own polemical purposes), there was not the will to start a civil war. The memories were too deep and too painful and the issues, although similar, were not so strongly felt.

In December 1641 Londoners had taken to the streets because they feared being shelled from the Tower. In November 1679 and November 1680 as many as two hundred thousand people watched processions carrying an effigy of the pope across the City, from Aldgate to Temple Bar, where it was burned. The floats carried familiar figures – Jesuits with bloody daggers, promiscuous nuns, papist plotters and 'papists in masquerade'. It was a great spectacle, rather like the lord mayor's show or a 'play'. There was a lot of free liquor, everyone had a good time, but when it was done the people did not storm Whitehall or the Tower, but tottered home to bed.[60] The French ambassador was amazed that the night had passed without bloodshed; it would not have been like that in Paris, he said. It seems probable that the public on balance thought that Exclusion was desirable, but not a matter of life and death. It related not to what could happen tonight or tomorrow, but what might happen if Charles died before his brother. There was not the immediacy, the gut fear, that had driven Londoners to riot in 1641–42. As one leading exclusionist, Lord Russell, remarked: 'I never found ... that there was the least disposition or tendency to [rebellion] in the people. And 'tis known rebellion cannot be now made here, as in former times, by a few great men'.[61]

One further similarity between 1640–42 and 1679–81 was the deep fissure that opened up within the nation, this time between the supporters and opponents of Exclusion. Divisions appeared especially on those occasions on which individuals had to make a clear and public choice: in votes in Parliament and in elections, in subscribing petitions and addresses. The terms used to describe the two 'parties' were 'petitioners' and 'abhorrers', soon adapted into 'Whigs' and 'Tories'. The former was a contraction of 'Whiggamore', an extreme Covenanter from south-west Scotland; the latter referred to Catholic Irish bandits. Terms originally coined as insults came in time to be acknowledged, even with pride. In January 1683 Ormond remarked 'if we have good luck, we shall be all Tories; if we have bad luck, we shall not be all Whigs'.[62]

The battles between the parties, in Parliament, elections and the press, were verbally and sometimes physically bruising. The Tories deeply resented being described as papists or favourers of popery. At the hustings the Anglican clergy, who voted in a general election for the first time in 1679, were insulted, jostled and worse. As in 1640–42 the conservative backlash against populist tactics (in this case more apparent than real) created vigorous potential support for firm action and strong monarchy. Charles I had been unable to harness the surge of Royalist support effectively because he was driven out of London. Charles II maintained control of London and of most of the machinery of government, and took advantage of the Tories' fear and anger to wreak revenge on the Whigs and their allies, the Protestant Dissenters, raising the Stuart monarchy to the zenith of its power.

Charles began to offer a firm lead to the Tories immediately after dissolving the last of the three Exclusion Parliaments, which was held at Oxford in March 1681. The Commons' behaviour had become increasingly extreme and outrageous. They had initiated frivolous or malicious impeachments, expelled MPs for subscribing abhorrences, and resolved that anybody lending money to the king was an enemy to the kingdom. Charles issued a declaration similar to his father's of 1629, condemning the extravagant behaviour of the Commons and promising to uphold the church and rule according to law. He ceased payments to Oates and his fellow informers, some of whom now were ready to testify against Shaftesbury and the Whigs. First, though, the Irish witnesses had to prove their credentials as defenders of the Protestant interest by giving evidence against Oliver Plunkett, the Catholic archbishop of Dublin, who was to be the last Catholic victim of the Popish Plot. Oates refused to turn his coat, insisting that his story had been true, but retribution was at hand. In 1683 the duke of York was awarded damages of £100,000 against him; Oates was to remain imprisoned until it was paid. In 1685 Oates was convicted of perjury. The offence did not carry the death penalty, so he was sentenced to a flogging that was intended to kill him; it did not.

The king's first priority in 1681 was to place the machinery of law and coercion in safe (Tory) hands. He had already started to weed out unreliable JPs and deputy lieutenants, but now the process gathered pace. Some of the more extreme Tories denounced any who were less zealous than themselves as 'Trimmers' or closet Whigs, but the king and his ministers refused to dismiss anyone on the basis of unsubstantiated allegations. Meanwhile, Tory lords lieutenant organised and drilled the militia and encouraged firm action against Whigs and dissenters.

Their activities intensified after the Rye House Plot of 1683, an alleged design to assassinate Charles and James on their way back from New-market to London. The subsequent investigations revealed more than one shadowy and half-formed conspiracy. Some involved assassination, and the extent of the conspiracies was exaggerated by the Tory press, but they had more substance than the Popish Plot.[63] Several of those implicated were convicted of treason, some on limited evidence. A treason conviction required two witnesses, but Algernon Sidney, the brother of an earl, was convicted on the evidence of one witness and a republican tract found in his study. This might seem unjust, but the judges believed it was vital for the safety of king and state to secure convictions. Other aristocratic casualties included Lord Russell, the son of the earl of Bedford, who was executed outside his London home, and the earl of Essex, who (almost certainly) cut his throat in the Tower, although there were allegations that he had been murdered. The treason trials of 1683–84, like the early Popish Plot trials, were intended to get across the message that treason was a sin, and a mortal sin at that. They showed that the loss of Star Chamber had not deprived the crown of the power to destroy its enemies.

The Rye House Plot led to more intense measures in the localities. The houses of Whigs, or suspected Whigs, were searched for arms. Many were confiscated and deposited in the magazines of the county militias. The duke of Beaufort, lord lieutenant of Wales, embarked on a progress around the principality. In town after town he put the militia through its paces, drilling and firing volleys. The musters, accompanied by bonfires and loyal toasts to the king and his brother, attracted large crowds. They provided entertainment for the people, but also empha-sised the military power of the state.[64] Meanwhile the persecution of dissenters, which had revived in 1681, intensified, as the king made it clear that he wished the laws to be enforced. In the Roundhead strong-hold of Taunton, the mayor closed the meeting houses and burned the seats and fittings in the market square, as the county gentry drank loyal toasts.[65] Increasingly, dissenters met clandestinely, or not at all. Only the Quakers stubbornly continued to meet – in the street, if their meeting houses were closed, even in the bitter winter of 1683–84. As far as the

Tories were concerned, nonconformist conventicles were a front for plotting against the state and they had to be suppressed. Where the civil authorities were unable to suppress them, they were backed up by the militia and the army. Whig morale crumbled and Whig dignitaries crept to make their peace with the king and his brother. 'I am an old sinner', Lord Wharton told the duke of York. 'So you are my lord', replied James affably.[66]

Similar policies were followed in Charles's other two kingdoms. In Ireland Ormond purged the army of dissenters and carefully watched the Ulster Scots. In Scotland, the duke of York played a leading role in strengthening royal power. He first arrived in 1679, soon after Bothwell Brig and the removal of Lauderdale. While continuing to connive at small-scale dissent, James addressed the political threat posed by Presbyterian extremists. He pushed through the Scottish Parliament a 'test', to be taken by office-holders and clergy, which recognised the king as head of the church and included a renunciation of any right of resistance and a promise to attempt no alteration of the government in church or state. The welcome James received in Scotland owed much to resentment of the English Parliament's attempts to exclude him from the English throne without any consideration of the repercussions in Scotland. He showed himself as tough and brutal as Lauderdale towards extremists and dissidents, but he built up a following among the magnates and Highland chiefs, clergy and people. Unlike Lauderdale, he came without Scottish alliances and entanglements; he was also heir presumptive to the Scottish throne, which made many nobles eager to seek his favour. His staunch defence of the established Episcopal Church won him friends in Scotland and did not go unnoticed in England. When he returned to England in 1682 he left Scotland quiet, its government in the hands of a loyal privy council.[67]

In England, the king controlled the machinery of government in the counties, but not in the corporate towns which, under their charters, had the right to elect their own magistrates and officers. In 1662–63 the Corporation Act commissioners had removed those they regarded as 'disaffected', but many had subsequently been re-elected and new men of similar views had joined them. Magistrates were often reluctant to persecute fellow townspeople; Tory peers and gentry complained that the towns were a dangerous gap in the machinery of law enforcement.

The most dangerous of all was London. Tories controlled the court of aldermen and the militia, but the sheriffs, who also served for Middlesex, were popularly elected. In 1680 and 1681 radical Whig sheriffs were chosen and selected juries that routinely acquitted Whigs and dissenters. Charles was furious when a London jury decided that Shaftesbury had no case to answer when charged with treason. The king decided that the City had to be brought to heel and the attorney general launched a legal challenge to its charter. The crown's case was not strong, but the king had chosen the judges and they knew what was expected of them. Eventually in June 1683 they declared that the London authorities had not observed the terms of their charter, which was forfeit to the king. Instead of issuing a new charter, the king appointed a group of commissioners to run the City.

Other towns anxiously watched these proceedings. If London, with all its resources, could not protect its charter, how could they? Some towns had already surrendered their charters in 1682. After the Rye House Plot and the judgment against the City, the trickle became a flood. Most towns received new charters allowing the king to remove members of the corporation at will. This was designed to exclude 'disaffected' magistrates from office, but it had the additional bonus (from the Tories' point of view) that it would strengthen their prospects in parliamentary elections. In many towns only the corporation had the vote, but even where the franchise was wider a strongly Tory mayor and corporation would help secure the election of Tory candidates.[68] The general election of 1685 produced an overwhelmingly Tory House of Commons.

The legal and political onslaught on the Whigs was accompanied by an ideological assault. Tory clergymen argued that both royal authority and the hereditary succession of the crown were divinely ordained. To resist the former or to try to alter the latter were offences against God. Many in their zeal to deny that resistance could ever be justifiable argued, or implied, that it was the Christian duty of subjects to do whatever the king commanded. Meanwhile, in 1683, the university of Oxford condemned a range of opinions expressed in printed books, almost all of them published between 1640 and 1660. These opinions related to the rights of subjects and limitations on the power of kings, such as 'all civil authority is derived originally from the people'.[69] Such views found little expression by 1683. Press censorship had been re-established, in fact if not in law. After condemning the Whigs' use of the press to stir up 'the rabble', the Tories countered with highly effective propaganda of their own;[70] Whig works were suppressed. Although the Whigs had claimed to represent 'the people', it is clear that there was a strong popular Toryism, just as there had been a strong popular Royalism during the civil wars.[71] The Exclusion Crisis had opened up divisions in English society reminiscent of those of the 1640s.

In the years after 1681 Charles II finally overcame his aversion to ruling as a partisan king. He was badly shaken by the crisis and by a serious illness, probably a stroke, in 1679. Convinced that the Whigs wished to destroy the monarchy and himself, he finally (if hesitantly) gave up trying to appease his enemies and resolved to rely on his 'old friends'. For the first time in his reign, he ruled as a large section of his people wanted and was able to live out his last years in relative comfort and peace. By falling 'into the vein of his people', and exploiting the backlash against the perceived threat of civil war, Charles had raised the Stuart monarchy to a position of unprecedented strength.[72] This was not something that he had consciously sought to do. Despite the suspicions of many of his subjects, he had no vision of absolute monarchy. He did not share his grandfather's theoretical belief in the godlike attributes of kings, nor the highly authoritarian mindset of his father and brother. Charles II's instincts had been to avoid trouble and in particular to avoid provoking those whom he saw as the enemies of the monarchy and of himself. He had therefore refused to become a partisan king or to keep alive the divisions of the civil war. But his foreign policy and the conversion of his brother created deep fears of 'popery and arbitrary government' which were to precipitate exactly the sort of crisis he had tried to avoid and the nation became almost as deeply divided as in 1642. Faced with a divided nation, Charles had no choice but to take sides and so was able at last to reap the benefits of the surge of support for strong monarchy that had developed in reaction to the civil wars. He understood, at last, that the Tories and Church of England men were the true friends of monarchy, but also that his new-found increase of power depended on his maintaining their support. His brother failed to appreciate this crucial point and was to demolish the strong position that he had inherited at almost breakneck speed.

Charles did not enjoy his position of peace and comfort for long. His new palace at Winchester, in many ways a symbol of the repose that he craved, was not quite finished when he died, after suffering another stroke, on 6 February 1685. There were rumours that his brother had had him poisoned. There were also rumours that he had died a Catholic, and these were true. The night before his death, James had cleared the bedchamber of bishops and councillors and then brought in John Huddleston, a Catholic priest who had helped Charles after Worcester. Charles told him that he had earlier saved his body and now he would save his soul. He confessed and received the eucharist and extreme unction; when the bishops returned, he refused Anglican communion. Not long after he died, James published two papers which purported to give his brother's reasons for his conversion.

For many dissenters and Whigs, the revelation of Charles's deathbed conversion confirmed their suspicions and compounded their belief in his malevolence and deceitfulness. The optimism of the Restoration seemed a world away and the trust and even generosity shown in the Restoration settlement now appeared to many to have been mistaken. The discovery many years later of the true contents of the Secret Treaty of Dover was to give his critics further ammunition. Others were not so negative. By 1685 many Tories were delighted that, having been misled by evil counsel earlier in the reign, Charles had at last seen the light and learned to support the church and to rely on his 'old friends'. The Tories' fondness for Charles grew with hindsight, as his successors (first James, then William) proved deeply disappointing. Like the very different reign of Elizabeth I, Charles II's was later seen as 'golden' in a way that had been far from apparent at the time.

Such a view was not confined to Tories. The marquis of Halifax had been a critic of the government under Danby; as the most determined proponent of moderation (or 'trimming') within the council in 1681–85, he had been at times an isolated and uncomfortable figure. Yet in his 'Character of King Charles II', written between 1689 and 1695, Halifax was far more inclined to forgive than to condemn. Whereas many were deeply critical of Charles's relentless promiscuity, Halifax wrote of 'a warmth and sweetness of the blood', 'an overflowing of good nature', commenting that 'if all who were akin to his vices should mourn for him, never prince would be better attended to his grave'.[73] Despite his misfortunes, wrote Halifax, Charles was never vindictive and his love of ease meant that his subjects were able to live at their ease as well. He concluded: 'Let his royal ashes then lie soft upon him, and cover him from harsh and unkind censures; which though they should not be unjust can never clear themselves from being indecent'.[74]

6

James II

Charles II and James II were both similar and dissimilar. Unlike their father, they were tall, around six foot, and very energetic, physically and sexually. Each had a string of mistresses, although Charles's were usually beautiful and voluptuous, while James's were so plain that it was maliciously suggested that they were given him by his priests as a penance. Charles was not in love with his wife, but usually treated her with kindness and respect, even though he clearly blamed her for the failure to produce a legitimate heir. He showed no remorse about his affairs. James was overawed by his first wife, who died in 1671, and loved his (much younger) second wife. He was racked by guilt at his inability to remain faithful to either of them and explained his expulsion from England as God's punishment for the sins of the flesh.

The brothers differed in appearance. Charles was dark, even swarthy, with full lips and a pencil moustache. He looked more Latin than Anglo-Saxon, whereas James looked increasingly sallow with age. But it was in intelligence and temperament that they differed most. Charles was not a scholar like James I, but he was quick and witty. He had a range of interests, which included theology, navigation, shipbuilding, chemistry and anatomy. His knowledge was wide rather than deep, not least because he had a limited attention span. He was easily bored, which meant that those who could keep him amused could wield considerable influence over him. Unlike his father, he was a king who liked to have fun. He had a lively, if coarse, sense of humour, at times shocking the relatively broad-minded Samuel Pepys.[1] He was bored by paperwork, hated sitting down and often conducted business while striding through the park.

James had little sense of humour. It was said of one of his mistresses that nobody understood what he saw in her, because her greatest attribute was her wit, which he was too dim to appreciate. He did not share his brother's intellectual interests. His sole contribution to the Royal Society, of which he was a founder member, was the information that a herb called 'star of the earth' could cure the bite of a mad dog.[2] In later life he acquired some knowledge of astronomy, as applied in navigation, and he shared Charles's interest in the navy. What he lacked in incisiveness and insight, James made up in diligence. Unlike his brother, he lived within his means and paid his bills. He kept an orderly court, having his women smuggled up the backstairs, instead of flaunting them for all to see. He was a conscientious – perhaps over-conscientious – administrator, and in times of crisis he became overwhelmed by petty details, losing track of the bigger picture.

The difference between the two brothers was epitomised by their religious outlook. Charles was something of a free spirit; it could be said of him, as of his grandfather, Henry IV of France, that his religion was one of the great mysteries of Europe. He claimed to be a connoisseur of sermons, but also confessed to sleeping through them. Piety and devotion seem to have meant nothing to him. James started out as a conventional rather than a convinced member of the Church of England, but his life changed when he converted to Catholicism, probably in 1668. The reason for his conversion is revealing. He was persuaded that the Roman Catholic Church alone could claim to be a true church, in the sense of having been founded by a direct commission from Christ: 'Thou art Peter and on this rock I shall build my church'.

James had been a soldier, trained by Marshal Turenne, and he conceived of authority and obedience in military terms: officers obeyed generals, soldiers obeyed officers. Having established to his own satisfaction where religious authority lay, he was impervious to other arguments. He told Gilbert Burnet that Burnet might be too clever for him but he would never change his mind.[3] James's willing acceptance of authority also made him embrace the full gamut of Catholic devotional life. One cannot imagine Charles submitting the direction of his spiritual and moral life to a confessor. James apparently did so willingly, although he was still unable to curb his libido. He also seems to have derived genuine satisfaction and edification from Catholic worship. Although he did not inherit his father's aesthetic sense, he was sensitive (as Charles II never was) to the beauty of holiness – or at least devotional routine. In his last years, an exile with little to fill his days, he was punctilious in performing his devotions and was forever looking at his watch so as not to be late for them.

Given the differences between them, it is not surprising that the brothers were never close. Charles, anticipating a joke made about several American vice-presidents, said that nobody would assassinate him if it meant putting James on the throne.[4] At times there was a real coolness between them, as James's enemies tried to turn his brother against him by suggesting that he was encouraging opposition to Charles's policies or perhaps even plotting to supplant him. James's most formidable rival for his brother's favour, at least in the first half of his reign, was Buckingham. The stolid James was no match for the dazzling duke, with his rapier wit. Charles found Buckingham by turns infuriating and intoxicating, but more often than not he was swept along by his briskness, wit and capacity for merry-making.

If the two brothers were not close, at bottom they remained loyal to one another. Despite Buckingham's malicious accusations, James, unlike the sons of the Hanoverian kings, never formed a 'reversionary interest', or served as a focus for those dissatisfied with his brother. Indeed, his record of dogged loyalty is hard to match in English history. His loyalty was reciprocated. Charles was deeply irritated by James's lack of political sense in converting to Catholicism and complained bitterly of the problems that his conversion created for both of them. However, when in 1679–81 the Commons tried to exclude James from the succession because of his Catholicism, Charles refused to agree. It may be that Charles feared that his enemies would turn on him, once James was out of the way, but there was also a sense of family solidarity. Charles might be outwardly informal, but he had a very keen sense of his dignity as king and of the royal status of the Stuart family. He indignantly rebutted suggestions, in 1660, that Parliament should be used to annul James's 'inappropriate' marriage to Anne Hyde.

The brothers' political attitudes and attributes were also different. They shared a common sense of kingly authority and a common suspicion of their subjects. Experience of civil war and exile led them to exaggerate greatly the extent of disaffection – the English did not in fact deserve their reputation as a rebellious and ungovernable people. But there the resemblance ended. James was in many ways similar to his father. He carried his military mindset into government and politics.

Life was a matter of simple polar opposites: good and bad, right and wrong, obedience and disobedience. Kings should command, subjects were duty bound to obey. A king was to be guided by his conscience, the law and his counsellors. It was not up to subjects to tell him what to do. Like his father, James was so convinced of his rightness and rectitude that he dismissed criticism as either ill-informed or malicious. He could be almost alarmingly straightforward. 'We cannot but heartily wish, as it will easily be believed, that all the people of our dominions were members of the Catholic Church', he declared in 1687.[5]

In particular, he was unable to comprehend, and refused to take into account, the anti-Catholic prejudices of his people. He believed that these were born of generations of ignorance and misinformation, for which the Protestant clergy were largely responsible. If only people could see Catholicism as it really was, as he had done, they would realise that it was the one true religion.[6] If only people were not constrained by fear of punishment or exclusion from office, they would become Catholics. Conversion, for James, had seemed natural and easy. He could not understand why others should not find it equally natural and easy – or why so many people remained stubbornly Protestant. Faced with opposition, it never occurred to him that he was being unwise or impolitic. He pressed on regardless, confident he was right and that he was carrying out God's will. As he pondered his and his family's deliverance from exile and his survival of the Exclusion Crisis, he became convinced that God had preserved him in order to advance the Catholic religion. He also believed that any show of weakness would encourage more opposition. Convinced that disaffection was rife and that republicans were plotting to overthrow the monarchy again, he argued that the only way to save the monarchy was through firmness and force. In the crisis of 1679–81, while his more supple brother ducked and weaved, James urged him to rely on the authority of the crown – and on the army.

However straightforward James might be, he often behaved in ways that his subjects regarded as dishonest or illegal. In part this was a product of anti-Catholicism. His Protestant subjects assumed that Catholicism was fundamentally dishonest and that Catholics were allowed to perjure themselves and break all the laws of God and man in order to advance the interests of their church. They therefore looked for hidden meanings and hidden agendas that perhaps were not there and put the most sinister constructions on all that James said and did. But he also gave them ample cause for suspicion. His religious zeal distorted his perceptions. It seemed to him natural justice that Magdalen College, Oxford, founded long before the Reformation, should be handed back to Catholics and filled with Catholic fellows. His Protestant subjects saw it as an attack on the Church of England and on property rights, as college fellowships were seen as equivalent to freeholds. He also tended to overcompensate for generations of discrimination against Catholics by appointing men to office simply because they were Catholics. Although he claimed to be even-handed, and called for a fair debate between Protestant and Catholic, in practice he promoted the production of Catholic pamphlets and tried to stop the Church of England clergy from preaching or writing against popery.

His understanding of the law was also both partial and flexible. Given his cast of mind, he was ill-equipped to grasp legal subtleties. He remarked that he believed that the law was what his judges said it was, but he dismissed judges whose view of law and justice differed from his.[7] Having secured a ruling from the judges that he had the right to dispense with the penalties of law in particular cases, in the interests of justice, he claimed that this gave him the right to dispense the whole nation from the penalties of the laws against Catholic and nonconformist worship. Although he said in 1688 that he did not claim the right to *suspend* laws,[8] that was precisely what he did. Like his grandfather, James I, he was impatient of legal niceties that seemed inconsistent with natural justice. Unlike his grandfather, he was not restrained by either caution or a sense of the politically possible. Confident of his rightness, and convinced that any sign of weakness would encourage his enemies, he pressed forward, uniting his subjects against him more quickly and more completely than even Charles I had been able to do.

James II's first act as king was to summon the privy council. He told the councillors that he believed that the laws 'are sufficient to make the king as great a monarch as I can wish' and promised that he would respect his subjects' property and preserve the government in church and state as established by law. He added, 'I know the principles of the Church of England are for monarchy and the members of it have shown themselves good and loyal subjects; therefore I shall always take care to defend and support it'.[9] The councillors asked permission to print his statement, which was granted. A more careful reading might have tempered their enthusiasm. His assurances included no reference to his subjects' liberties and his commitment to the church was conditional. He would defend and protect the church *because* its members were loyal, but *only so long as* they continued loyal. The church had no claim to legitimacy in itself, so it deserved protection for its political loyalty alone.

It was soon to become apparent that James's understanding of 'loyalty' differed from that of the Tories and the Anglican clergy. For James non-resistance implied unquestioning and unconditional obedience, particularly in the measures that he was to take on behalf of the Catholics. Anglicans and Catholics were, in his eyes, little different. He had found conversion from one church to the other very easy and they had fought on the same side in the civil wars. Years before Burnet had tried, and failed, to explain to James that non-resistance was not the same as passive obedience.[10] The clergy taught that resistance was wrong, but also that Christians should obey God rather than man. If the king commanded something contrary to the Word of God, they should refuse to obey – and suffer the consequences. The clergy, in particular, should be prepared to suffer, and even to face martyrdom, for the church's sake.[11]

Much of the tragedy of James II can to be traced to this fundamental failure of understanding. The Tories had rallied to him in the Exclusion Crisis on the assumption that he would defend the church, just as the clergy were defending his right to the throne. Until 1686 he did so, in Scotland as well as in England. The Tories assumed that he would continue to rule as if he were an Anglican, even if he had worshipped openly as a Catholic from the very beginning of his reign. But James regarded such dissembling as unmanly, just as he had resisted pleas from the bishops and his brother to conform outwardly to the Church of England. He believed that God wanted him to advance and promote His one true church.[12]

James believed that he was on a mission from God and that he did not have much time. He was already fifty-one and, although Mary Beatrice had borne him several children, none had lived and so he had no Catholic heir. His elder daughter, Mary, remained the heir apparent. Both daughters had been brought up as Protestants and both had married Protestants. Anne, the younger, had married Prince George of Denmark, an amiable nonentity. By contrast Mary's husband, William of Orange, was the uncontested leader of European Protestantism and the most determined adversary of Louis XIV. James had to assume that, unless God blessed him with a son, he would be succeeded by a Protestant. He consistently rejected proposals from Catholic courtiers that he should tamper with the succession, using the standard Tory argument that 'where the crown is hereditary (as it is in these kingdoms, thanks be to God) His Almighty power alone can dispose of it'.[13] He aimed, therefore, to strengthen the position of the English Catholics to a point where his successor would have no choice but to allow them toleration. As Catholics were few, he needed to encourage converts from Protestantism, who would not come forward while the penal laws penalised every aspect of Catholic life (including recusancy) and the Test Acts denied Catholics access to Parliament and public office. James needed to remove these laws, as barriers to conversion. Once Catholics were able to compete freely for converts, in James's view there could be only one winner.

James's whole strategy as king rested on this single, naïve assumption. Had his Protestant subjects known of it, they would not have taken it seriously, because in their view nobody in their right mind would convert to Catholicism. It was assumed that the Roman Catholic Church relied on force to make converts, a point hammered home in 1685 by Louis XIV's use of dragoons to 'convert' his Protestant subjects to Catholicism. Many Huguenots fled to England, where their accounts of their suffering added to Protestants' fear and loathing of popery. But James did not intend to use force. He believed it would be unnecessary, but also counter-productive, because any force used by Catholics in his reign would be repaid with interest in the next. His army, although large, remained predominantly Protestant until some Catholic units were raised late in 1688. On the other hand, James made full use of his authority in pursuing his religious policy and dealt sternly with criticism or disobedience. Although a Catholic, he was legally supreme head of the Church of England and exercised his right to appoint bishops. In 1686 he delegated his disciplinary powers as supreme head to an 'ecclesiastical commission', whose main function was to punish clerics and academics who expressed views that the king did not like. This body removed the Protestant fellows from Magdalen College and suspended Bishop Compton of London for refusing to discipline one of his clergy for an anti-Catholic sermon.[14] The main qualification for new bishops was an unconditional willingness to do the king's bidding.

If converts were to come forward, James needed to remove the penal laws and Test Acts. They would have to be removed legally, in other words repealed by a Parliament. If the repeal was legally questionable, few would risk converting and a Protestant successor would easily be able to reverse it. At the start of his reign, James assumed that a Tory Parliament would make no difficulty about repealing the penal laws and Test Acts, but in that respect the Parliament elected in 1685 disappointed him. It started well, voting him all his brother's revenues and more and actively supported him against the rebellion that summer of the duke of Monmouth.

After leading the army that defeated the Covenanters at Bothwell Brig in 1679, Monmouth had become increasingly identified with the Whigs and with exclusion. Although many Whigs regarded Mary (and William) as the obvious Protestant alternative to James, many others distrusted William, who was regarded in his own country as ruthless, authoritarian and very possibly planning to turn the Dutch Republic into an absolute monarchy. Monmouth, by contrast, was English, handsome and charismatic. There were repeated rumours that there existed proof that Charles had really been married to Lucy Walter, placed for safekeeping in a mysterious black box. Although Charles continued to deny that he had married Lucy, Monmouth's supporters continued to insist that he had.

By the end of 1679, Monmouth had emerged as the 'Protestant Duke', the obvious alternative to the Catholic James, and the people's hero. Charles's affection for his wayward son turned to irritation and then to anger. Monmouth's Whig connections were increasingly with the more radical wing of the party. In 1682 he went on a quasi-royal 'progress' around Cheshire and was similarly feted at Lichfield and Chichester. Everywhere crowds cheered him; at Chester they also lit bonfires and broke the windows of the local Tories. Monmouth was keeping dangerous company and the investigations into the Rye House Plot suggested that he had been implicated. At the end of 1683 Monmouth came to court and confessed to his father that he had indeed been involved, although not in any design to kill the king. Charles gleefully published the news, Monmouth's Whig friends denied that he had confessed, and the duke shamefacedly retracted his confession.

Charles was furious and Monmouth decided to follow other Whig dissidents into exile. William III, for reasons which remain unclear, received him royally and continued to treat him with the most conspicuous favour, despite repeated curt messages from Charles that he disapproved strongly of such treatment. It may be that William believed that, in his heart of hearts, Charles still had a fondness for his son. Certainly the kindness stopped abruptly when Charles died. Monmouth and his Whig friends began to prepare for a rebellion, gathering money and arms and hiring ships. At the same time the earl of Argyll, another political exile, planned a rising in Scotland, which was quickly suppressed. Both Monmouth and Argyll were helped by the reluctance of the Dutch urban authorities to respond to the requests of the English ambassador that they should arrest the conspirators and impound their ships. Monmouth was able to sail unmolested and landed at Lyme Regis on 11 June 1685.

The south west of England had a tradition of puritanism and Dissent, and many of the towns had a record of support for Parliament in the civil war and for the Whigs in the exclusion crisis. Monmouth brought few men and relied on recruiting followers. He issued a declaration in which he claimed to be the rightful king and attempted to prove it by touching for the King's Evil. Although some of his supporters had little fondness for monarchy, others seem genuinely to have believed that Monmouth was legitimate and that James II was a usurper. As James struggled to gather an army from the various garrisons, Monmouth recruited peasants and craftsmen and attempted to train them. He was encouraged when, in an encounter with the Somerset militia, many militiamen fled or defected to the enemy. For more than a fortnight the king's forces, commanded by the earl of Feversham, shadowed Monmouth's motley army around the west country. At last on 5 July Monmouth attempted a night attack at Sedgemoor. He had the advantage of surprise and it nearly worked, but once the regular troops rallied the combat degenerated into a slaughter. Hundreds of prisoners were convicted of treason and hanged or, more often, sentenced to transportation. Monmouth himself did not face trial. The fact of his treason was obvious and Parliament passed an Act of Attainder against him.

After days on the run, the man who would be king was captured, cowering in a ditch, hungry and filthy. He had less luck than Charles I with his executioner and it took five blows to sever his head from his body. Despite the very public nature of the execution, and the displaying of his head on a spike, many ordinary people believed that he was still alive and would return to free the English from Catholic rule.[15]

The English Parliament gave the king active support against Monmouth, voting money for additional forces, but when Parliament reconvened in November both Houses protested that James had kept on some of the new regiments, almost doubling the size of the army, and commissioned nearly a hundred Catholic officers. It was unfortunate, for James, that these actions coincided with the final phase of Louis XIV's campaign against the Huguenots, which culminated in the revocation of the Edict of Nantes. James did not like the Huguenots, whom he regarded as being (like English dissenters) no friends to monarchy, but he thought Louis's violent methods were 'unchristian and not to be equalled in any history since Christianity'. However, he was reluctant to condemn the persecution publicly, because he saw it as a French domestic issue.[16] So it was not surprising that many suspected James of supporting Louis's action and of wishing to replicate it in England.

James was angry and disappointed by Parliament's behaviour and by what he saw as the Tories' betrayal of their principles, but he had an alternative strategy. Back in the 1670s, when Danby had persuaded Charles to order the enforcement of the laws against dissenters and Catholics, James had cooperated in the House of Lords with peers who supported toleration for dissenters. In the first month of his reign, James responded to Anglican sermons against Catholicism by warning some of the bishops that they should not expect his protection if they failed to do their duty towards him. 'I will ... undertake nothing against the religion which is established by law', he told them, 'unless you first break your word to me.' 'You may be sure', he added, 'that I shall find means to do my business without you.'[17] James's preference was to work with the Anglicans. He still tended to see Dissent as the religious wing of an English republican movement. He also, in 1685, had a strongly Tory Parliament in being.

By the end of the year, he was disillusioned with the Tories and his disillusionment grew in 1686. Despite his warnings, Anglican ministers continued to write and preach against popery. He was also infuriated by the refusal of the fellows of Magdalen to accept his nominee as the new president of their college. It was nothing unusual for kings to nominate heads of houses in the two universities; such nominations were usually accepted without demur. In this case, the man proposed, Anthony Farmer, had an unsavoury personal reputation and was believed to have undertaken to declare himself a Catholic. He was also ineligible under the statutes and the fellows used this as a pretext not to obey the king and to elect one of their number in his place. The king ordered the fellows to elect the newly-appointed bishop of Oxford instead, but the fellows argued that they could not because the post was already full. James was livid. 'Is this your Church of England loyalty?', he asked, adding 'I will be obeyed'. The fellows remained obdurate, leading James to complain that he had 'no enemy ... but among those who call themselves Church of England men'. A 'new spirit' had grown up among them since the civil wars, when Anglicans and Catholics 'loved each other and were ... all one'.[18]

James's impatience with the Tories' scruples was reflected in his council. He had removed Halifax before the end of 1685. A year later, he gave his brother-in-law, and lord treasurer, the earl of Rochester, the choice of converting to Catholicism or losing his office. Rochester chose the latter. Meanwhile Rochester's elder brother, the second earl of Clarendon, was experiencing at first hand James's changing policy towards Ireland. In the last months of Charles II's reign a few Catholics had been granted military commissions. The immediate impetus for this came from James, but the original instigator was Richard Talbot, a member of an Old English family; his brother had been Catholic archbishop of Dublin. The Talbots had links with James that went back to the 1650s. Under Charles II, Richard Talbot had lobbied energetically on behalf of Old English landowners and in the interests of the Catholics of Ireland generally; he had been one of the two Catholic army officers commissioned in 1672. In the early 1680s he worked to undermine Ormond's position as lord lieutenant. It was not easy. Charles had great respect for Ormond and to some extent was in awe of him. But Talbot plugged away, claiming that the bulk of the officers in the Irish army were 'Cromwellians' (by which he meant New English Protestants) and as such not loyal to the king. Only the Catholics, he argued were truly loyal. Charles was not entirely convinced but he did agree to grant a few commissions to Catholics.

The process accelerated under James II.[19] James sympathised with the plight of Catholics in Ireland, but he regarded England and the English as superior to Ireland and the Irish, and his first concern was to maintain his authority in England, against what he perceived as widespread disaffection. He was also determined to maintain the Navigation Acts, which subordinated Ireland's economic interests, and those of the American colonies, to England's.[20] He wished to avoid measures in Ireland that would upset or provoke Protestant opinion in England – in other words, measures that would materially strengthen Catholics and weaken Protestants. Gradually Talbot wore down the king's resistance, harping on the loyalty of the Catholics and the alleged disloyalty of the Protestants. While the notional viceroy, Clarendon, sent letter after letter of bleating protest to London, Talbot removed Protestant army officers and installed Catholics in their places.

Early in 1687 Talbot (now earl of Tyrconnell) was made lord lieutenant in place of the disgraced Clarendon and continued to change the officer corps, so that by 1688 the army was 90 per cent Catholic. He extended his operations, suppressing the Protestant militia (the main means by which the Protestants could defend themselves) and putting Catholics into government and legal offices as well. He also, unbeknown to the king, approached the French ambassador in London, asking if Louis XIV would take Ireland under his protection, should James be succeeded by Mary. The ambassador was non-committal, but Tyrconnell saw clearly that the only way a Catholic Ireland would survive was by breaking its ties with the English crown and by finding a powerful ally to guarantee its independence.

Tyrconnell's measures in Ireland naturally pleased the Catholic majority, although some (especially among the Old English) worried that he was proceeding too far too fast. They naturally added to the anxieties of Protestants in England, and in Scotland where, early in 1687, James granted full toleration to Catholics and a limited toleration to Protestant Dissenters (which in practice meant mainly Presbyterians). In Scotland, as in England and Ireland, adherents of the established church were

alienated, but James was unconcerned. He built up his armies in all
three kingdoms. By the end of 1685 the English army numbered 20,000
men, a much larger force than had been present in England for most
of the 1650s. He also, in all three kingdoms, allowed the militia to decay,
preferring to rely on professionals rather than on the goodwill of his
subjects – or at least those of his subjects who had comprised the
dominant ruling elite under Charles II.[21]

As James had rejected the existing dominant elites – or, as he might
have put it, they had abandoned him – he needed to find support
elsewhere. In Ireland Catholics were superior to Protestants in numbers,
if not in landed wealth or military and administrative experience. While
James might doubt the wisdom of proceeding at Tyrconnell's breakneck
pace, he harboured no doubts about the Catholics' loyalty. But the Scots
Presbyterians and the English dissenters had a record, at least in James's
eyes, of plotting and subversion. James had a longstanding aversion to
religious persecution as such, which he showed in his reaction to Louis's
treatment of the Huguenots. His initial intention had been to secure
toleration for Catholics (alongside the Church of England and the
Episcopal Church of Scotland), but not for the English dissenters or
Scots Presbyterians, who continued to be persecuted. The alternative
was a toleration embracing both dissenters and Catholics. As his animus
towards the Church of England became more obvious, he seems to have
convinced himself that the dissenters had defied authority only because
they had been goaded beyond endurance by persecution. He was encouraged in this conviction by the Quaker, William Penn. He began to
pardon various groups of dissenters, particularly Quakers and Baptists,
but he was more reluctant to think better of the Scottish Presbyterians.
When in February 1687 he issued a declaration of indulgence in Scotland,
it allowed Catholics to worship freely and Presbyterians to worship in
private houses only. Field conventicles continued to be suppressed.

On 4 April 1687 he issued a declaration of indulgence in England. In it
he declared that he believed that conscience should not be constrained
and that persecution always failed, citing the experience of 'the four last
reigns' – interestingly, not including that of Mary. He ordered that the
penalties of all penal laws in matters of religion 'be immediately suspended'. There were to be no licences, although James expected that no

sedition would be preached and that meetings should be open to all. He also stated his intention to admit subjects of all religious views to his service and to dispense them individually from taking the oaths and tests required by law.[22]

The liberty that James granted was more extensive than that of 1672 (or that which he had just granted in Scotland). He gave full freedom of worship to Catholics and imposed fewer conditions on Protestant dissenters, although a certain residual suspicion remained. The indulgence also extended to the laws concerning office-holding. Whereas Charles II had based his declaration on the crown's ecclesiastical prerogative, James issued his simply 'by virtue of our royal prerogative'. In the test case, Godden versus Hales, in 1686, a Catholic army officer was prosecuted for holding office contrary to law. He pleaded a dispensation from the king and the judges ruled that the king could dispense with the penalties of law if he judged it necessary. James seems to have seen this as confirming that he possessed the power to suspend laws and that the dispensing and suspending powers were one and the same. Maybe he did: one could see the latter as following from the former. But whoever drafted the declaration made a distinction. Freedom of worship was granted to the whole country and rested on a suspending power, but office-holders were to receive individual dispensations. This may have been designed to give them a document that they could produce if challenged; or it may reflect a sense that the two aspects of the declaration were legally distinct. Whatever the legal niceties, the king's Protestant subjects, and especially the Anglican clergy, were alarmed. If a king, especially a popish king, could suspend laws, what protection did the subject have? Apart from giving liberty to dissenters and papists, the declaration destroyed the claim of the Church of England to be the national church. The Anglican clergy and laity were allowed freedom of worship and peaceful enjoyment of their property, but the authority of the hierarchy and clergy was swept away.

The declaration, for James, was only a first step. He stated that he was confident that its provisions would be confirmed by Parliament, but what sort of Parliament? The Tory Parliament of 1685 was eventually dissolved in July 1687. James soon made it clear that he expected the Dissenters to show their gratitude for their freedom by repealing the penal laws and Test Acts. The Catholics might well support this too, but until the Test Acts were repealed they could not legally sit in Parliament. The dissenters were happy to enjoy their freedom, and to see the Anglican clergy discomfited, but they were wary of papists bearing gifts and had no wish to put Catholics into positions of power, from which they might oppress Protestants. Their anxieties were reinforced by pamphlets and James and his opponents battled in print to win the hearts and minds of the dissenters. Halifax's *Letter to a Dissenter* argued that it was against the fundamental principles of the Catholic Church to grant toleration and reminded the Dissenters that the Catholics had turned to them only after being rebuffed by the Anglicans. 'You are therefore to be hugged now', it warned, 'only that you may be the better squeezed at another time.'[23]

Their reluctance to comply with James was reinforced when William and Mary made it clear that they supported the repeal of the penal laws – even those affecting Catholics – but not the Test Acts. Dissenters could therefore be confident that they would enjoy toleration and civil equality in the next reign, without putting papists into power. Meanwhile, the bishops and Anglican clergy began to woo the dissenters, claiming to see the error of persecution and suggesting talks about broadening the church and allowing liberty to those Protestants who chose to remain outside. The proposals were vague and guarded, but they still represented a sudden, and (to dissenters) gratifying, change of heart.

Dissenters were divided, as in much else, in their response to the declaration. Some were enthusiastic, especially when James set up a commission to claw back fines paid by dissenters.[24] More were wary. James's hopes of securing an amenable Parliament depended on the cooperation of dissenters and compliant Anglicans, but the signs were not good. James sent orders to canvass county JPs about the forthcoming elections: those who refused to promise to support candidates committed to repeal were dismissed. The towns looked more promising.[25] Many parliamentary boroughs had significant dissenting populations and the electorates were often small. James began to use the powers in his brother's charters to remove aldermen and councillors whom he regarded as unreliable and to replace them with men who (he thought) would vote as he wished. The charters gave him no power to appoint members of corporations, but James claimed to be only making recommendations – which he expected to be obeyed.

In the general election of 1685 the king and his agents had put considerable pressure on candidates to stand, or not to stand; the Tories, as the beneficiaries of his efforts, had not complained much. Now he extended the pressure to the electors: his agents bullied, wheedled and menaced, and in some garrison towns the military threatened to take over the electoral process.[26] Halifax remarked airily that these frantic efforts were doomed to failure. 'Here is rapid motion', he wrote, 'without moving a step, which is the only miracle that church hath yet shown to us.'[27] Others on the ground were not so sure. If they *did* succeed, James would have secured a House of Commons that, unlike that of 1685, did not represent any major sector of English opinion. The Tories were numerous and powerful; the minority of Dissenters who supported James, with their hangers-on (Catholics and Anglican fellow-travellers) were neither. Such an unrepresentative body would be a much more insidious and dangerous threat to Parliaments than Charles I's attempt to rule without them, as it would give the illusion of consent without the substance. A king who could suspend laws at will and who could secure a 'Parliament' that would rubber-stamp his decisions would be absolute indeed.

We do not know whether James's campaign to 'pack' Parliament would have succeeded, because it was never put to the test; but it was alarming enough. Late in 1687 came another cause for alarm when it was announced that the queen was pregnant. Fearful and suspicious Protestants predicted that, whatever happened, the Jesuits would produce a boy. Few were more fearful and suspicious than William III. He had married Mary in order to strengthen his claim to the English throne. As the son of James's sister Mary, he was third in line, but his wife was first – so long as the queen did not have a son. The mainspring of William's life was his struggle against Louis XIV's France. He had improved his claim to the English throne because he wished to bring England's navy into the next great war, which he believed would be only a matter of time. He warned the rulers of the Dutch Republic that they would have to fight, sooner rather than later, for their trade and their religion. He was also convinced, wrongly as it happens, that there was a secret alliance between James and Louis and that they aimed (as in 1672) to attack the Dutch. His warnings, at first greeted with scepticism, were from 1685 taken increasingly seriously in the Dutch Republic. News of the queen's pregnancy drove William to intervene in England, confident that he would have the backing of the Dutch States General. In May 1688, before the queen had given birth, he decided to invade England.

James remained blissfully ignorant of William's plans. Delighted that the pregnancy was going well and praying that God would bless him with a son, he pressed on with his electoral preparations. Irked by the bishops' approaches to the dissenters, he told them to order their clergy to read the declaration of indulgence in their churches. It seemed a shrewd move. If they complied they would seem to endorse the indulgence; if they refused it would suggest that their assurances to the dissenters were insincere. The plan backfired. Seven bishops drew up a petition to the king saying that they believed they could not order the reading of the declaration because the power on which it rested had been declared illegal in Parliament (notably in 1663 and 1673). They stressed that this did not imply any lack of goodwill towards Protestant Dissent.[28] The petition was presented privately to the king, but an earlier version appeared in print almost immediately.[29] James was furious: 'this is a standard of rebellion', he declared.[30] He ordered that the bishops be arrested and prosecuted for seditious libel. The bishops found themselves popular heroes, widely seen (even by dissenters) as martyrs for the Protestant religion. The trial was designed to vindicate the dispensing and suspending powers, but the bishops were acquitted, amid wild public rejoicing, on 30 June. That night seven men (Danby, Bishop Compton and five Whigs) drafted a letter to William, inviting him to England. They assured him that nineteen people in twenty wanted a change and that James's army would refuse to fight for him.[31]

The invitation was not spontaneous – William had asked his English contacts to procure one. His determination was reinforced by the birth of James's son on 10 June. Rumours circulated that the queen's child had died and that a healthy baby had been smuggled in in a warming-pan (in June?). The child, christened James Francis Edward, seemed sickly, perhaps because the royal doctors advised against milk and urged that he be given gruel and canary wine (which may help to explain his later fondness for the bottle). Even the pope expressed concern at the eccentricities of English paediatrics. At last, the baby was given a wet-nurse and grew apace. Cynics remarked that the people would believe he was really the king's son only if he died. The stories of deceit multiplied.

William, who had more reason than most to want to believe them, ordered that prayers should no longer be said for the Prince of Wales in his chapel. In England, few royal births (especially of a Prince of Wales) can have given rise to less rejoicing. This, and the celebrations at the bishops' acquittal, showed how isolated James had become.

As in 1639, however, there was little sign of disorder. There were occasional attacks on Catholic chapels, a number of which had opened since the start of the reign and were widely seen as illegal, but no more serious disorders. James, unlike his father, had a substantial standing army. It was far from certain, or even probable, that his electoral plans would succeed. But there was little sign of rebellion against him in any of his three kingdoms, least of all in Ireland, where Tyrconnell's Catholic army offered reinforcements in the unlikely event of trouble in England. In Scotland, James had wooed the Presbyterians by gradually relaxing the restrictions in his declaration of indulgence. The regime would come under serious threat only if there were to be an invasion, with an army sufficiently large to challenge James's. James was aware that William might want to seize the English throne, but did not believe that he would be able to gather sufficient forces. In the summer of 1688 war seemed inevitable in the northern Rhineland and James could not imagine that the States General would allow William to denude the Dutch Republic of troops when there was a danger of French attack. And James had (or thought he had) a powerful ally in Louis XIV. When Louis made his move that year in the Rhineland, however, it was too far south to threaten the Dutch. He also kept his fleet in the Mediterranean, where it could be of no help to James, rather than bringing it round to Brest. The States General, relieved, authorised William to make a pre-emptive strike against England.

It was only in mid September 1688 that James became seriously alarmed and began to augment his army. The election plans were put on hold as he tried to rally his subjects. Tory magnates were invited to resume their lord lieutenancies and revitalise the militia, but few showed any eagerness. Leading Tories hoped to exploit the king's predicament to extort concessions. Ideally they wanted him to reverse what he had done in favour of Catholics (and Dissenters) and to rely on the Tories, as in 1685.[32] An increasingly desperate king did as they wished, but the momentum of events was too rapid. After his first attempt to sail was scattered by a storm, William's fleet set out again, avoided the English navy and sailed south west, landing in Torbay on 5 November. William had wisely ignored his contacts' assurances that the English would not fight. His fleet was considerably larger than the Armada of 1588. Although his army of 21,000 was smaller on paper than James's, it was more experienced and better equipped.[33] William had been careful to prepare English opinion. Dutch publications had been disseminated in English and William brought over his own printing press. He had already issued a declaration, which recited the misdeeds of James's reign, focusing on those that affected the Tories, such as the maltreatment of the church. The statement of grievances culminated in the suspicious circumstances surrounding the birth of the 'pretended' Prince of Wales. William claimed to have been invited by 'a great many' peers, gentlemen and others to secure the liberties and religion of the nation and declared that he intended to summon a free Parliament, the remedy for all ills.[34]

The declaration was a shrewd document. It was published in several languages and was aimed at William's continental allies (who included Catholic monarchs, such as the king of Spain and the emperor) as well as the English. William was careful not to say that he intended to overthrow James or to seize the throne, although both possibilities must have occurred to him. Instead, he said, he wished to help the English remedy their own grievances in their own way. Faced with the declaration, even the loyallest of Tories could see little reason to oppose William's army. James was on his own, forced to rely on his army. As William advanced slowly from the south west, James prepared to march to meet him. Substantial riots against Catholic chapels and ugly rumours that he was bringing over French or Irish Catholic soldiers to butcher his English Protestant subjects showed how isolated and unpopular he was.

News came that Protestant magnates, including Danby, had risen in the north and midlands, ostensibly to defend themselves against the papists. James advanced as far as Salisbury Plain, in far from easy conditions in a wet November. As he waited for William, news came that some units had defected to the enemy. Scouts who were sent out did not come back. Rumours spread that William's army was advancing rapidly. James's advisers dithered, while the king wore himself out on matters of detail. He could not sleep without opiates and suffered from nosebleeds; a contemporary found his high command in chaos while James wandered around trying to find something to stop the bleeding. His nerve broke. There was no guarantee that he would be able to engage William's army or, if he did, that his men would fight. He retreated towards London.

James's pessimism was understandable. Although few soldiers defected, they included his nephew, Clarendon's son Lord Cornbury. His daughter Anne and his favourite, Lord Churchill, joined the lords in the midlands. If James could not rely on his nearest and dearest, whom could he trust? Reluctantly, he agreed to negotiate with William, but only to gain time. He knew from William's declaration that he would expect a free Parliament to reverse all that James had done and, above all, to declare that the Prince of Wales was not his son – and that, of all things, James could never agree to.

Meanwhile, William maintained the pressure by advancing slowly but steadily towards London. James succeeded in sending his wife and son to France and prepared to follow them. On 10 December he received three emissaries from William. He read their proposals and said that he would give an answer in the morning. In the small hours he slipped down the backstairs of Whitehall Palace to the river, where a boat was waiting. He threw the great seal (used, among other things, to validate writs for elections) into the Thames and ordered his commander in chief to disband his men, without telling him to disarm them first. So he slipped away like a thief in the night, determined to leave as much chaos behind him as possible. News of his departure triggered major anti-Catholic riots in London: chapels were smashed and the Spanish embassy rased to the ground.[35] In the provinces rumours spread that Irish Catholic regiments, brought over to strengthen the army, were marching home, burning, killing and pillaging. As a group of peers, meeting in Guildhall, struggled to re-establish order, news came that James had been captured near Faversham by some fishermen. The lords in the Guildhall brought him back to London, where he received a surprisingly sympathetic welcome.

William had been quietly pleased at the new of James's flight – it was so cowardly and furtive. He was far less pleased at his return. William had no wish to have James as his prisoner, or to harm him, so next time more obvious pressure would be needed to make him go. In the middle of the night James's guards at Whitehall were replaced by Dutchmen and it was suggested that he should go to Ham, for his own safety. James asked if he could go to Rochester instead, to which William agreed with alacrity. On 18 December James left London by boat, with an escort of Dutch soldiers; it was very apparent this time that he was being taken away by force. Some of his Tory friends, alarmed at the course of events, urged him to stay and defend his rights, but he had no wish to do so. The confidence that God was with him had been shattered by the events of the last few weeks. Members of his own family, his closest foreign ally and his people had all betrayed him. He talked mournfully of Richard II and other murdered kings, and was convinced that William wanted him dead. He said that if he stayed he was sure he would be sent to the Tower 'and no king ever went out of that place but to his grave'.[36]

In fact William wanted him out of the kingdom, alive and unharmed, as soon as possible and ordered that the back door of the house in Rochester should be left unguarded. On Christmas Eve a small boat carried James to France, where (after a long and unpleasant crossing) he landed the following day. It was an ignominious end to a reign that had started with such promise and with so many advantages, but he was not inclined to dwell on his own failings. Louis provided James and his court with comfortable lodgings in the château of St-Germain-en-Laye, west of Paris. There the exiled king settled down to ponder on the providence of God and prepared to meet his Maker.

Sophia, electress of Hanover, the mother of George I. (*National Portrait Gallery*)

7

William and Mary

Despite his public pronouncements, William III clearly wanted the English crown, the sooner the better. He was a remarkably determined man, driven not by personal or dynastic ambition (by 1688 it was most unlikely that Mary would have children) but by a sense of mission, rooted in a firm Calvinist faith and a belief in divine providence. Like Charles I, Cromwell and James II, William was convinced that he was acting out God's will, a belief shared by the historian Gilbert Burnet. 'I considered him', he wrote, 'as a person raised up by God to resist the power of France and the progress of tyranny and persecution.'[1] This sense of mission rested on the perception that Louis XIV aimed to establish a 'universal monarchy' and on long experience of French aggression, against the Dutch Republic, France's weaker neighbours and William's own principality of Orange, on the Rhône.

Holding lands in Germany as well as France and the Netherlands, William was accustomed to thinking in European terms, but his family had also played a unique role in the formation and government of the Dutch Republic. He had learned the arts of politics the hard way. His father had died before he was born, his mother when he was ten. The House of Orange had many enemies in the republic, who feared that successive princes were trying to establish themselves as monarchs, indeed absolute monarchs, and to destroy the traditional autonomy of Dutch provinces and cities. The key to any such attempt was their command of the army, so the republicans (or 'States Party') were especially suspicious of their attempts to enlarge it. Following William II's abortive coup in 1650, just before his death, the States Party seized power and excluded his son from the key offices of *stadhouder* (literally 'lieutenant', more accurately chief executive) and captain general.

The regime of the States Party collapsed in the face of the French invasion in 1672 and William III was called on to lead the resistance to

France. At first he enjoyed almost universal support, but after the French had been driven out of Dutch territory the old suspicions and allegations revived. The States Party accused him of exaggerating the threat from France and keeping the war going in order to maintain and extend his own power. The backing he received from the national assembly, the States General, became increasingly fitful. In 1678–79 William unsuccessfully opposed making peace with France, partly because Louis was to be allowed to keep many of his ill-gotten gains, partly because William was convinced that Louis would soon resume his aggression. When he did so, in 1682, William tried unavailingly to persuade the States General to respond; instead the army was substantially reduced. Only from 1685, with the persecution of the Huguenots and swingeing new French tariffs on Dutch goods, did William begin to persuade the Dutch of the need to rearm and that war with France was inevitable.

William had had a much tougher political education than any other Stuart monarch, apart from James VI and I. Dutch politics could be brutal and violent, as well as extraordinarily complex. As *stadhouder* and captain general, he was an elected servant of the federation and the States General, not a ruler in his own right. Moreover, all major decisions had to be approved by all seven provinces (which also had their own assemblies) and all the major towns of the province of Holland; on occasions Amsterdam effectively vetoed decisions made by the other six provinces. Working within such a system called for considerable political skills as well as a certain ruthlessness. Often for William it involved appealing to the five mainly agricultural inland provinces (and their nobilities) against the two maritime provinces of Holland and Zeeland. William developed skills of manipulation and persuasion, but also learned to be pragmatic; he had little choice but to confine himself to the possible.

There was thus a tension between his clear sense of mission and the need to be flexible or devious in order to achieve as much as he realistically could. His sense of mission made it difficult for him to compromise, but his common sense told him that he had to. He drove himself harder than was wise. He always had respiratory problems – including asthma – and had a hoarse voice and a continual dry cough. His physical condition did nothing to improve his temper. He could never understand why others did not see the threat from France as starkly as he did (although in fact, had William but known it, from 1685 Louis's main concern was to hang on to what he had, not to expand further). He found both the Dutch and the English blind to what was going on beyond their borders, too quick to moan in wartime about high taxes and the disruption of trade, and prone to unfounded fears that he was seeking to become a military despot. He did not suffer fools gladly and tended to be impatient. As Burnet (who knew him very well) put it:

> His designs were always great and good: but it was thought he trusted too much to that and that he did not descend enough to the humours of his people, to make himself and his notions more acceptable to them: this in a government that has so much freedom in it as ours, was more necessary than he was inclined to believe; his reservedness grew on him so that it disgusted most of those who served him: but he had observed the errors of too much talking more than those of too cold a silence.[2]

In all his difficulties in the years leading up to 1688, William derived great strength from the love and support of his wife. When William came over to England to ask for her hand in 1677, Mary had been so shocked and upset that she had cried for a day and a half. William lacked small talk or obvious charm, was nearly twelve years her senior, and stood four inches shorter (at five feet eleven inches Mary was almost as tall as her father). He suffered from a constant hacking cough and, although his mother had insisted that he speak English as a child, his grasp of the language was rusty. At the age of fifteen, Mary had found herself transported to a strange land with a husband she hardly knew. As with her young stepmother, Mary Beatrice, a marriage that began inauspiciously turned out to be a happy one. Mary came to accept that there were certain areas of her husband's life that were closed to her, including the very masculine worlds of soldiering and hunting. Like James I, William felt most able to unwind in the company of a small group of aristocratic hunting companions.

In time, Mary came to appreciate that William's apparent coldness and reserve covered a painful shyness, particularly in the presence of women. Compared with his Stuart uncles, William showed little interest in the opposite sex. His relationship with his one recorded mistress, Elizabeth Villiers, seems to have been based on common intellectual interests as much as physical attraction. Mary was careful not to intrude in what William regarded as men's business and in time won his trust, respect and eventually love. Their one great sadness was that they had no children, although Mary suffered a miscarriage in 1678. She came to appreciate the virtues of the Dutch, their piety, politeness and cleanliness; it was a far cry from the promiscuity and dissimulation of Charles II's court. She shared with William an interest in architecture, gardening and interior decoration, as well as a firm Protestant faith and strict personal morality. Apart from William's relationship with Elizabeth Villiers, theirs was a court untainted by scandal, in which even the Dutch Reformed clergy could find little to criticise.

The accession of Mary's father to the English throne did not initially create a conflict of loyalties for Mary. William sent Monmouth away as soon as James came to the throne and offered military assistance against the duke's rebellion. There can be no doubting William's sincerity in this. He had no wish to see Mary's claim to the throne nullified by a usurper. James was duly grateful, but gradually their relationship turned sour. William was worried by James's apparent friendship with France and failure to condemn the persecution of the Huguenots. Above all, he was angered by James's seeming unconcern about Louis's annexation of the family principality of Orange. James also demanded that William should expel English and Scots radicals from the republic and send back the English and Scots regiments that had long been in the Dutch service.

Mary watched anxiously as the relationship between her husband and her father deteriorated. She was unimpressed when James sent her his reasons for converting to Catholicism and declined his suggestion that she might follow his example. She was alarmed at the news that came from England and the rumours that James had urged her sister Anne to change her religion and that he was planning to alter the succession in favour of a Catholic. Much of the information from England came via English and Scots exiles, who naturally put an unfavourable gloss on James's actions. The most important of these was Gilbert Burnet, who left England in 1684. Aware that James wanted to have him extradited to face charges of allegedly treasonable writings in Scotland, where he was likely to be tortured, tried and executed, Burnet was hardly a dispassionate observer. He was, however, a historian of European reputation and his ability to win the confidence of Charles, James, William and Mary suggests that he was not devoid of charm.

Burnet's role at William's court was not confined to his status as an expert on English affairs. He wrote numerous propagandist pamphlets denouncing James's government and persuaded Mary to address the issues raised by her conflict of loyalties; the fact that he was a clergyman doubtless made her more willing to listen. In particular, he asked her what William's status would be when she inherited the English crown. She was shocked when he explained that Philip II had been a mere consort to Mary Tudor and agreed with his suggestion that she should raise the matter with William. She told William that she thought it unnatural and against the laws of God that a husband should ever be subordinate to his wife, and that she 'would give him the real authority as soon as it came into her hands and endeavour effectually to get it to be legally vested in him during life'.[3]

By early 1688 Mary was as convinced as William that Mary Beatrice's alleged pregnancy was a trick designed to shut them out of the succession. Faced with what seemed mounting evidence of her father's duplicity, she sided with her husband. She did not do so lightly and was deeply concerned for both of them when William sailed for England – another reason why William did not wish any harm to befall his father-in-law. Mary came over to London after James had gone. Some accused her of seeming unconcerned about her father, as she was said to have skipped from room to room in Whitehall as if she did not have a care in the world. She may just have been relieved that the conflict had been resolved without bloodshed – or excited at taking possession of a palace.

William had shown his dedication and determination by organising an invasion fleet in 1688 about four times the size of the largest of the Spanish armadas – a stupendous logistical, political and diplomatic achievement. But tact and caution had also been necessary, to avoid alienating his Catholic allies and the English public. This was seen most clearly in the declaration in which he explained and justified his invasion. He had been careful to solicit an invitation to invade. When James first left London in December, the City authorities invited William to the capital. It was suggested that there should be a meeting of the 1681 Parliament, the last of Charles II's reign, together with the corporation of London, to decide what to do next. James's second flight simplified matters. The meeting invited William to take over the civil and military government for the time being and to call a Convention, as in 1660, to consider how to resolve the problems created by James's departure.

There could be little doubt that William would have to be given control of the government: nobody else could prevent the country collapsing into chaos. The remnants of James's army were mutinous, Ireland was out of English control, and the position in Scotland was uncertain, with the Catholic duke of Gordon holding Edinburgh Castle. William made his military power abundantly clear, quartering large numbers of his troops around London and the south east.[4] He was careful not to interfere in the elections for the Convention, ordering his troops to withdraw from towns on election days. But by the time the Convention met, on 22 January 1689, he was already king in all but name.

The Tories in the Convention were reluctant to recognise this. Many had welcomed the invasion, thinking it would force James to reverse his unpopular policies and make a fresh start; if that included disinheriting the Prince of Wales, so much the better. They had not expected James to run away, nor had they expected William to be biased towards Whigs and Dissenters – some of his closest confidants, initially, were radical Whigs who had been in exile in the Dutch Republic.[5] If James's first flight could be blamed only on himself, his second could be blamed on William; James had been driven out of London. Tories began to suspect that William had intended from the start to seize the crown and that they had been duped by his declaration into betraying their principles. In failing to oppose his invasion, they had aided and abetted an act of resistance. And with James gone, and likely to be replaced by William, they were being asked to alter the hereditary succession, which they had defended so vigorously in the Exclusion Crisis.

They did their utmost to prevent this. The Commons resolved that James, by the advice of Jesuits and other wicked persons, had broken the fundamental laws and the original contract between king and people and had deserted his kingdom; he had abdicated and the throne was therefore vacant. This was a messy, composite resolution. Was the 'abdication' a consequence of breaking the fundamental laws or the 'original contract'?[6] Some chose to believe that James had been deposed for breaking the laws. Others preferred to link abdication with desertion – a voluntary act – or stated that he had deposed himself.[7]

The ambiguities of the resolution may have been designed to make it acceptable to both Tories and Whigs in the Commons, but in the Lords the Tories, who were in the majority, opposed it vigorously. They claimed that the terms 'abdication' and 'original contract' did not exist in English law and there was considerable debate about what the latter meant.[8] Some argued that such questions were better left alone: 'should you go to the beginning of government, we should be much in the dark'.[9] Tory peers also insisted that the throne could not be vacant, because when a king died he was immediately succeeded by his heir.

Such arguments were ingenious but not ingenuous. The Tories' real aim was to deny William the crown. They proposed that William and Mary should serve as regents for James, as if the latter were under age or mad, but he was patently neither. They then claimed that, when James left, Mary (the next heir) had become queen in her own right. But William was not having that. 'He could not think of holding anything by apron strings ... Also he could not resolve to accept of a dignity so as to hold it for the life of another.'[10] Although his poor health made it unlikely that he would outlive Mary, he had to consider that possibility. As a mere consort, he would lose all claim to the throne when his wife died. William had not made such Herculean efforts and taken such huge risks to be, in his phrase, his wife's gentleman usher. He needed the fullest possible control over England's resources – more particularly the navy – for his great struggle against France. He made it known to some leading peers that unless he was made king in his own right, for life, he would return to Holland. Faced with the prospect of civil war in all three kingdoms, the Tories caved in. The crown was offered jointly to William and Mary, but with William alone wielding executive power. An Act had to be passed in 1690 giving Mary the power to exercise regal power in his absence.[11]

This response to the problems created by William's expulsion of James could be seen in two ways. It could be seen as establishing that the right to the crown was now conferred by Parliament and that divine hereditary right was dead; or as an untidy exercise in pragmatism that resolved the issue in the way that was perhaps least unacceptable to all concerned. The second seems the more plausible. In the debates between the Houses, the Commons' spokesmen went out of their way to stress that they were *not* making the crown elective and MPs were well aware that they had to carry the Lords with them.[12] 'All they mean by this matter is to provide a supply for this defect in the government brought upon it by the late king's maladministration.' As one MP said of the 'vacancy', 'we found it so, we have not made it so'.[13]

In settling the future *transmission* of the crown, the Houses were careful to maintain the hereditary principle. William and Mary were to be succeeded by any children they might have, then by Anne and her children, and finally by any children William might have by a subsequent marriage. As Anne had been pregnant several times already, and was to give birth to a son, William Henry, duke of Gloucester, in 1689, the Protestant Stuart succession seemed secure. In other words the change of rulers could be seen as a temporary violation of the hereditary principle: after William and James were dead, the succession would flow back into its proper channel.

Tory attachment to the hereditary succession had been shaken but not broken, with the important caveat that they were now committed to the hereditary *Protestant* succession. On 29 January, before agreement was reached on who was to have the crown, the two Houses resolved, without a dissenting voice, that experience showed that it was inconsistent with the safety of a Protestant kingdom to be governed by a Catholic prince.[14] The Tories here conceded that the Whigs' fears, as expressed in the exclusion bills, had been well founded, but the key word was 'experience'. The Tories had given James the benefit of the doubt and he had proved them wrong. The principle enshrined in this resolution was later included in the Bill of Rights of 1689 and the Act of Settlement of 1701, which declared that no Catholic (or spouse of a Catholic) could be king or queen of England. This provision is still in force. After that, there was no need to investigate the birth of James's son. His Catholicism excluded him from the throne.

The resolution against Catholic rulers originated in the Lords and offered a means for the Tories to preserve their commitment to the hereditary succession, albeit in a modified form. The Lords also proposed, unsuccessfully, to push the principle one stage further by recognising the right of Sophia, electress of Hanover, the nearest Protestant claimant, to succeed to the throne if Anne died without issue. In 1689 that seemed unlikely, but by 1701, after the death of the duke of Gloucester, it was more than probable. The Act of Settlement therefore also decreed that Sophia, or her heirs, would succeed to the throne after Anne's death. The Commons did agree to another proposal from the Lords, also designed to salve Tory consciences and make the new rulers more acceptable. Many Tories were prepared to accept that William and Mary were king and queen *de facto*, but not by right. The oath of allegiance was modified, to be a bare promise of loyalty, with no reference to William and Mary as 'rightful and lawful' monarchs.[15]

The overwhelming lack of support for James in England in 1688–89 ensured that in England what was later known as the 'Glorious Revolution' was largely bloodless. Jacobite opposition to the new regime was far stronger in Scotland and Ireland and there was far more bloodshed. The Jacobites in Scotland remained a real military threat until their leader, Viscount Dundee, was killed at Killiecrankie in July 1689, in a battle which, ironically, the Jacobites won. The magnitude of this threat strengthened the hand of the Scottish Whig nobles. In March 1689 William called a Convention at Edinburgh. It drew up a Claim of Right, which (unlike the English Declaration of Rights) declared forthrightly that James had forfeited the throne for his misgovernment. It also offered the crown to William, with the clear implication that he was expected to respect the laws and heed the advice of Parliament.

William was usually sensitive to attempts to restrict his powers, but he regarded Scotland as far less important than England and the continued Jacobite resistance made him more willing to humour his own supporters. The identification of the bishops with James – most refused to acknowledge William as king – enabled the Whigs and Presbyterians to claim that they alone were truly loyal. The Claim said that the people did not want episcopacy and in July 1689 the Scottish Parliament passed an Act abolishing it. Presbyterians began to seize control of parishes, at least in the Lowlands and South, driving out Episcopalians and moderates by force. Many of the aristocracy favoured episcopacy, if only as a means to keeping the clergy in a suitable position of subordination, but Parliament reduced landowners' powers of patronage.

In 1690 William was persuaded to recall the general assembly, dominated by ministers removed in 1662, who promptly claimed to be the rightful governors of the established church. His representatives also agreed to the abolition of bishops, the repeal of the 1669 Act of

Supremacy and the re-establishment of Presbyterianism. More than half of the parish clergy were removed. In 1694 William conceded that the general assembly could regulate its own affairs and direct those of the church. The Presbyterian leadership established a church order as oppressive as that of the 1650s – indeed too oppressive for many who described themselves as Presbyterians, with rigorous moral discipline and Sabbath observance. In 1696 an Edinburgh student was executed for blasphemy.[16]

William also, in 1690, agreed to abolish the lords of the articles and so lost the power to determine which bills went before Parliament. The Scottish Parliament had now recovered many of the powers that it had wrested from Charles I in 1640–41 and lost at the Restoration.[17] It became increasingly difficult to manage. Several groups of magnates, each with their blocs of client MPs, competed for power, but none proved strong enough to impose its will on the others and proceedings drifted aimlessly amid squabbling and acrimony. To make matters worse, Scottish grievances against the English government multiplied. Scots merchants had long complained of being treated as foreigners and excluded from trade with English colonies, and their trade suffered badly in the war against France. In 1692 William's government was blamed for allowing or authorising (the circumstances are very obscure) the massacre of the Macdonalds of Glencoe by their traditional enemies, the Campbells. Later in the decade, the Scots attempted to found a colony at Darien, in the isthmus of Panama. It failed, thanks to heat, disease and the hostility of the Spanish, but the Scots also blamed the English, who had proved less than friendly towards the venture. Finally, the Scots were livid about the provisions for the succession in the Act of Settlement. As in 1649 the English were disposing of the crown, blithely forgetting that the Stuarts were also monarchs of Scotland.

The Jacobite threat in Ireland was much more serious and lasting. After James fled, Tyrconnell was sure that it was only a matter of time before William tried to re-establish English rule over Ireland, so he set out to extend his power over the whole of the island. Protestant merchants and clergy fled to England, amid rumours of impending massacre. There were numerous attacks on Protestant clergymen and their churches, and (according to William King) systematic plunder of Protestants, urged on by the priests, but even King admitted that there were few murders. 1689 was not a repeat of 1641, although the Protestant refugees and the English assumed that it would be.[18] Meanwhile, Tyrconnell increased the size of his army, raising many new regiments, with no prospect of money to pay them. Trade had collapsed, merchants carried away their valuables, and many farmers failed to plant their fields, fearing yet another destructive war; as one Protestant bishop put it, the Irish had turned their ploughshares into swords.[19]

Tyrconnell also approached the French, with some prospect of success. Louis was eager to encourage the Jacobites in Ireland, to divert English resources from the war on the Continent. James, traumatised by his expulsion, had no wish to go to Ireland, but Louis was adamant that he should; so in March 1689 he landed at Kinsale with a modest sum of money and a group of French military advisers.

The French were not impressed by the Irish. Tyrconnell had raised far more men than the country could afford. They were poorly armed – one regiment had only seven serviceable muskets – and poorly disciplined. Often landlords had enlisted their tenants and they would fight for nobody else. Soldiers stole from the civilian population and each other – the French called them 'mutineers' and 'wild bears'.[20] Ever since James's accession, Catholics had been talking of recovering their lost lands and power. The level of banditry increased and took on a religious and political edge. So-called 'rapparees', armed with half-pikes and daggers, preyed primarily on Protestants and English. They were treated at times, by James and Tyrconnell, as auxiliaries to the regular forces, something that the French, accustomed to a clear distinction between regular armies and civilians, were unable to understand.[21]

The French urged Tyrconnell to form a smaller, better-equipped army and disband the rest, but he replied that the officers would not disband their men until they had been paid – and there was no money. Brass cannon were melted down to make coins. Meanwhile, the officers bickered among themselves and the Gaelic Irish accused Tyrconnell of favouring the Old English. Despite these difficulties, Tyrconnell managed to gain control of the whole island except for Enniskillen and Derry. James himself appeared before Derry on 18 April, but the inhabitants refused to surrender and the siege dragged on until James was persuaded to abandon it on 22 July. A week later provisions arrived from England.

The siege of Derry (or as they called it Londonderry) occupies a prominent place in Ulster Unionist mythology. Had the besiegers been properly armed and equipped with artillery the outcome would have been very different, but the failure of James's army to take the city was a psychological as well as a military blow. Meanwhile friction developed between the king and his Irish allies. James's priority was always to regain England; Ireland was just a convenient jumping off point. He was also determined to avoid measures in Ireland that might upset the English. He was, wrote one Irishman, 'infatuated with this rotten principle, provoke not your Protestant subjects'.[22] But the Irish wanted to reverse a century and more of expropriation and oppression. James summoned a Parliament, almost wholly Catholic, which met in Dublin on 7 May. Against his wishes it repealed the Acts of Settlement and Explanation and passed an Act of Attainder that declared forfeit the life and property of just about every significant Protestant in Ireland. He also had to agree to an Act declaring that the English Parliament could not legislate for Ireland and it was only with difficulty that he blocked a bill to repeal Poynings' law, by which all bills put before the Irish Parliament had to be approved by the English privy council. The Navigation Acts were suspended.

None of these measures was likely to go down well in England and meanwhile the siege of Derry prevented any thought of an expedition across the Irish Sea. To make matters worse, James's troops were routed at Newtown Butler as they retreated from Derry. James, once a brave soldier and leader of men, was only a shadow of his former self. He dithered, fussed over details and was often overwhelmed by pessimism. On 13 August an expeditionary force from England landed in Ulster. It contained a motley collection of nationalities and was commanded by the duke of Schomberg, a German who had served for many years in the French armies. Its arrival removed any lingering hope of James's taking an army to England, but it achieved little over a long wet winter, in which many men died of disease or were picked off by Irish irregulars.

In the spring of 1690, William became impatient. The stalemate in Ireland was tying up troops and draining valuable resources that were urgently needed for the war effort against France on the Continent. He was determined to defeat James's army as quickly as possible and on 14 June he landed himself at Carrickfergus with an additional 15,000 men and £200,000 in cash: coin was chronically scarce in Ireland, which was why the brass cannon had been melted down. He headed towards Dublin; James marched to meet him, but with little confidence of success. On 29 June James drew his men up on the southern bank of the River Boyne, west of Drogheda. It was not an ideal defensive position but there was nothing better between there and Dublin. On 1 July, after securing a bridgehead upstream, William's main army forded the river in the face of heavy fire. They encountered fierce resistance on the other bank, until William's cavalry came to their aid. Meanwhile, a large part of James's army was prevented by the terrain from engaging the enemy, but on the news that William's cavalry had crossed the river more and more of James's army broke and fled. Although they had not suffered heavy casualties, the road to Dublin was open.

James himself moved more quickly than most, pausing in Dublin only to order the privy council to deliver the city to William before riding post haste to Dungannon and taking ship for France. James had the distinction, unique among the Stuarts, of having visited all three of his kingdoms. He had also lost all three, but he did not seem unduly concerned. He blamed the Boyne on the folly and cowardice of the Irish, which was less than fair. He had come to terms with his expulsion from England by explaining it as God's punishment for his sins, especially sins of the flesh, so he accepted defeat in Ireland as a further necessary dose of divine retribution. He embarked on a regime of austerity and devotion. In 1692 and 1696, when Louis planned to invade England, James dutifully made his way to the seaside, but responded to the failure of the plans with equanimity and returned to his hair shirt and his prayers.[23]

Having taken Dublin without resistance, William assumed that the campaign was over. Like Cromwell forty years before, he issued a declaration promising pardon to those peasants and common soldiers who surrendered, but not many did. Instead the Jacobites took refuge in fortified towns. The rapparees plundered Protestants and English and picked off small detachments of soldiers. Their depredations were matched by regular troops on both sides, the Jacobites because they were not paid, the Williamites because they were fighting in an alien, and hostile, land. One Englishman commented that they had plundered and devastated the country as ruthlessly as the Turks had the Balkans.[24] The Williamites found it hard to cope with the rapparees, who enjoyed considerable support among the Irish and who were adept at hiding their weapons and melting back into the civilian population. The Williamite soldiers responded by looting, demanding compensation from the people, and by savage reprisals, killing civilians, including priests, women and children, which merely strengthened the rapparees' claim that they were protecting a defenceless populace against brutal invaders.[25]

William was impatient to return to England, but was made aware of the realities of warfare in Ireland when his army besieged Limerick. The rains came, carts and artillery sank into the mud, soldiers fell sick and died. Some time after William had returned to England, his commander in Ireland, Ginkel, was forced to lift the siege. Reluctantly, William continued the war into 1691. There were successes, notably the capture of Athlone and victory at Aughrim, but a second siege of Limerick proved as difficult as the first. By now William was eager to get out of Ireland on the best conditions he could get. In October Limerick surrendered on terms.[26]

The treaty of Limerick was drawn up by William and his Dutch advisers, with little consultation with Irish Protestants.[27] It allowed all members of the Jacobite army to leave Ireland, with their weapons and valuables. The Catholics were to 'enjoy such privileges in their exercise of their religion as are consistent with the laws of Ireland, or as they did enjoy in the reign of king Charles II'. William also promised to try to persuade the Irish Parliament to allow further security to Catholics.[28] His record suggests that he was probably sincere in wanting this. He had powerful Catholic allies and had consistently supported freedom of worship for Catholics, in the Dutch Republic and in England.[29] But he was also optimistic to the point of naïvety. His experience of Irish Protestants must have made him aware that they had no intention of allowing any liberty to Catholics, especially after the attacks on Protestants in 1688–89, the behaviour of James's Dublin Parliament and almost three years of vicious civil war.

When the Dublin Parliament met in 1692 it was once again solidly Protestant. It interpreted the clauses in the treaty relating to land as restrictively as possible, so that many more estates passed from Catholics to Protestants.[30] It also passed the first of a series of new penal laws against Catholics, aimed against Catholic worship but also designed to eliminate Catholic landownership altogether. It was laid down that estates belonging to Catholics were to be divided among all their sons, which in time would make them too small to be viable. If one son turned Protestant, however, he would receive the whole estate. Slowly but surely, such measures reduced the amount of land in Catholic hands to a mere 5 per cent by 1776.[31] In 1698 the Dublin Parliament formally repudiated the treaty of Limerick. It was already, in most respects, a dead letter.

The accession of new monarchs in 1689 gave the English House of Commons an opportunity to raise questions about what they could and could not do. The Declaration of Rights, which was read to William and Mary on 13 February, stated that certain powers abused by James II (for example the dispensing and suspending powers) were illegal and made certain stipulations for the future: for example, parliamentary elections ought to be 'free'. Many of its clauses clarified grey areas and restated what many believed to be the law. The most novel was the assertion that it was illegal to keep a standing army in peacetime without the consent of Parliament. Hitherto Parliament had neither recognised the legality of the army nor condemned it as illegal.[32] Parliament also at last recognised the dangers of mutiny and desertion, after a mutiny at Ipswich, passing an Act allowing for the punishment of mutineers by court martial. The Act was, however, temporary and was to be the first of many. The monarch's need to renew the Act each year gave the Commons the power to enforce the provision in the declaration against standing armies in peacetime. By failing to renew the Act, they could deprive him of the means to discipline his army.[33]

The Declaration, later passed into law as the Bill of Rights, did not impose sweeping new restrictions on the monarchy, for the very good reason that William would not have stood for it. In the early months of 1689, the Dutch forces quartered in the south east were all that stood between England and civil war. Some MPs expressed fears of 'the mob', others feared an attempt to establish a republic.[34] William was able to resist moves to limit the king's powers further, although he privately thought that those powers were inadequate.[35] He did not openly oppose attempts to restrict his authority, but (as with the offer of the crown) privately he made his wishes very clear.

In many respects the key question was not the extent of the king's powers but the extent to which he could use them. One major constraint was Parliament and the effectiveness of that constraint, as always, depended on money. In a debate on 29 January, before the offer of the crown or the completion of the Declaration of Rights, William Harbord stressed to the Commons that this was the crucial issue. 'All the revenue is in your own hands, which fell with the last king and you may keep that back. Can he whom you place on the throne support the government without the revenue?' [36] Others argued that the Commons had been far too generous at the Restoration and should not make the same mistake again. They should now ensure that 'Parliaments be duly chosen and not kicked out at pleasure'.[37] Whigs fearful of strong monarchy joined with Tories resentful of William to propose that key revenues like the customs should be granted only for a term of years: 'If you give the crown too little you may add at any time; if once you give too much you will never have it back again.' [38]

The refusal to grant William a sufficient revenue for life was the key decision of the Revolution.[39] William was able to prevent new restrictions on his power, but he could not force the Commons to vote him money. To compound his financial problems, England was soon at war with France. William's accession as king, and James's taking refuge in France, inevitably brought England into the war that had started on the Continent in 1688. The Commons voted unprecedented sums for the war, but never enough, and the crown sank further and further into debt. By the end of the war, in 1697, the Commons were voting annual 'estimates' for the army and navy, while separate provision was made for the court and civil government in the 'civil list', which still exists today.[40]

Although William was voted the civil list for life in 1698, he still had to come to Parliament each year for money for the army and navy. His financial dependence on Parliament was much greater than that of Charles II, who had had a substantial independent revenue and became wholly dependent on Parliament only in wartime. It transformed the relationship between king and Parliament. Parliament now met every year for several months (which encouraged the development of the London 'Season'). But 1689 also marked the start of a slow and subtle process whereby monarchs found it harder and harder to use their acknowledged prerogatives. Those prerogatives were to some extent reduced by legislation. The Triennial Act of 1694 forced the king to call a general election at least once every three years. The Act of Settlement of 1701, besides excluding Catholics from the throne and settling the succession, imposed restrictions on a future foreign king that showed the resentment of many MPs against their current Dutch king. He was not to appoint any foreigner to office, or engage England in a war involving any continental territory, or even leave the country, without Parliament's consent.[41] But most of the constraints under which monarchs laboured owed less to legislation than to the practical difficulties of working with Parliament.[42]

These first became apparent under William III. The war against France was long and expensive. English trade suffered heavily from French privateers, the shortage of coin gave rise to hardship and riots, yet at the same time City financiers grew rich from lending money to the government and there were frequent accusations of profiteering and corruption. For all this, the war on land did not produce a single major victory. William insisted that the key theatre of war had to be the Southern Netherlands, which led to accusations that he put Dutch interests before English. (The reverse accusation was made in the Dutch Republic.) To make matters worse, the Commons were riven with partisan divisions. Whigs accused Tories of wishing to restore James II and blamed military and naval failure on treachery. They tried repeatedly to force the Tories to show their distaste for William and his regime by reinstating the phrase 'rightful and lawful' in the oath of allegiance and requiring MPs and office-holders to subscribe the Association. Modelled on the Bond of Association of 1584, this was drawn up in 1696, following a plot to assassinate the king. Subscribers undertook to stand by William (described as the 'rightful and lawful king') and promised that if any harm became him they would wreak revenge on his enemies. A similar 'association' had been used by the Whigs late in 1688 to try to show that the Tories were not fully committed to William. Now some Tories initially refused to subscribe, but most eventually did and later took an oath abjuring the Pretender that was imposed in 1702.[43]

The Tories were also unhappy with William's sympathy for Dissent, shown when he suggested at the start of 1689 that Parliament might repeal the Corporation Act. But here again, as in their collusion with William's invasion, the Tories had painted themselves into a corner.

The church leaders' offers to the dissenters in 1687–88 may have been unspecific, but they had been too public and too repeated to be quietly forgotten. They had to deliver either a broader church, to accommodate the Presbyterians, or toleration, or both.

The bishops and Tory politicians resolved to agree to toleration in order to prevent the dilution, or destruction, of the pure spirit of Anglicanism, or, even worse, a schism within the church. The Toleration Act of 1689 was the product of a cynical political deal, clinched (appropriately enough) in the Devil tavern.[44] It was a grudging measure. It did not repeal any of the laws against Dissent, but laid down that those against dissenting meetings should not be enforced against mainstream Protestant dissenters. There was to be no freedom of worship for Catholics, Unitarians or Jews. Meeting houses had to be registered with the local JPs and had to keep their doors open during meetings, as there was still the explicit suspicion that dissenters were plotting sedition. The laws against dissenters holding office (including the Test and Corporation Acts) were to remain in force, as was the ban on dissenters attending England's two universities. Public office and higher education were to remain Anglican monopolies.

The Toleration Act, for the Tories, was an attempt at damage limitation, and it failed. The Act decreed that everyone should attend either their parish church or a licensed meeting house every Sunday, but that proved impossible to enforce and church attendance fell sharply. Dissenters gained access to office, as they had under Charles II, by the practice of occasional conformity – taking communion in an Anglican church in order to qualify. Although dissenters could not attend the universities, they opened their own schools and academies, whose curricula were far more modern and practical than those of Oxford and Cambridge. And, if they really wanted to go to university, they could go to Scotland or the Dutch Republic.

The Tories soon found that they had paid a heavy price for keeping the church pure. Its power and moral influence in society declined. In the 1690s standards of public morality seemed to plummet – a Speaker of the Commons was expelled for taking bribes – and London was believed to be in the grip of a crime wave. Press censorship, revived in 1685, proved increasingly ineffectual and in 1695 lapsed altogether. Works appeared that challenged conventional revealed religion. John Locke, by no means the most radical, denied the existence of original sin and declared that the only essential Christian truth was that Jesus was the Messiah. Tories and Churchmen were quick to blame these evils on the weakening of the church. The crunch came in 1697 when the lord mayor of London, having received communion in order to qualify for office, went in state to a Presbyterian meeting. Tory MPs and clergymen called for a ban on occasional conformity. Meanwhile, the death of the duke of Gloucester and the Act of Settlement revived differences about the succession that had remained dormant since 1689. During the 1690s many of the divisions in Parliament had occurred on issues other than those that divided Whig from Tory – corruption, the cost of the war and, from 1697, fear of a standing army. By 1702 the Houses were once more sharply divided on party lines.

William was not convinced by Whig claims that the Tories preferred King James to himself and indeed he regarded the Whigs as too inclined to republicanism.[45] He expressed distaste for parties, describing himself as a trimmer, and was angry that the English seemed more interested in pursuing their own vendettas than in winning the war.[46] He found them insular, xenophobic, ignorant and at times spiteful. He had to work with the Commons, but it was not easy. The House developed the habit of 'tacking' extraneous clauses to money bills. As the Lords could not amend money bills, but only accept or reject them, this was a way of pushing through measures that the Lords would otherwise have rejected, leaving William with the choice of passing the bill or losing the money.[47] In 1699 he was forced to give his assent to a bill reducing the standing army to what he saw as dangerously small proportions, at a time when he believed that a new war against France might break out at any time; to add insult to injury, the first regiment to be disbanded was his own Dutch guards. 'Tacks' forced William to send out convoys for merchant shipping (at the expense of the battle fleet) and to agree to claw back estates granted in Ireland to Dutch and Huguenot officers. Meanwhile, the Commons established a committee of public accounts. Chosen by ballot each year, it subjected government spending to unprecedented scrutiny, interrogating civil servants and demanding to see documents. Its appointment owed much to suspicions of waste and mismanagement, but to William it marked yet another device to strip him of the power to govern effectively.[48]

William was not a patient man, but he was an experienced politician. As head of state in both England and the Dutch Republic he had advantages. He used the Dutch diplomatic corps so that the English did not know what he was up to and refused to involve English generals or politicians in major war decisions.[49] He had also suffered enough bruising defeats in Dutch politics to know that it was sometimes better to give in than to fight to a finish. He did not enjoy being king of England. He said the 'Commons used him like a dog'.[50] He disliked the ceremonial and rejected the mystical aspects of monarchy, dismissing pageantry and ceremony as 'whipped cream' – all air and no substance – and he refused to touch for the King's Evil. Partly because of his asthma, he hated crowds, withdrawing from Whitehall Palace (which burned down in 1698) to the more secluded Kensington Palace and Hampton Court. As a military leader, for whom warfare was a way of life, he found the very unmilitary English nobility uninteresting – all they could talk about, he said, was horses and farming. Like James I, he felt that he was a foreigner in an alien land.

Faced with the chauvinism of the English, he found some comfort in Dutch friends and confidants, like Hans Willem Bentinck and Arnold van Keppel, raised to the peerage as earl of Portland and earl of Albemarle respectively. This merely added to the malevolent comments, including allegations (seemingly unfounded) that his relationship with Keppel was homosexual. William appointed many Englishmen to senior positions in the navy, but few in the army, on what seemed to him the sound grounds that the foreigners who had come over with him were more able, experienced and reliable. This led to complaints (orchestrated by John Churchill, earl of Marlborough) that William was biased against the English and was unconcerned about English interests. To all these reasons for unhappiness was added the personal tragedy of Mary's death from smallpox on 28 December 1694. She was thirty-two. William was devastated; her death left a permanent void in his life and he never remarried. Her passing also removed one of the few reasons for spending time in England. Each year from 1690 to 1697 he travelled to Flanders to lead the allied war effort against France. After the war was over he would still spend the summer in the Dutch Republic, which he found more congenial than England.

Although William was driven to distraction by the small-mindedness and bloody-mindedness of the English Parliament, he was enough of a pragmatist to realise that he could not ignore it. In 1701 there was outrage when the Commons discovered that William had signed secret treaties with Louis XIV and the emperor to partition the Spanish empire on the death of Carlos II. Four of his ministers were impeached for their alleged part in this. Portland had been actively involved, but the other three had known little or nothing. Of all the aspects of kingship, high-level diplomacy was the one which kings regarded as their own special preserve – and the one where secrecy was the most necessary. Nevertheless, William started laying some treaties with foreign allies before Parliament, as a way of winning trust and securing money. In the last years of his reign, this became normal practice.[51]

In 1700 Carlos II finally died. In his will, he left the entire Spanish empire to Louis XIV's grandson, Philip of Anjou, on condition that he must never succeed to the French throne and that the two crowns had to remain separate. After some hesitation, Louis accepted. The will was naturally denounced as invalid by the Austrians and hostilities soon started between France and Austria. William feared a Franco-Spanish 'universal monarchy' and believed it was vital that England should support the Austrians. But the Dutch and English saw Carlos's will as a way of peacefully resolving the question of the Spanish succession, until Louis provoked them by occupying 'barrier' fortresses on the Dutch border and by recognising the Pretender as 'James III' when his father died in 1701, reopening the question of the English succession which had seemingly been resolved when Louis had recognised William as king in 1697.

William exploited these gaffes as he patiently built up another anti-French coalition. This time he was careful to take the Commons into his confidence by showing them all relevant treaties. If he wanted them to provide the money for war, he had to persuade them that the war was necessary. Aware that he might not live to see the end of what was likely to be another long war, he groomed Marlborough, whose abilities he had finally recognised, to be his successor as the military leader of the allies. In the event, he did not live to see even the start of the war. On 21 February 1702, his horse stumbled on a molehill, throwing him and breaking his collarbone. Two weeks later he fell seriously ill. He told Portland that he did not fear death and in some ways looked upon it as a release. When he died on 8 March, his lungs were found to have wasted away: his chest problems had probably owed much to tuberculosis. He was wearing a lock of Mary's hair around his neck.

William III is perhaps best remembered and commemorated today in Northern Ireland, where he is revered by Ulster Unionists as a Protestant icon and Orange lodges are key features of Unionist organisation and sociability. But the Orange order was founded only in the 1790s and William himself favoured toleration for Catholics and tried to deliver on the promises he had made in the treaty of Limerick. In England, he is remembered less well, perhaps because the history of the seventeenth century has not retained the sense of immediate contemporary relevance – real or reinvented – that it has in Ireland. While the wars against France continued and the Revolution of 1688 was seen as Glorious, William was revered, at least by Whigs, as the man who saved England from popery and slavery. His birthday (4 November) was for a while celebrated with almost as much fervour as the following day.

In England, as in Ireland, William was very much a Protestant hero and his star faded as English history came to be viewed in less explicitly denominational terms. Burnet, however, was in no doubt as to his importance.

> I considered him as a person raised up by God to resist the power of France and the progress of tyranny and persecution ... After all the abatements that may be allowed for his errors and faults, he ought still be reckoned among the greatest princes that our history, or indeed any other, can afford.[52]

8

Anne

When Anne came to the throne it was clear to all that she would be the last Protestant Stuart monarch of England. For much of her life, it had been far from certain that she would be queen. As the second daughter of James II, her sister Mary was first in line for the succession and there was always the possibility that her father's second wife would have a son, who would take precedence over both of them. However, by the time Mary Beatrice gave birth to James Francis Edward, in June 1688, Anne was as convinced as most of her fellow Protestants that there was much that was suspicious about the birth. The Catholics had been too confident that it was a boy and, after all this time, it seemed a little too good to be true. Besides, like her sister, Anne had a vested interest in believing that the child was not really the queen's.

Anne's upbringing had done little to prepare her for government. Despite the best efforts of French and English surgeons, from early childhood she suffered from chronic short sight. Difficulty in seeing clearly the faces of those with whom she was speaking exacerbated her innate shyness. She had a disjointed upbringing, spending two years in France with her grandmother, Henrietta Maria, and aunt ('Madame'); after their deaths, she returned to England to find her mother terminally ill. Not long afterwards she found herself with a stepmother only a few years older than herself. Like her sister Mary, her formal education was relatively neglected, although both were fluent in French. (Anne's written English contained numerous errors.) By contrast, their tutor Bishop Compton instilled in his charges a rooted commitment to the Church of England as a primitive and apostolic church. This did not mean, as it did for some churchmen, that Compton dissociated himself from non-episcopal churches on the Continent; indeed, he was one of the leading supporters of Huguenot refugees in England. Mary continued to worship as an Anglican in the Dutch Republic, while earning the respect of the pastors of the Dutch Reformed Church. As queen it was Mary, rather than William, who chose bishops – good pastors and scholars, who concentrated on running their dioceses and showed no animus towards dissenters or even occasional conformists. Anne, who never went abroad after her childhood sojourn in France, retained a deeper sense of the uniqueness of the Church of England, without wishing to repeal the Toleration Act or renew the persecution of dissenters. Both sisters deplored what was widely seen as the rise of deism and atheism and eagerly supported the Societies for the Reformation of Manners, which strove to suppress drunkenness, prostitution, gambling and a range of other evils, including the perceived licentiousness of the stage.

Anne married Prince George of Denmark in 1683. He was a man of few words and little wit, of whom Charles II famously remarked that he had tried him drunk and tried him sober and either way there was nothing in him. The marriage was happy, without a hint of scandal, but a long series of pregnancies and miscarriages – perhaps as many as seventeen – played havoc with the princess's already fragile health. She found walking difficult and could no longer ride – one of the pleasures of her youth. The accession of her father in 1685 added to Anne's problems. She greatly missed her sister and asked permission to visit her, which was denied. Anne blamed her stepmother, who was emerging as a patron of the more militant Catholics at court. Anne feared that she would be pressed to convert, which she was determined never to do. In 1687 she began a secret correspondence with Mary, in which each fed the suspicions and anxieties of the other about the way in which their father's policies were developing.

In the short term the Revolution of 1688–89 did little serious damage to the principle of royal hereditary succession. The initial adjustment within the existing royal family was no more dramatic than those of 1399 and 1461, and much less startling than that of 1485, when Henry VII (whose claim to the throne was highly questionable) ousted Richard III. The death of the duke of Gloucester in 1700 transformed the situation. Despite her many pregnancies, Anne had produced no children who had survived. Now, although she was still only thirty-five, her poor health made it improbable, and undesirable, that she should conceive again. The nearest heirs by blood, headed by Anne's half-brother James Francis Edward, 'the Old Pretender', were all Catholics, so Parliament, in the Act of Settlement, vested the succession, after Anne, in Sophia and her heirs.

Sophia was the youngest daughter of James I's daughter Elizabeth, the 'Winter Queen' of Bohemia. All the senior branches of the family were Catholic. By passing over so many closer relatives, this did far more damage than 1689 to the hereditary principle. In the eyes of many Tories (and Scots) this took the crown away from the Stuart family and vested it in one that was doubly undesirable, as a German and a Lutheran. Tory attitudes had changed since 1689. Experience of a foreign, non-Anglican king had made them hostile to the prospect of a foreign, non-Anglican dynasty. William was denounced for allegedly putting Dutch interests before English and presiding over a regime that was widely seen as extravagant and corrupt. It was feared that the Hanoverians would put their German principality first and would see England merely as a source of money.

It was hard to see Sophia (who died just before Anne, in 1714) or her son George, who succeeded to the throne in that year, as worthy of the throne of Charles I. For a substantial part of the population, emotional attachment to the monarchy had been heightened by the civil war and by Charles's 'martyrdom', which continued to be commemorated each year. Faced with the hostility of the Whigs and Dissenters, many post-Restoration Anglican clergymen emphasised the sacred attributes of monarchy, seen pre-eminently in the ceremony of the 'royal touch', discontinued by William but revived, for the last time, by Anne. Neither Charles II nor James II was seen during his reign as either a king worthy of their 'martyred' father or a friend of the church, but perceptions softened after 1689. By comparison with William's reign, 'Good King Charles's' days did indeed seem 'golden', while those who had bid good riddance to James II subsequently began to feel a sense of loss that became greater with time.

Under Queen Anne, the Tories enjoyed a wallow in emotional royalism, all the more intense and poignant because it was doomed to end with her lifetime. All the time, there was the gloomy prospect of an alien king, whose hereditary claim was weak and who was not surrounded by an aura of majesty or divine approval. Small wonder that some Tories flirted, or more than flirted, with Jacobitism, seeing in the unlovely person of 'James VIII and III' the charisma and magical power that the Hanoverians lacked. The one almost insuperable drawback about the Pretender was that he was a Catholic. Many Tories hoped fervently that he would become a Protestant and claim his rightful inheritance, but he never did, forcing the Tories (as under James II) to choose between their loyalty to monarchy and their loyalty to the church. As under James II, most eventually chose the church, but this did not stop them deeply regretting the death of hereditary, divine-right monarchy at George I's accession. For some, the exiled Stuarts became the epitome of ultimate justice and of lost monarchical ideals and values. Much Jacobite writing, indeed, was pervaded by a sense of loss, of a vanished royalist, chivalric and even magical past that could be restored only by the special providence of God. This sense of loss was essentially emotional. It cannot be explained rationally, but it underlay much of the bitterness and anger displayed by the Tories after 1689, and especially in the last years of Anne's reign.

Anne, who did not make friends easily, had for some years enjoyed a close friendship with one of James's leading protégés, John Churchill, and his wife, Sarah. In November 1688, when James's army marched westwards, Anne and the Churchills headed north, accompanied by Bishop Compton, reliving his past as a cavalry officer in the civil war. Under William, the Churchills helped to sour Anne's relationship with the king and queen. She complained that her financial allowance was inadequate and that William had failed to give Churchill, now earl of Marlborough, the military promotion that he deserved. Only towards the end of the reign did William's attitude towards Marlborough soften, as he groomed the earl to take his place as leader of the war effort against France.

Anne inherited a war with France, a monarchy financially dependent on Parliament, and a Parliament (and nation) deeply divided between Whig and Tory. She, nevertheless, enjoyed the affection and respect of the nation. For the Tories she was, unlike William, the rightful heir to the throne and a devout member of the Church of England. She was, as she stressed in her first speech to Parliament, truly and wholly English – she and Mary were the only Stuart monarchs who had two English parents. She also lacked William's talent, experience of government and alternative power-base in the Dutch Republic. And she was a woman, in a political world that was outwardly, if not in reality, exclusively male.

Anne tried to present herself as a new Elizabeth but did not quite succeed. She lacked Elizabeth's presence and charisma and she was chronically overweight. Like Elizabeth, she had to contend with men who patronised or tried to bully her, but she lacked Elizabeth's political intelligence and steely resolution. In their place, she offered dogged determination and a sense of duty. Having failed to produce a child who survived to adulthood, she became a 'nursing mother' to her people. She attended the privy council assiduously, even when her health deteriorated to the point where she had to be carried to meetings. Her court was decent but dull, her conversation at the tea table – tea was becoming fashionable among ladies of quality – was stolid and uninspired; unfortunately, she had inherited her father's lack of wit. Nevertheless, she provided a focus for national unity and pride during the war with France that lasted almost all of her reign: peace was made only in 1713. It was a successful war in which, unlike William, Marlborough delivered a series of great military victories: Blenheim, Ramillies, Oudenarde, Malplaquet. Under Queen Anne, England became unquestionably a major military as well as naval power.

In the course of Anne's reign, England became part of the larger entity of Great Britain, thanks to the Union between England and Scotland. Since the union of crowns in 1603, there had been various schemes to unite the two old enemies. These had generally foundered on English unwillingness to join with a nation that they regarded as impoverished and backward. The Scots were likely to gain economically, but what benefit could England derive? After the Act of Settlement of 1701 the picture changed. English ministers feared that the Scots might refuse to accept the Hanoverian succession and choose a monarch of their own. The most obvious candidate was the Pretender, who could be assured of French backing, because Louis XIV had recognised him as the rightful king of England. The French had already opened up a second front in Ireland in 1689–91. Now they threatened to do the same in Scotland, installing a Stuart puppet ruler in Edinburgh.

The Jacobites (or 'Cavaliers') were not the only group within the Scottish Parliament critical of the Act of Settlement. The 'Country'

party wanted no truck with the Pretender but hoped to use the uncertainty about the succession to secure a greater degree of autonomy
for Scotland. The interests of the two parties were ultimately incompatible, but they joined to pass two provocative pieces of legislation in
1703. The Act of Security and Succession laid down that a Hanoverian
could succeed to the Scottish throne only if Scotland's government was
freed from 'English or any foreign influence'. The Act anent Peace and
War decreed that Scotland should make neither war nor peace without
the consent of its Parliament. These might seem to be intended simply
to annoy the London government, but in fact they were part of a wider
package of proposed reforms designed to give the Scottish Parliament
greater control over the government of Scotland and to prevent 'corruption', especially in the form of English ministerial influence. These
reforms aimed to restore the powers that the Scottish Parliament had
secured in 1640–41. They included an Act to limit the length of Parliaments to a maximum of three years, a parliamentary committee to
direct the government during recesses, and parliamentary appointment
of royal officials. Bills to secure the first and third of these were approved
by the Scottish Parliament in 1705 – but did not receive the royal
assent.[1]

For Anne's English ministers, embroiled in a massive war against
France, the behaviour of the Scottish Parliament was both irritating and
threatening. By 1704 they had decided that the best way to deal with the
Scottish Parliament was by subsuming it in the Parliament at Westminster by means of an 'incorporating union'. They used a mixture of stick
and carrot. They threatened to confiscate all property in England belonging to Scots and to ban all imports from Scotland. This was a serious
threat because Scotland's most buoyant export industries – notably coal
and linen – were heavily dependent on the English market. They also
reassured two of the most powerful interest groups in Scotland, the
clergy and lawyers, by promising that the Scots would retain their own
church and law. Scots merchants were to be allowed to trade throughout
England's colonial empire, which also promised greater prosperity to
manufacturers and landowners. As for the politicians who had proved
so turbulent since 1689, they would have access to the far greater patronage resources available to ministers in London. Despite these
assurances and attractions, there was still much hostility in Scotland to

the idea of union. Anti-English feeling was strong and giving up the Edinburgh Parliament was seen by many as an abandonment of national identity. The treaty was nevertheless concluded in 1707. The Scots were to choose forty-five MPs (about one twelfth of the House of Commons) and sixteen representative Scottish peers were to sit in the Lords.[2]

For decades the Act of Union has been a live issue in Scottish politics. It has been depicted as a shameful betrayal of nationhood, in which interest groups and powerful individuals allowed themselves to be won over by bribery. In this view the English appear as devious and cynical, offering only membership of a Parliament in which the Scots would be heavily outnumbered; and their offers were backed up with the implied threat of economic ruin and military force. But if some Scots were bribed, many were not. The English ministers were careful to address concerns about the law and above all the church, which contributed at least as much as the Edinburgh Parliament to Scotland's sense of identity.

Moreover, many Scots saw England as a country to be emulated, a more ordered, economically advanced and civilised society. Advocates of progress looked to England for inspiration; landlords adopted English agricultural methods, even if they were unsuitable for their soil. Just as Lowland influence (and the English language) gradually permeated the Highlands, so English influence gradually spread into the Lowlands, not through military or economic power, but by a subtler process, a form of cultural imperialism.[3] Ambitious Scots saw England as a bigger stage on which to display their talents and called themselves North Britons rather than Scots.[4] In the short run, their optimism seemed ill-founded. The new British Parliament interpreted some points of the treaty in ways that displeased the Scots, and the Presbyterian clergy bitterly resented the passing of an Act allowing freedom of worship to Scottish Episcopalians. The Scottish privy council was wound up; decisions were now taken in London, in which Scots had only a limited voice. Scottish affairs and Scottish interests were neglected. Scots felt that in the new world of 'Britain' they had been not so much subsumed as submerged.

Yet the Union brought benefits as well. Neglect could prove irritating but it also allowed Scotland to develop with little interference from London. The Union had secured the Scottish succession for the House of Hanover. Although Jacobitism was stronger in Scotland than in England, the majority of Scots had no wish to return to Stuart rule, especially as the Pretender and his son remained stubbornly Catholic. Meanwhile, Scotland prospered. Trade boomed and cities grew. Daniel Defoe described Glasgow as one of the cleanest and handsomest cities he had seen.[5] Culturally, too, Scotland flourished, producing philosophers and scientists of European reputation – David Hume, Adam Smith, James Watt. Scotland's four universities – England still had only two – enjoyed a golden age, while Oxford and Cambridge subsided into comfortable well-fed torpor. With prosperity and a flourishing intellectual life went increased national self-confidence; Scotland was no longer a backwater on the periphery of Europe. The Presbyterian clergy gradually lost the power to control – and stifle – intellectual life; increasingly, they did not attempt to do so. Meanwhile, Scottish architects, designers, painters and even lawyers made their mark in England.

Admittedly, English prejudice against Scots (and for that matter the Irish) remained vigorous. When George III appointed a Scot, the earl of Bute, as his prime minister, the same Scottish stereotypes appeared that had been current in the reign of James VI, including references to 'the itch'. But for all their lingering prejudices, Englishmen shared with Scots the sense of belonging to an entity called Great Britain. During the eighteenth century they constructed an identity as 'Britons', born partly of common enemies – France and Catholicism – but also of common attributes – the English language, Protestantism, a shared culture and pride in the Empire and in English (now British) 'liberties'.[6] The Union, which remained contentious in the last years of Anne's reign, ceased to be an issue. 'Britain' was a problem at the time of the union of crowns in 1603 and on the eve of the Act of Union; by the middle of the eighteenth century it was a fact.

A similar self-confidence could be found among the ruling English Protestant minority in Ireland. The treaty of Limerick – and its subsequent reinterpretation by Parliament – brought to an end the stubborn resistance of Catholic Ireland to English Protestant rule. In the eighteenth century the Catholic population remained outwardly sullen and cowed. The peasantry were wretchedly poor and already dependent on the potato. Hunger was endemic and there was a major famine in 1741. Many landlords were negligent or oppressive. One English observer described them as 'lazy, trifling, negligent, inattentive, slobbering, profligate'; another declared 'the poor people of Ireland are used worse than negroes'.[7]

Desperate though their situation was, there was little serious rural crime before the 1760s. The rapparees continued active under William and Anne and their activity even increased for a while after George I's accession. The methods used by the authorities against the rapparees ensured that they continued to enjoy the sympathy of the Catholic population. But that population posed only a limited threat to Protestant rule. The power of the Catholic nobility was only a shadow of its former self. Those people who seemed to pose any threat were disarmed by the army and militia, and the rapparees' knives were no match for the soldiers' guns.[8] There was much popular support for the Jacobite movement and the exiled Stuarts. Initially James II had been denounced by the native Irish as 'James the Shite', with one Irish and one English shoe, for his precipitate flight after the Boyne. In time, the animus faded and he and the Pretenders came to be seen in an almost messianic light, as the godly princes who could free the Irish from English rule. This vision was particularly expounded by the Catholic clergy; between 1687 and 1765, the pope even allowed the head of the Catholic house of Stuart to nominate Irish bishops. But it was a vision that depended on liberation from outside: by France or another continental power; or by the 'Wild Geese', the Irish brigades serving on the Continent. The standing army, lodged in barracks throughout Ireland, usually numbered little more than six thousand, but it was sufficient to keep the native population more or less under control. Although the Protestant elite became extremely nervous at times, Jacobite risings in Scotland and England did not trigger similar revolts in Ireland.[9] Only in the late eighteenth century, with the rise of Catholic nationalism, did the majority once again find its voice and develop the confidence in its numbers that led to Roman Catholic Emancipation and eventually to Home Rule.

In the meantime, the English Protestant elite prospered. Dublin became a fine city, with squares and streets as elegant as any in the British Isles. It should be stressed that this elite was *English*. Its members referred to themselves as 'the king's English subjects of Ireland', dissociating themselves from the Ulster Scots, who numbered 200,000 by the middle of the eighteenth century.[10] An Act of the Irish Parliament had re-established full episcopacy in 1666 and had imposed the English prayer book, but local practice varied considerably and the Church of Ireland was firmly controlled by the English Protestant laity.[11] Membership of the Church of Ireland became an essential qualification for office. A sacramental test on office-holders, imposed in 1704, was designed against Catholics but had the additional effect of excluding Presbyterians, who remained poor, second-class citizens, little better off than the Catholics.[12]

If the Protestant elite saw themselves as 'English', they also in some senses saw themselves (and were perceived in England) as 'Irish'. One historian has distinguished between 'Anglo-Irish', with extensive estates on both sides of the Irish Sea but based primarily in England, and 'Irish Protestants', men and women of English extraction whose lands, and interests, were predominantly or exclusively in Ireland. They might see themselves as subjects of the English crown living in one of the monarch's three kingdoms; they were often seen in England as the inhabitants of a colony, who (by emigration) had lost their rights as English people. For the English, the Irish economy, like that of other colonies, was something to be managed and restricted for the profit of the mother country.[13]

The relationship between the Irish Protestants and the London government was delicate and based on mutual dependence. Although there was still a substantial army in Ireland, the Irish Protestants well knew that if there were ever to be a major rebellion they would need military help from England to suppress it, as in 1649–52 and 1689–91. Similarly the London government, engaged in two great wars against Catholic France between 1689 and 1713, relied on the Protestant elite in Ireland to keep the Catholics quiet and to prevent Ireland from becoming the base for a French assault on England. Common Protestantism did not necessarily make for harmony. Irish Protestants denounced economic legislation, such as the ban in 1666 on importing Irish cattle into England, that sacrificed Irish agriculture, industry and trade for the benefit of England. One reason for the development of the Irish linen industry was that the English Parliament would not allow an Irish woollen industry that would compete with that of England.

Irish Protestants also fiercely resisted attempts by the Westminster Parliament to legislate for Ireland, which it occasionally attempted to do. Not until 1782 did Westminster concede that it could not do so.[14]

The Irish Protestants' often acrimonious exchanges with the London government (and its representatives in Dublin Castle) were increasingly focused on the Dublin Parliament. This had met very irregularly – in the hundred years up to 1691 only in 1613–15, 1634–41, 1662–66 and 1689. It met in 1692 and from 1695 it met every two years. The reasons for this were essentially financial. The 'hereditary' revenues voted in 1662–66 had then seemed generous, but they proved less than sufficient to meet the demands of war after 1689. The Irish Parliament voted relatively small sums each session, usually for two years, so the monarch was forced to call it regularly and to pay heed to what it said. Its financial bargaining power enabled it to secure the redress of grievances and to circumvent Poynings' Law. Draft bills were sent over by the privy council in London, but they often incorporated 'heads of bills' drawn up in Dublin after discussion in Parliament.[15]

The relatively modest sums demanded of the Irish Parliament, compared to that of England, showed how cautious London was when dealing with the Irish Protestants, and the Dublin Parliament was only once asked to underwrite a loan. Irish Protestant politicians feasted on government patronage and luxuriated in the Dublin Season. On the rare occasions when London got it wrong, it was quick to make amends. After a furious row about a patent to coin halfpennies, the London government built a fine new Parliament House, opposite Trinity College.[16] No new Parliament was built at Westminster until the old complex of buildings was destroyed by fire in 1834. On the other hand, the threat of rebellion had gone and Ireland could be managed using money, of which the London government had plenty, rather than force. Irish independence was understood only in terms of absence of interference from Westminster. Before the 1780s there was barely a hint of the nationalism, and particularly the Catholic nationalism, that was to be so powerful in nineteenth-century Ireland.

William had found the English Parliament difficult – critical, xenophobic and factious. Anne did not have to face the problem of xenophobia, but she had to face a Parliament that, since 1700, had become even more sharply divided on party lines.[17] In the Exclusion Crisis Whigs and Tories differed mainly on the issues of the nature of monarchy (and the succession) and the relationship between Church and Dissent. Those divisions were blurred, but not entirely obliterated, by the extraordinary behaviour of James II, but resurfaced after William's invasion. The Whigs claimed that they alone were truly loyal to William and that the Tories hankered after the return of James. This was largely untrue, but it was given credibility by the Tories' reluctance to offer William the crown or to recognise him as 'rightful and lawful' monarch. As has been seen, the crown's new-found financial dependence on Parliament gave the Commons real power. Sometimes this was exercised by disgruntled 'Country' backbenchers, as in the measures against corruption and the standing army, promoted by a mixture of Whigs and Tories. The thinking behind such measures was essentially negative and those who promoted them wished to prevent the misuse of power, not to exercise power themselves.

The cohesion given to the Commons by the resurgence of party divisions gave the leaders of the majority party the chance to use their control of the Commons to force their way into office and to force their wishes on the monarch. To put it simply, they could tell the monarch that, unless he or she adopted the policies and made the appointments that they demanded, they would not push through the money bills on which the government depended. Within the executive, real power was passing from the monarch to the politicians who governed in the monarch's name. 'Ministers', remarked George II sourly in 1744, 'are the kings in this country.' [18]

William III had been able to resist the pressure from the politicians to some extent, partly because party divisions were less clear cut and deep in his reign than they were to be in Anne's, partly because he was tougher and abler. He had employed 'managers' to act as buffers and links between the politicians and himself; this had been all the more necessary as he was abroad for so much of the time. Anne, less tough, less able and a woman, was even more dependent on 'managers'. For much of her reign the duke of Marlborough and Lord Godolphin played key roles in government. Both were long-standing personal friends of the queen. Marlborough continued William's role as the linchpin of the coalition against France and the commander in chief of the allied armies. Godolphin was responsible for providing resources for the war, above all money, which also involved him in the management of Parliament. Marlborough's victories gave the regime a solid underpinning of success, which made it easier for the nation to bear an even heavier tax burden than in the 1690s. (In addition, trade was less badly disrupted in this war.) Even so, by 1709 war weariness was setting in, especially when the queen's Whig ministers brushed aside Louis XIV's offers of peace, making the quite unreasonable demand that he should join the allies in driving his grandson, now securely installed as King Philip V, out of Spain ('No peace without Spain').

In the early part of the reign, Marlborough and Godolphin had worked together with Robert Harley. Harley came of a Presbyterian and Whig family, but emerged as the leader of the Tory party. An astute politician, he had been a prominent member of the commission for public accounts and started Anne's reign as Speaker of the Commons. Dismissed at the behest of Whig politicians in 1708, he returned as lord treasurer when the Whigs fell in 1710. Harley was far from a typical Tory. He was attached to the church as a moral force, not as a sacred institution, and he was valued by the queen for his essentially non-partisan approach to politics.

Anne, like William, was by nature a moderate, or 'trimmer'. Unlike Harley, she had a deep and genuine spiritual commitment to the Church of England, which initially inclined her to rely on the Tories. In William's reign, she said, 'though there was no violent thing done [to the church], everything was leaning towards the Whigs and whenever that is I shall think the Church beginning to be in danger'.[19] But she recoiled from the extremism and irresponsibility of the High Tories. In 1702 and 1703 the Commons passed bills against occasional conformity, which were rejected by the Lords. In 1704 the Commons drew up another bill and it was proposed to tack it to a major money bill. Anne was outraged that the Tories were prepared to jeopardise supply, and the war effort, for such a partisan measure. In the end, enough Tories were persuaded not to support the tack and it failed to pass the Commons.

But for Anne the Whigs were even worse. Not only were they hostile to the church, but the morals and religious orthodoxy of some of their leaders left much to be desired. They also showed greater solidarity than the Tories, working together to impose their will on the hapless queen, 'designing ... to tear that little prerogative the crown has to pieces'. All she wanted was 'to keep me out of the power of the merciless men of both parties'.[20] 'Why', she asked, 'for God's sake must I who have no interest, no end, no thought but for the good of my country be made so miserable as to be brought into the power of one set of men?'[21] Harley, for his part, argued that 'persons or parties are to come in to the queen and not the queen to them'. 'If the gentlemen of England are made sensible that the queen is the head and not a party, everything will be easy and the queen will be courted and not a party.'[22]

The concept of a queen above party was a worthy ideal, but it failed to survive the tough realities of partisan politics. Neither Marlborough nor Godolphin was a party politician – their overriding concern was to win the war. After the 'tack', they doubted the Tories' commitment to the war and became increasingly convinced that only the Whigs could provide sufficient resources and competence. The House of Commons elected in 1705 was fairly evenly balanced, but the Whigs were more diligent and organised; the election of 1708 produced the only clear Whig majority of the reign. From 1706, and still more 1708, Marlborough and Godolphin pressed and bullied the queen into dismissing Harley and appointing Whig ministers whom she personally disliked.[23] She regarded Lord Wharton as a rake and an atheist and was deeply resentful when Wharton and his colleagues tried to make her appoint to bishoprics men she regarded as wildly unsuitable, in order to goad the High Tory clergy. The years of the Whig ministry, 1708–10, were very painful for Anne, especially as her husband had died in 1708.

The Tory landslides in the elections of 1710 and 1713 created equally intractable problems. Anne dismissed Godolphin in 1710 and Marlborough (reluctantly) at the end of 1711. The Tories were as eager as the Whigs to enjoy a monopoly of office and patronage, and had the added incentive of wishing to be fully in control of the government when Anne died, so that the incoming (and probably hostile) Hanoverian would have little option but to work with them. This was the avowed strategy of the dashing young Tory leader, Viscount Bolingbroke, and the years after 1710 saw a bitter struggle between Bolingbroke and Harley, the latter still determined to avoid single-party government.[24] Anne cannot have relished this jockeying for position in anticipation of her death, or the partisan measures passed by the Tories, including Acts against occasional conformity and dissenting schools.

Although Anne was devoted to her stolid but well-meaning husband, she also needed female company. For many years her most important confidante had been Sarah, countess and later duchess of Marlborough, whom she treated as an equal. In their correspondence they addressed each other as 'Mrs Morley' and 'Mrs Freeman'. Sarah was a strong-minded woman, with strongly Whig political views, and she was far more of a party political animal than her husband. She was convinced that all Tories were Jacobites and urged Anne to rely on the Whigs. She exploited Anne's need for friendship and chivvied and bullied her mercilessly when she did not get her way. Although Anne's affection and respect for the duke continued, once she became queen Anne wearied of the duchess's tirades and tantrums. Although she held a variety of court offices, and was Anne's most senior female servant, the duchess rarely came to court, a serious dereliction of duty as the queen became more and more of an invalid. The vacuum left by the duchess came to be filled by Abigail Masham, soothing and gentle by comparison. She was also a kinswoman of Harley's, but was less politi-cally involved than the duchess, who made none too subtle hints that this was a lesbian relationship. Sarah went off to revel in the wealth that a grateful nation had bestowed on her husband – and to ruin the lives of her children and grandchildren.[25] Anne had valued Sarah as a friend before she became queen, but as queen she found her as demanding and domineering as the male politicians she had to contend with.

The increased power of Parliament had its positive side as well. Between 1641 and 1643 the Long Parliament had swept away the accu-mulated detritus of feudal and other ancient royal revenues and created a tax system that raised revenue quickly and efficiently, so providing security for systematic government borrowing. Charles II had benefited from this to some extent, notably in the huge vote of £2,500,000 for the Second Dutch War; he had also refined the system he inherited, making the collection of revenue more professional. But his difficulties with Parliament ensured that he was never given another grant as large as that of 1664 and he received no money at all from Parliament after 1679. Moreover, having improved his credit by undertaking to repay loans in strict chronological order, he wrecked it by stopping repayments in 1672. It took the best part of a decade to repair the damage.[26] After 1689 the situation changed. Whatever their differences, Whigs and Tories agreed that the war with France had to be fought and won, because the alternative would be the return of James II as a French puppet. The same was true of the war of 1702–13. Once Louis had recognised James's son as 'James III', the War of the Spanish Succession became also a war of the English succession.

As in the 1640s, the Commons, usually suspicious of royal requests for money, accepted that it was vital to raise as much money as possible as quickly as possible. The result was an enormous increase in royal revenue. Charles I's annual income was less than £1,000,000. James II's (which was larger than his brother's) was about £2,000,000. During the war of 1689–97 the average annual revenue was £3,500,000; between 1702 and 1713 it was £6,000,000. And this was a real increase: price levels remained fairly stable between the 1630s and the 1710s. Much of this additional revenue consisted of excises which, like all indirect taxes, fell proportionately more heavily on the poor than on the rich. But from 1689 to 1713 approximately £2,000,000 a year was raised by the land tax, which showed that the landowners who comprised the majority of members of Parliament were prepared to tax themselves.

Heavy though these taxes were, they did not bring in enough to meet the demands of war. As in the 1640s and 1650s, money had to be raised by borrowing and here again the Commons proved constructive. Their attitude in the 1690s owed much to the committee of public accounts. King, ministers and civil servants saw this as an unwarranted intrusion into the mysteries of government, but the commission found much less waste and mismanagement than MPs had expected. It also had the unexpected (and perhaps unintended) effect of educating MPs about the true costs of war. In time some of the longer-serving members, notably Robert Harley, began to make constructive proposals about raising money and presenting government demands to the House. The Commons also began to vote money to pay the interest on loans, rather than for spending immediately on the war. In this way much larger sums could be mobilised.

The most important single step was the Tonnage Act of 1694, which provided for a loan of £1,200,000 and for the subscribers to be formed into a corporation, the Bank of England, which could also deal in bills of exchange, which were promissory notes, more easily transportable than gold and silver coins. The bank soon began to issue its own notes – promises to pay the bearer a certain sum, initially £100 but soon as little as £5. The bank also welcomed deposits (at interest) from small investors, which created funds that could then be lent to the government at somewhat higher interest. Before the 1690s, government borrowing (except in the 1640s and 1650s) had depended on the personal credit of kings, which was often poor. Tradesmen presented James I with inflated bills, because they knew it would be a long time before they were paid.[27] 'Banks' too had depended on the creditworthiness of individual bankers and some went bankrupt, especially those who lent too much to the crown. The Bank of England was the first institutional bank in England (as so often following Dutch models). Its foundation by Act of Parliament and the extensive wealth and expertise of its board members made it a far safer investment than any family bank. Certain other City corporations, notably the East India Company and the South Sea Company, also received investments from the public and made loans to the government. Meanwhile, individual investors were encouraged to lend directly to the government through loans whose interest was secured by Act of Parliament, which offered much better security than the word of a king. As a result, interest rates fell from around 10 per cent in the 1690s (the original Bank subscription paid 8 per cent) to 3 per cent or less in the 1730s.[28]

The ability to mobilise such large sums of money for war meant that by 1714, like the Dutch Republic in the previous century, England wielded naval and military power out of all proportion to its population. France's population was nearly four times as great as England's, but Louis XIV's fiscal system remained essentially medieval and he borrowed at interest rates so exorbitant that the royal accounts were doctored to conceal the true figures. The Bourbon kings of the eighteenth century were to accumulate greater and greater debts, which eventually were to bring the monarchy crashing down. Even under Louis XIV the burden of taxation was becoming insupportable, so that whole villages in Languedoc gave up tilling the soil because they could not make enough money to pay the taxman. England, with its much smaller population, coped remarkably well. While famine stalked the land in France (and in Scotland) in 1709, and later in Ireland, few if any starved in England.

By 1714 it was accepted that the debts accumulated during the wars could never be paid back, so ministers set out to reduce the interest paid on what, for lenders, had become a secure long-term investment.

Overseas trade, interrupted by war (especially in the 1690s), continued to grow and with it the nation's prosperity. Although the English grumbled about the taxes they paid, a growing proportion of the population was able to buy an increasing range of consumer goods from around the world. Tea and coffee, once exotic luxuries, were now items of everyday consumption. More and more people bought textiles from India and ceramics from China. English manufacturers catered for the growing taste for the exotic and the stylish and became far more concerned with design and fashion. England's emergence as a great power did not come at the expense of the creature comforts of its people.

Nor did it come at the expense of their liberties. As the volume and range of taxation grew, so did the administration that collected it. The developments of Charles II's reign continued, as the revenue service was made more structured and professional, with effective supervision of local collectors and clear criteria for promotion. Nevertheless, in an age of ferocious party competition, party leaders were always on the lookout for rewards for loyal supporters – or for those who might become loyal supporters. Places in the administration, especially sinecures in the more ancient branches, were valuable plums of patronage and there was a danger, widely perceived in the 1690s, that the expansion of the revenue administration (and armed forces) could increase the rewards at the disposal of ministers. The Revolution had effectively removed the threat from the royal prerogative. Kings had to rule as Parliament expected, unless they could raise a large enough army to rule by force; hence the anxiety about the standing army in 1697–99.

William III was too sensible to dream of establishing a military despotism and Anne clearly was not cut out for it. But there was the more insidious possibility that ministers might exploit the 'influence' of the crown, its ability to buy support through offices and pensions, to subvert the independence of Parliament and make it ineffectual as a check on the crown. This danger had first become apparent under Danby in the 1670s and it led to a clause in the Act of Settlement against placemen sitting in the Commons, as well as several place bills. It also led to the Triennial Act of 1694, which laid down that there had to be a general election at least every three years. This, like the similar but abortive measure in Scotland, was intended to deny ministers the time to build up a substantial 'court party' in the Commons. In fact the danger was never quite as great as it appeared. William, Anne and their managers did not want either party to win sweeping electoral victories. An evenly balanced House of Commons was easier to manage than a heavily partisan one and allowed the monarch more scope to appoint moderates and neutrals to office.

Only after 1714 did one party, the Whigs, gain a monopoly of patronage. Before 1714 the English state became substantially more powerful, but this did not lead to a strengthening of the monarchy because Parliament both implemented and controlled the process, watching vigilantly for attempts to extend either the prerogative or the influence of the crown. It should be added that the main thrust of this more powerful state was directed outside England, in foreign war and in defending and extending England's colonial empire. Within England day to day government remained much as before, in the hands of the 'better sort' of county, town and parish. The army was available to be used against riots and disorders, but in fact it rarely was.

After 1689, England displayed the slightly odd phenomenon (by the standards of eighteenth-century Europe) of a weak monarchy presiding over a strong state; elsewhere, the need to mobilise forces for war led to a concentration of power in the king. Within the 'crown', the monarch exercised less and less personal power as ministers ruled in his or her name. These ministers derived their power over the monarch from their ability to push government bills (especially money bills) through Parliament, but also from the support that they enjoyed in the wider society. The eighteenth-century electoral system has become a byword for corruption and aristocratic influence, and later Sir Robert Walpole was to secure repeated majorities in the Commons because of the number of 'rotten boroughs' that the Whigs controlled. He could afford to lose most of the counties and the larger towns and still win overall.[29] But neither party possessed such electoral control under William and Anne and both monarchs were determined that it should stay that way.

Following the Triennial Act, the period 1695–1715 saw ten general elections. Although many MPs were returned without a contest, many constituencies, large and small, were vigorously contested. The electorate was large, probably larger (in percentage terms) than it was to be even after the 1832 Reform Bill, although electors were much less equitably distributed between constituencies. It has been estimated that one adult male in three had the right to vote in 1715.³⁰ Candidates had to contend with a large and volatile electorate and even the unenfranchised could make their presence felt, flinging stones, dirt and insults. The divisions between Whig and Tory bit almost as deep as those of the civil war and the Tories in particular often harked back to the 1640s. The divisions spilled over from parliamentary to municipal elections. Whigs and Tories read different newspapers and attended different clubs, pubs, race meetings and even doctors.³¹ Their rivalries could lead to violence and not only at elections; the celebration of royal birthdays and anniversaries bred demonstrations and counter-demonstrations.

As in the Exclusion Crisis, the parties were divided under Anne on the monarchy and the church. The Whigs were coming to espouse a more contractual view of monarchy and to see the Revolution of 1688 as an example of successful popular resistance to a tyrant – which had secured English liberties once and for all, so that no such act of resistance would ever be necessary again. The Tories' view of monarchy was much more emotional despite, or perhaps because of, the fact that monarchy as they knew it would die with Queen Anne. Even so, they still clung to the shibboleths of divine hereditary right and non-resistance. In religion, the Whigs wanted at least to preserve the Toleration Act; some wanted to give dissenters (who mostly voted Whig) full civil rights as well. Many Tories would have liked to repeal the Toleration Act; most wanted to prevent what they saw as abuses of the Act, notably occasional conformity and dissenting schools. Occasional conformity was finally declared illegal in 1711; the significantly named Schism Act outlawed dissenting schools in 1714. In addition, although Whigs and Tories had initially agreed on the necessity of the war, from 1709 the Tories denounced the Whig insistence on 'no peace without Spain' as a cynical device to prolong the war, from which their allies among the monied men in the City (many of them dissenters or men of continental origin) were profiting so handsomely.³²

Dr Henry Sacheverell tapped into the full gamut of Tory anger and resentment. He was an Oxford don who already had a considerable track record as a scourge of Whigs and dissenters when he was asked by the High Tory lord mayor of London to preach the 5 November sermon in 1709. He launched into a splenetic (if not very coherent) diatribe that centred on three allegations: that the Revolution of 1688 had not involved popular resistance; that the Toleration Act was 'un-warrantable'; and that the church was 'in danger' under the present Whig ministry. The lord mayor eagerly ordered that it should be printed ¹ ʰe ministry rose to the bait. The Commons resolved to impeach ₂verell on a charge of sedition.³³

ₐis decision might savour of overreaction, but this had been a ₋profile sermon by a famous preacher and it had aroused enormous vocal public interest. It had aimed to spread disaffection and to ₙate people from the government. Admittedly it was hard to pin this ᵥn. Sacheverell had taken legal advice before giving the sermon and ₗ chosen his words carefully. But the implications of the sermon ₗ the intention behind it were clearly seditious. The trial began on February 1710 in Westminster Hall. Competition for seats was intense ₗd aristocratic ladies fought for places. The wider public followed with ₚt attention and preachers vilified or prayed for the doctor, depending n their point of view. Because of the evasive wording of the sermon, ₕe arguments in court were complex and the trial lasted almost a month.

A few days into the trial, on the night of 1 March, there were the most serious riots seen in London since 1688. Urged on by high church parsons, large Tory crowds rampaged through the western suburbs of London, attacking meeting houses and the homes of leading Whigs. Men equipped with crowbars and axes stripped all the timber, even the floors, from Daniel Burgess's Presbyterian meeting house in Carey Street and consigned them to a huge bonfire. Later the crowd surged towards the City, threatening to burn the Bank of England, but they were dispersed by the lord mayor.³⁴ Minor disorders continued through the remainder of the trial and large guards of the City militia patrolled every night.

On 21 March the Lords found Sacheverell guilty, but then, to the amazement of the Commons, handed down a sentence of one year's suspension from officiating as a priest and three years' suspension from preaching. For the Commons this was a ludicrously light sentence, little better than an acquittal. For the doctor, it was a triumph and he milked it for all it was worth. A former pupil gave him a living in Shropshire and his journey to take possession took on many of the trappings of a royal progress. He rode sedately from one civic reception to another and cheering crowds greeted him wherever he went. Meanwhile, his picture and his story appeared in the press, in prints and on playing cards. The Whigs countered as best they could, notably with Sacheverell chamber pots, but there could be no doubt that popular sympathy was with the doctor, who had become a Tory icon. In the hotly contested mayoral election in Norwich in 1710, Sacheverell's picture appeared between those of Charles I and Charles II. The doctor was indeed in exalted company.[35]

The Sacheverell trial had its elements of farce, but it aroused intense public emotion and there was nothing farcical about the riots. This was indeed a divided society, but it was not on the verge of civil war. Loyalty to the queen was a strong unifying and restraining factor, but so was the fundamental orderliness and governability of the English people. The Sacheverell riots were directed against objects rather than people and had their own internal discipline; the gutting of Burgess's meeting house was carried out with almost military precision. The battles between the customers of Whig and Tory taverns (or 'mughouses') had an air of ritualised violence, like fighting between rival football supporters.

English respect for law and order was shown in the summer of 1714. Towards the end of July Queen Anne finally succumbed to her many ailments. As she lay dying an enlarged privy council assembled, including leading figures from both parties and representatives of the elector of Hanover, who had recently succeeded his mother, Sophia, to put the finishing touches to well prepared plans for a smooth transfer of power. Anne died on the morning of 1 August. A regency council, appointed to direct the government until George could arrive, ordered that the new king be proclaimed throughout the three kingdoms. There was no disorder, but rejoicings were muted, except among Dissenters, who were confident that the recently passed Schism Act would not now take effect. The queen was buried with full pomp in Westminster Abbey, beneath the tomb of Mary Queen of Scots and alongside Charles II, William and Mary, and Prince George.[36] (Her father had been buried at St-Germain-en-Laye.) With her died the Protestant branch of the House of Stuart.

Loyalty to the Stuarts continued long after Anne's death. The new Hanoverian regime was deeply unpopular and was seen by Tories as biased towards Whiggism and Dissent. George I was an unappealing

ruler and not just because he was German. He provided over a sordid
court and an administration that was widely seen as corrupt, even before
it was rocked by the financial scandal of the South Sea Bubble in 1720.
The party animosities of Anne's last years continued. There were widespread riots against dissenting chapels in 1715 and the anniversaries of
George's accession and coronation were often marked by demonstrations and worse. George's accession could be seen in the long run to
have marked the triumph of the Whig view of monarchy, as limited,
constitutional and without charisma. The Georges did not practise the
royal touch and generally kept royal ceremonial to a minimum, until
George III set out to revive it.[37]

The Tory view of monarchy – mystical and magical, containing
elements of the divine and the sacred – died with the last Protestant
Stuart, or rather it increasingly became the property of the Jacobites. In
England, as in Ireland, there were many Jacobite sympathisers, but too
few of them were prepared to turn Jacobite sympathy into Jacobite
action. They would drink the health of 'the king over the water', but
when sober they would do nothing to aid his cause. For most, Jacobitism
was an exercise in nostalgia, romantic and melancholy, rather than a
call to arms. They dreamed of a lost prince coming to claim his crown,
but did nothing to hasten his arrival. A significant number of Jacobites
became freemasons and some Scottish Episcopalian ministers believed
in fairies.[38]

It is easy with hindsight to belittle the Jacobite threat. The authorities
in all three kingdoms took it very seriously indeed. In Ireland the
rapparees and conspirators were seen as the tip of an iceberg of popular
Jacobitism, whose true dimensions were hidden from the authorities by
the fact that they did not speak the same language as the people. The
English, as they had shown in 1640 and 1688, were most unlikely to
rebel without the protection provided by a substantial invading army,
so the best chance of a successful Jacobite rising was in Scotland. There,
in the Highlands and north east, there were nobles who still possessed
real military power and smouldering resentment of the Union created
a wider potential for disaffection. In 1708 the Old Pretender sailed for
Scotland, but his advisers judged the prospects so slim that he did not
leave his ship and returned to France. The 1715 rising in Scotland was
a much more serious affair. The earl of Mar gathered forces from

sympathetic clans in the Highlands and proclaimed 'James III' in the principal towns from Dundee to Inverness. But after failing to defeat the duke of Argyll at Sheriffmuir, the momentum was lost. The Highlanders drifted home and, when the Pretender arrived, Mar advised him to return to France. Meanwhile, an attempted revolt of (mainly Catholic) Jacobite gentry in the north of England was defeated at Preston. Despite some sympathy for the rebellion further south, few were prepared to risk their necks. The Whigs tried to discredit the rebellion by depicting the Jacobites as poverty-stricken and verminous Scots, eager to plunder the wealth of England.

The most serious challenge of all to the Hanoverians came in 1745, when the Young Pretender, Charles Edward Stuart, arrived in Scotland to find minimal opposition. Normally the Highlands were guarded by the Black Watch, consisting of clansmen loyal to the House of Hanover, but they were fighting in Germany, allowing the Pretender to establish control over Scotland and sweep south into England. The Hanoverian authorities were gripped by something approaching panic but, fortunately for them, Charles's Highland followers became more and more uneasy the further south they came. When they reached Derby, he was persuaded to turn back. He was pursued by George II's brother, the duke of Cumberland, nicknamed 'the Butcher'. The Highlanders made their final stand at Culloden, near Inverness, on 16 April 1746. Charles's poorly armed clansmen were slaughtered by superior weapons; the Pretender made his escape over the sea to Skye. Although much of his Scots support had come from the north east and even the Lowlands, the authorities decided that now was the time to destroy Gaelic society in the Highlands. A system of military roads and forts had been established there after 1715. Now such symbols of clan life as the kilt and the bagpipes were forbidden and clansmen were not allowed to carry swords. Heritable jurisdictions were abolished and the authorities in London and Edinburgh set out to bring English industry, English customs and the English language to the last Gaelic fastnesses in mainland Britain, but with only limited success until the Highland Clearances dispersed much of the population.

In one sense, the demise of the centuries-old view of the monarchy cannot be blamed on the House of Stuart. Any hereditary monarchy is at the mercy of accidents of birth and death and it was not inevitable that Charles II would have no legitimate children, or that Mary would be childless, or that none of Anne's children would reach adulthood. Had any of the three left an heir, the line of the Protestant Stuarts would have continued and with it, presumably, the old, or Tory, view of monarchy. Ironically, Charles I had in the long run done far more good than harm to the monarchy, leaving behind the image not of an inept ruler but of a Christlike martyr. The real damage was done by James II, whose conversion to Catholicism split the family. It was unfortunate that it was the Catholic side that produced the heirs, the direct male line only dying out with 'Henry IX', alias 'Cardinal York', in 1807.

It is easy to write the Stuart kings and queens of England off as an inadequate or unfortunate dynasty. They certainly suffer in English historiography when compared to the Tudors (or at least Henry VIII and Elizabeth). To paraphrase Oscar Wilde, for one Stuart to lose his throne was unfortunate; for two to do so looked like carelessness. Yet the century of Stuart rule over Britain saw major achievements, not least an extension of order and civility across all three kingdoms. By 1714 differences were resolved through political channels or the law courts, not by violence. Citizens enjoyed a liberty under the law far more extensive than in most continental countries, although such liberty was not extended to all. With peace came prosperity, although Scotland and Ireland were to reap the full benefits only after 1714. No longer needing to defend themselves against attack, wealthy landowners, first in England and then in Scotland and Ireland, built elegant country houses, with landscaped parks and ornate interiors.

There were losers as well as winners, of course, headed by Catholics in general and Irish Catholics in particular. The triumph of order was in part a triumph of English power and English values. With it came the eclipse of the native cultures of Ireland and Scotland – not just the Gaelic culture of the Highlands, but also the Scots culture of the Lowlands, as burghers affected English accents and followed English fashions. Only in Wales did the native language stubbornly hang on – and indeed flourish.

The triumph of England within Britain was matched by the triumph of Britain within the world, in terms of trade and empire, but also of military and naval power. One could argue that the Stuarts contributed little to these processes and if anything hampered them. The first important phase in state-building came during the civil wars and interregnum and was driven by Parliament, as was the second phase from 1689. But the Stuarts had their achievements. James VI and I brought greater order to Scotland and began the process of union between England and Scotland; Charles II actively encouraged naval and imperial expansion; William III brought England into the mainstream of European power politics and actively promoted religious toleration; Queen Anne acted as a focus of unity and loyalty in difficult times and completed the union with Scotland.

There is much about eighteenth-century Britain that may seem repugnant to modern eyes, such as the arrogant assumption of British superiority to other nations; the extent to which Britain's trade and empire were based on slavery and the slave trade; the grotesque inequalities of wealth and material comfort; and the casual acceptance of cruelty, to both people and animals. Such phenomena were not unique to Britain and aroused little criticism at the time. By the standards of eighteenth-century Europe, Britons enjoyed an almost unrivalled liberty and a broadly based prosperity, seen in the acquisition of consumer goods, improving standards of comfort and an ever growing range of amusements. They were better fed, better dressed and better informed than their forebears, more conscious of style and fashion in clothes, novels and architecture. They were expected to behave with restraint and decorum, and politeness was an essential aspect of gentility. Architecture, whether of houses or cities, showed a greater concern for proportion, taste and refinement. People of fashion strolled in squares or tree-lined walks. There was a confidence about eighteenth-century London, Dublin, and Edinburgh that had been absent a century before. Here was a society that believed in progress and enjoyed material comfort. For many, life was no longer a painful pilgrimage; it was possible to speak, with approval, of the pursuit of happiness.

Glossary

Arminian: A follower of the Dutch theologian Arminius (1560–1609), who challenged Calvin's theology of double predestination. Used more widely, as a term of abuse, of those like Archbishop Laud who placed added emphasis on ceremonies and the beauty of holiness.

Articles, Lords of the: A committee, appointed by the king, to prepare bills for the Scottish Parliament. Established by James VI, it was abolished in 1640, re-established at the Restoration and abolished again in 1690.

Cabal: A small, secretive and conspiratorial group. Applied to five of Charles II's ministers, between 1667 and 1673, whose initials spelled the word: Clifford, Arlington, Buckingham, Ashley (later Shaftesbury) and Lauderdale.

Canons: Ecclesiastical laws, of the Church of England, passed by the Convocation of Canterbury.

Conventicle: An illegal religious meeting of people who refused to conform to the established church. Under the English Conventicle Acts of 1664 and 1670, it consisted of five people or more over and above the immediate family.

Convocation: The representative assembly of one of the two provinces of the Church of England (Canterbury and York), which passed canons (ecclesiastical laws) for the church and also, until 1664, voted taxes to be paid by the clergy. The upper House consisted of the bishops, the lower of representatives of the lower clergy.

Deputy lieutenants: Commissioned by the king to organise and command the county militia, under the direction of a lord lieutenant.

Episcopacy: The government of a church by bishops.

Feudalism: A system in which land is granted by a king to noblemen and knights in return for military service. In England it survived mainly as a means whereby the king raised money from the greater landowners, until feudal tenures were abolished in 1660.

General assembly: The supreme body of the Scottish church, consisting of representatives of the parishes and regions.

Gentry: Owners of sufficient land to enable them to live off their rents and to live the life of a gentleman. The gentry included knights, and later baronets, but not noblemen (the holders of peerage titles).

Graces: A series of concessions offered by Charles I to Irish Catholics in return for money, but never actually granted.

Heritable jurisdictions: In Scotland, the right of landowners to hold courts that would dispense justice (of a sort) to those living on their lands.

Impositions: Non-parliamentary customs duties collected after Bate's case of 1606 and declared illegal in 1641.

Jacobite: Used after 1688 for supporters of the exiled Catholic branch of the house of Stuart – first James II (died 1701), then the Old Pretender (James Francis Edward, 1688–1766) and then his son, the Young Pretender (Charles Edward, 1720–88). The name comes from Jacobus, the Latin for James.

Kirk session: In Scotland, a meeting for parish government and especially moral discipline.

Laird: A member of the Scottish gentry.

Patent: A grant by the monarch to a person or persons to perform a 'public' service and to receive payment for it.

Poynings' Law: An Act of the English Parliament in 1494, which laid down that all bills to be put before the Irish Parliament had first to be approved by the English privy council.

Prelacy: A hostile term for episcopacy.

Presbyterian: A form of church order, in which power ostensibly flowed up from the parishes to regional assemblies and ultimately a national general assembly, as in Scotland. The term came to be used in England in a political sense in the 1640s to describe moderate Parliamentarians and proponents of a puritan, parish-based national church, but without the clerical dominance apparent in Scotland.

Privy council: In England and Scotland, the most important body advising the king and including his leading ministers and some of the chief nobility. The word privy meant secret.

Rapparees: Catholic Irish bandits who were seen to some extent as protectors or heroes by the native Irish.

Recusants: Roman Catholics who refused to obey the laws requiring them to attend Protestant parish churches.

Servitors: In Ireland, English soldiers and officials (mainly in Elizabeth's reign).

Star Chamber: The king's privy council sitting as a court, assisted by one or two judges. The Irish equivalent was Castle Chamber.

Surplice: A white gown which the clergy of the Church of England were required to wear.

Tacking: The practice whereby the English House of Commons added extraneous clauses to money bills in order to force the Lords to consent to them. (The Lords were unable to amend money bills.)

Tonnage and poundage: Import duties, voted by Parliament, mainly on luxury items such as wine or brandy.

Tories: Catholic Irish bandits. Used, originally as a term of abuse, to describe opponents of the exclusion of James, duke of York, from the succession in 1680–81.

Wardship: Under feudal law, the king had the right to appoint a guardian for anyone holding land from him whose father died while he was under age. In fact, the guardianship was usually sold to the family, so became a form of death duty. In Ireland the king assumed the guardianship of some young Catholic lords in order to convert them to Protestantism.

Whig: A contraction of 'Whiggamore', a radical Scots Presbyterian, the term was coined *c.* 1680 as a term of abuse for supporters of the exclusion of James, duke of York, for the succession. Whigs came to be identified with commitment to toleration for Protestant dissenters and to limited and (in some cases) contractual monarchy. In the nineteenth century the 'Whig Interpretation of History' saw English history as an inevitable progress from personal monarchy and attempts to impose religious uniformity to constitutioonal monarchy, liberal parliamentary democracy and religious toleration.

Notes

Notes to Chapter 1: Inheritance

1. S. R. Gardiner, *History of England, 1603–42* (10 vols, London, 1883–84), i, p. 43.
2. R. Ashton (ed.), *James I by his Contemporaries* (London, 1969), pp. 7–8.
3. See in general K. B. Macfarlane, *The Nobility of Later Medieval England* (Oxford, 1973); R. L. Storey, *The End of the House of Lancaster* (Gloucester, 1986).
4. A. Fletcher, 'The Coming of War', in J. S. Morrill (ed.), *Reactions to the English Civil War* (London, 1982), p. 36. See also M. E. James, *Society, Politics and Culture: Studies in Early Modern England* (Cambridge, 1986), ch. 7; J. H. Hexter, *Reappraisals in History* (London, 1961), pp. 143–46; L. Stone, *The Crisis of the Aristocracy, 1558–1641* (Oxford, 1965), ch. 5.
5. H. Miller, *Henry VIII and the English Nobility* (Oxford, 1986).
6. James, *Society, Politics and Culture*, ch. 8.
7. *CSPD, 1670*, pp. 611–12; R. North, *Lives of the Norths*, ed. A. Jessopp (3 vols, London, 1890), i, pp. 179–80.
8. See J. Brewer and J. Styles (eds), *An Ungovernable People? The English and their Law in the Seventeenth and Eighteenth Centuries* (London, 1980).
9. C. Hill, *Change and Continuity in Seventeenth-Century England* (London, 1974) ch. 8.
10. J. P. Kenyon, *The Stuart Constitution* (Cambridge, 1966), p. 23.
11. Norfolk Record Office, Norwich Civic Records, case 16a, 24, fol. 41; 25, fol. 73.
12. B. Sharp, *In Defiance of All Authority : Rural Artisans and Riot in the West of England, 1586–1660* (Berkeley, California, 1980); K. J. Lindley, *Fenland Riots and the English Revolution* (London, 1982).
13. K. J. Lindley, 'Riot Prevention and Control in Early Stuart London', *TRHS*, 5th series, 33 (1983), pp. 109–26, especially pp. 109–11.
14. James I, *Letters*, ed. G. P. V. Akrigg (Berkeley, California, 1984), p. 297.

15. K. Wrightson and J. Walter, 'Dearth and the Social Order in Early Modern England', *P & P*, 71 (1976), pp. 22–42.

16. Lindley, *Fenland Riots and the English Revolution*, pp. 26–27 and passim.

17. J. Walter, 'Grain Riots and Popular Attitudes to the Law: Maldon and the Crisis of 1629', in Brewer and Styles (eds), *An Ungovernable People?*, pp. 47–52, 60–69.

18. Lindley, *Fenland Riots and the English Revolution*, ch. 2, especially pp. 57–60.

19. See the important essay by M. Goldie, 'The Unacknowledged Republic: Office-Holding in Early Modern England', in T. Harris (ed.) *The Politics of the Excluded, c. 1500–1850* (Basingstoke, 2001), ch. 6.

20. S. Hindle, 'Hierarchy and Community in an English Parish: The Swallowfield Articles of 1596', *HJ*, 42 (1999), pp. 835–51.

21. P. Collinson, 'The Monarchical Republic of Elizabeth I', in J. Guy (ed.), *The Tudor Monarchy* (London, 1997), pp. 123–29.

22. Sir W. Temple, *Works, 1672–9* (London, 1692), p. 154; A. Browning, *Thomas, Earl of Danby* (3 vols, Glasgow, 1951), ii, p. 70.

23. J. Macpherson, *Original Papers Containing the Secret History of Great Britain* (2 vols, London, 1775), i, p. 211n.

24. T. C. Smout, *A History of the Scottish People, 1560–1830* (London, 1972), pp. 303–4.

25. *NHI*, iii, p. 357.

26. The following paragraphs owe a great deal to Smout, *History of the Scottish People*.

27. D. Hirst, 'The English Republic and the Meaning of Britain', in B. Bradshaw and J. S. Morrill (eds), *The British Problem, c. 1534–1707* (Basingstoke, 1996), pp. 198–99.

28. Smout, *History of the Scottish People*, p. 32.

29. For the early history of the House of Stuart, see C. Bingham, *The Stewart Kingdom of Scotland, 1371–1603* (London, 1974).

30. Smout, *History of the Scottish People*, p. 98

31. S. Ellis, 'Tudor State Formation and the Shaping of the British Isles', in S. Ellis and S. Barber (eds), *Conquest and Union: Fashioning a British State, 1475–1725* (Harlow, 1995), ch. 2.

32. M. Watts, *The Dissenters* (Oxford, 1978), p. 59; G. C. Bolam et al., *The English Presbyterians* (London, 1968), pp. 19–21; Smout, *History of the Scottish People*, pp. 59–60.

33. For a rather more pessimistic account of the effectiveness of Scots Presbyterianism, see M. Lynch, 'Scotland', in M. Prestwich (ed.), *International Calvinism* (Oxford, 1985), pp. 236–55.

34. See C. Brady, 'Comparable Histories? The Tudor Reformation in Wales and Ireland', in Ellis and Barber (eds), *Conquest and Union*, ch. 3.

35. See S. G. Ellis, *Tudor Ireland* (Harlow, 1985), pp. 292–97; *NHI*, iii, pp. 113–15.

36. Ellis, *Tudor Ireland*, pp. 291–92.

37. For the complex history of the wars, see Ellis, *Tudor Ireland*, pp. 297–311; *NHI*, iii, pp. 115–37.

38. N. Canny, *Making Ireland British, 1580–1650* (Oxford, 2001), p. 66.

39. This paragraph owes much to C Russell, 'The British Problem and the English Civil War', *History*, 72 (1987), pp. 395–415.

40. See M. J. Braddick, *Nerves of State: Taxation and the Financing of the English State, 1558–1714* (Manchester, 1996).

41. C. Russell, 'Parliamentary History in Perspective, 1604–29', *History*, 61 (1976), pp. 12, 16; Braddick, *Nerves of State*, pp. 93–95; Russell, *The Crisis of Parliaments: English History, 1509–1660* (Oxford, 1971), p. 38.

42. Gardiner, *History of England*, ii, pp. 1–14; Russell, 'Parliamentary History in Perspective', pp. 9–10.

43. C. Marsh, 'Common Prayer in England, 1590–1640: The View from the Pew', *P & P*, 171 (2001), pp. 66–94.

44. See C. Haigh, *English Reformations* (Oxford, 1993); C. Haigh, 'Success and Failure in the English Reformation', *P & P*, 173 (2001), pp. 28–49.

45. The best account of Elizabethan Puritanism remains P. Collinson, *The Elizabethan Puritan Movement* (London, 1967).

46. See P. Collinson, *The Religion of Protestants: The Church in English Society, 1559–1625* (Oxford, 1982); K. Fincham and P. Lake, 'The Ecclesiastical Policy of James I', *JBS*, 24 (1985), pp. 171–82, 186–96; James I, *Letters*, p. 216.

47. Lecture given by K. Fincham to the Royal Historical Society in 2002; this will be published in *TRHS* for 2003.

48. See K. Fincham (ed.), *The Early Stuart Church, 1603–42* (London, 1993).

49. Victoria and Albert Museum, C62–1927 (from Hampton Court, Herefordshire).

50. See D. Underdown, *Revel, Riot and Rebellion: Popular Politics and Culture in England, 1603–60* (Oxford, 1985).

51. W. Hunt, *The Puritan Moment: The Coming of Revolution in an English County* (Cambridge, Massachusetts, 1983), pp. 118–23, 125–27.

52. D. Underdown, *Fire from Heaven: Life in an English Town in the Seventeenth Century* (London, 1993), pp. 2–5 and passim.

53. See C. Haigh, 'The Taming of Reformation: Preachers, Pastors and Parishioners in Elizabethan and Early Stuart England', *History*, 85 (2000), pp. 572–88; Haigh, 'Success and Failure in the English Reformation', passim.

Notes to Chapter 2: James I

1. J. Chamberlain, *Letters*, ed. N. McClure (2 vols, Philadelphia, 1939), ii, pp. 338, 493.

2. Sir W. Scott, *Secret History of the Court of James I* (2 vols, Edinburgh, 1811), ii, pp. 2–5.

3. Scott, *Secret History*, ii, pp. 75–76. See J. Wormald, 'James VI and I: Two Kings or One?', *History*, 68 (1983), pp. 190–91.

4. D. H. Willson, *James VI and I* (London, 1956), pp. 194, 336, 378–79, 404–5, 412, 415, 423–24.

5. Willson, *James VI and I*, pp. 167–68; R. Ashton, *James I by his Contemporaries* (London, 1969), p. 4; S. R. Gardiner, *History of England, 1603–42* (10 vols, London, 1883–84), i, p. 87 and n.; James I, *Letters*, ed. G. P. V. Akrigg (Berkeley, California, 1984), pp. 242–43.

6. Scott, *Secret History*, ii, p. 10.

7. R. Lockyer, *Buckingham* (London, 1981), p. 22.

8. D. Bergeron, *King James and Letters of Homoerotic Desire* (Iowa City, Iowa, 1999), p. 143. Their correspondence is printed in ibid., pp. 148–219.

9. James I, *Letters*, p. 338; Gardiner, *History of England*, ii, p. 325.

10. James I, *Letters*, p. 315.

11. Gardiner, *History of England*, iii, p. 98.

12. James I, *Letters*, pp. 374, 431.

13. Ashton, *James I*, p. 114; Scott, *Secret History*, i, p. 404. (Women were believed – at least by men – to be more lustful than men.)

14. Willson, *James VI and I*, pp. 303–5; T. Birch, *The Court and Times of James I* (2 vols, London, 1849), ii, p. 136; Chamberlain, *Letters*, ii, pp. 286–87. In letters to Buckingham he referred to women as 'cunts': James I, *Letters*, pp. 436, 440, 442.

15. Chamberlain, *Letters*, ii, p. 121; Willson, *James VI and I*, pp. 336, 378–79, 404–5.

16. A. Wilson, *The Secret History of Great Britain* (London, 1653), pp. 54–55, 65–66, 83; Sir J. Harington, *Nugae Antiquae*, ed. T. Park (2 vols, London, 1804), i, pp. 392, 395–97.

17. Wilson, *Secret History*, pp. 79, 105; G. Goodman, *The Court of King James*, ed. J. S. Brewer (2 vols, London, 1839), i, pp. 225–26; Ashton, *James I*, p. 241.

18. Scott, *Secret History*, i, p. 447.

19. Scott, *Secret History*, i, pp. 442–43; Wilson, *Secret History*, p. 149; James I, *Letters*, pp. 376, 440–42; Birch, *Court and Times of James I*, ii, pp. 78–79.

20. Harington, *Nugae Antiquae*, i. 367–70; Willson, *James VI and I*, p. 290.
21. Goodman, *Court of King James*, i, p. 168. Weldon also described the king as not very uxorious: Scott, *Secret History*, ii, p. 6.
22. Harington, *Nugae Antiquae*, i, pp. 348–52.
23. Goodman, *Court of King James*, i, p. 165; Scott, *Secret History*, ii, p. 1.
24. Ashton, *James I*, pp. 95–96, 98–100.
25. J. Nichols, *The Progresses of James I* (4 vols, London, 1828), i, pp. 460–61; Gardiner, *History of England*, iv, p. 366.
26. C. Carlton, *Charles I: The Personal Monarch* (London, 1984), p. 10.
27. Scott, *Secret History*, i, pp. 456, 459–60.
28. See Wormald, 'Two Kings or One?', pp. 187–201.
29. Ashton, *James I*, pp. 174–75.
30. Smout, *History of the Scottish People*, pp. 95–106; Wormald, 'Two Kings or One?', pp. 193–94, 197–98.
31. C. Russell, *The Fall of the British Monarchies, 1637–42* (Oxford, 1991), pp. 29, 32–36; Wormald, 'Two Kings or One?', pp. 194–97, 203–4.
32. J. P. Kenyon, *The Stuart Constitution* (Cambridge, 1966), pp. 12–14; Ashton, *James I*, pp. 67–68.
33. Gardiner, *History of England*, ii, pp. 70–72, 338–41; Chamberlain, *Letters*, i, pp. 300–1, 532–33.
34. A. Cromartie, 'The Constitutionalist Revolution: The Transformation of Political Culture in Early Stuart England', *P & P*, 163 (1999), pp. 86–87; Gardiner, *History of England*, ii, p. 277.
35. See A. Hassell Smith, *County and Court: Government and Politics in Norfolk, 1558–1603* (Oxford, 1974), chs 11–12; J. Thirsk, *Economic Policy and Projects* (Oxford, 1978), ch. 3; L. Stone, *The Crisis of the Aristocracy* (Oxford, 1965), pp. 424–45.
36. See G. R. Elton, 'Tudor Government, the Points of Contact: I. Parliament', *TRHS*, 5th series, 24 (1974), pp. 183–200.
37. Hassell Smith, *County and Court*, pp. 314–32.
38. See B. P. Levack, 'Towards a More Perfect Union', in B. C. Malament (ed.), *After the Reformation* (Manchester, 1980), pp. 57–74.
39. Birch, *Court and Times of James I*, i, p. 346.
40. Wormald, 'Two Kings or One?', p. 205.
41. Wilson, *Secret History*, pp. 12–13; Ashton, *James I*, p. 10; James I, *Letters*, p. 221; Willson, *James VI and I*, p. 165.
42. Scott, *Secret History*, ii, p. 61.
43. Wilson, *Secret History*, pp. 92–94; Goodman, *Court of King James*, i, pp. 202–4; James I, *Letters*, p. 240; R. Schreiber, *The First Carlisle: Sir James Hay, First Earl of Carlisle*, Transactions of the American Philosophical

Society, 74 (1984), p. 6; H. R. Trevor-Roper, *The Gentry, 1540–1640* (EcHR Supplement, 1953), p. 54.

44. Chamberlain, *Letters*, i, p. 581.

45. Gardiner, *History of England*, iv, pp. 1–23, 42–60; Wilson, *Secret History*, p. 155.

46. Chamberlain, *Letters*, ii, pp. 168, 227, 243, 310–11, 325, 357–58; Wilson, *Secret History*, pp. 157–58.

47. Wilson, *Secret History*, p. 157; Chamberlain, *Letters*, i, p. 223.

48. Ashton, *James I*, p. 242; Wilson, *Secret History*, pp. 106, 218–19; Nichols, *Progresses of James I*, i, p. 473.

49. Chamberlain, *Letters*, i, p. 601; C. R. Mayes, 'The Sale of Peerages in Early Stuart England', *Journal of Modern History*, 29 (1957), pp. 21–37; Stone, *Crisis of the Aristocracy*, pp. 105–17.

50. Chamberlain, *Letters*, ii, pp. 57, 290. See also ibid., ii, pp. 13, 333–34.

51. James I, *Letters*, p. 319.

52. Birch, *Court and Times of James I*, ii, p. 232; Chamberlain, *Letters*, ii, p. 418; Gardiner, *History of England*, ii, pp. 249–50.

53. James I, *Letters*, p. 339.

54. Birch, *Court and Times of James I*, ii, p. 289.

55. Ibid., i, p. 346.

56. Edward Hyde, Earl of Clarendon, *History of the Rebellion*, ed. W. D. Macray (6 vols, Oxford, 1888), i, p. 124.

57. Chamberlain, *Letters*, ii, p. 460.

58. Lockyer, *Buckingham*, ch. 5.

59. Chamberlain, *Letters*, ii, pp. 515–16.

60. James I, *Letters*, p. 433.

61. Clarendon, *History of the Rebellion*, i, p. 28; Willson, *James VI and I*, p. 443.

62. Clarendon, *History of the Rebellion*, i, pp. 27–29; Chamberlain, *Letters*, ii, pp. 555, 559, 564.

63. Gardiner, *History of England*, v, p. 332.

64. Chamberlain, *Letters*, ii, pp. 449, 508, 558, 582; Gardiner, *History of England*, v, pp. 99–100, 278–79.

65. Gardiner, *History of England*, v, pp. 280–90.

66. S. G. Ellis, *Tudor Ireland* (Harlow, 1985), pp. 311–12.

67. James I, *Letters*, pp. 204–5, 207.

68. *NHI*, iii, pp. 195–97; N. Canny, *Making Ireland British* (Oxford, 2001), pp. 180–84.

69. See M. MacCarthy-Morrogh, *The Munster Plantation* (Oxford, 1986).

70. See P. S. Robinson, *The Plantation of Ulster* (Dublin, 1984); *NHI*, iii, pp. 196–205.

71. *NHI*, iii, pp. 206–8; Canny, *Making Ireland British*, p. 177.

72. See H. Pawlisch, *Sir John Davies and the Conquest of Ireland: A Study of Legal Imperialism* (Cambridge, 1985).

73. *NHI*, iii, p. 227. See also ibid., pp. 190–92, 208–10, 224–25.

74. Scott, *Secret History*, ii, pp. 8, 12.

Notes to Chapter 3: Charles I

1. Cardinal Richelieu, *Testament politique*, ed. L. André (7th edn, Paris, 1947), pp. 279–86.

2. J. Richards, *Popular Memory and the Construction of English History* (London, 1998), pp. 19, 23–24.

3. W. C. Sellar and R. J. Yeatman, *1066 and All That* (Harmondsworth, 1960), p. 71.

4. Edward Hyde, earl of Clarendon, *History of the Rebellion*, ed. W. D. Macray (6 vols, Oxford, 1888), i, p. 95.

5. See K. Sharpe, 'Private Conscience and Public Duty in the Writings of Charles I', *HJ*, 40 (1997), pp. 643–65.

6. See C. Haigh, *English Reformations* (Oxford, 1993), pp. 290–91.

7. See the shrewd comments of S. R. Gardiner, *History of England, 1603–42* (10 vols, London, 1883–84), v, pp. 317–19.

8. P. Lake and K. Fincham, 'Ecclesiastical Policy of James I', *JBS*, 24 (1985), pp. 197–202; P. Lake, 'The Laudian Style' in Fincham (ed.), *Early Stuart Church*, ch. 7, especially pp. 168–71; N. Tyacke, *Anti-Calvinists* (Oxford, 1987).

9. Gardiner, *History of England*, vii, pp. 20–24, 131–32.

10. A. Fletcher, *A County Community in Peace and War: Sussex, 1600–60* (Harlow, 1975), pp. 85–86.

11. See N. Tyacke, 'Puritanism, Arminianism and Counter Revolution', in C. Russell (ed)., *Origins of the English Civil War* (London, 1973); N. Tyacke, 'Anglican Attitudes: Some Recent Writings on English Religious History from the Reformation to the Civil War', *JBS*, 35 (1996), pp. 156–67.

12. See J. Maltby, *Prayer Book and People in Elizabethan and Early Stuart England* (Cambridge, 1998).

13. Clarendon, *History of the Rebellion*, i, pp. 126–30.

14. Collinson, *Religion of Protestants*, pp. 144–45.

15. P. Collinson, 'Elizabethan and Jacobean Puritanism as Forms of Popular Religious Culture', in C. Durston and J. Eales (eds), *The Culture of English Puritanism* (Basingstoke, 1996), pp. 46–56.

16. P. Lake, '"A Charitable Christian Hatred": The Godly and their Enemies

in the 1630s', in Durston and Eales (eds), *Culture of English Puritanism*, ch. 5; P. Collinson, 'The Cohabitation of the Faithful and the Unfaithful', in O. Grell, J. Israel and N. Tyacke (eds), *From Persecution to Toleration* (Oxford, 1991), ch. 3, especially pp. 66–67.

17. Clarendon, *History of the Rebellion*, i, pp. 194–95; M. J. Havran, *The Catholics in Caroline England* (Stanford, California, 1962), chs 6–7.

18. C. Hibbard, *Charles I and the Popish Plot* (Chapel Hill, North Carolina, 1983).

19. D. Underdown, *Revel, Riot and Rebellion* (Oxford, 1985) passim.

20. C. Russell, *The Fall of the British Monarchies* (Oxford, 1991), pp. 30–31.

21. Gardiner, *History of England*, vii, p. 110.

22. Gardiner, *History of England*, vii, p. 112; T. Birch, *The Court and Times of Charles I* (2 vols, 1848), ii, p. 18.

23. W. J. Jones, *Politics and the Bench: The Judges and the English Civil War* (London, 1971), p. 39; Gardiner, *History of England*, vi, p. 149; vii, pp. 112–13, 361.

24. Gardiner, *History of England*, vi, p. 359. For one later example see ibid., ix, p. 141.

25. J. Guy, 'The Origins of the Petition of Right Reconsidered', *HJ*, 25 (1982), pp. 289–312; Gardiner, *History of England*, vii, pp. 88–96, 110–20. For an attempt to dispute Guy's claims, and to examine these events from the king's perspective, see M. Kishlansky, 'Tyranny Denied: Charles I, Attorney General Heath and the Five Knights' Case', *HJ*, 42 (1999), pp. 53–83.

26. J. Chamberlain, *Letters*, ed. N. McClure (2 vols, Philadelphia, 1939), ii, p. 310.

27. Clarendon, *History of the Rebellion*, i, p. 86.

28. K. Sharpe, *The Personal Rule of Charles I* (New Haven, 1992), pp. 585–90, 593–94.

29. Jones, *Politics and the Bench*, pp. 123–29.

30. Clarendon, *History of the Rebellion*, i, pp. 85, 130–31.

31. Birch, *Court of Charles I*, ii, pp. 283.

32. Gardiner, *History of England*, vii, pp. 167, 362–66; viii, pp. 86–87, 282; Jones, *Politics and the Bench*, pp. 96–98.

33. R. Ashton, *The City and the Court, 1603–43* (Cambridge, 1979), pp. 158–63.

34. Birch, *Court of Charles I*, ii, pp. 189–90, 237–38.

35. Gardiner, *History of England*, vii, pp. 71–76, 273–76; Birch, *Court of Charles I*, ii, pp. 230–31; Russell, *Crisis of Parliaments*, p. 317.

36. Clarendon, *History of the Rebellion*, i, p. 87.

37. See Jones, *Politics and the Bench*, ch. 2; A. Cromartie, 'The Constitutionalist Revolution', *P & P*, 163 (1999), passim.

38. Clarendon, *History of the Rebellion*, i, pp. 87–90.
39. Gardiner, *History of England*, v, p. 424; Russell, *Crisis of Parliaments*, title page.
40. Gardiner, *History of England*, vii, pp. 276–80; K. Brown, *Kingdom or Province? Scotland and the Regal Union, 1603–1715* (London, 1992), pp. 101–3.
41. Gardiner, *History of England*, vii, pp. 293–97; Brown, *Kingdom or Province?*, p. 108.
42. *NHI*, iii, pp. 253–56, 262–63.
43. *CSPV, 1626–28*, pp. 78, 105–6, 154.
44. Russell, *Fall of the British Monarchies*, pp. 32, 37–39.
45. Russell, *Fall of the British Monarchies*, pp. 39–42.
46. Russell, *Crisis of Parliaments*, p. 325.
47. Russell, *Fall of the British Monarchies*, pp. 52–53.
48. Chamberlain, *Letters*, ii, pp. 629–30.
49. R. Lockyer, *Buckingham* (Harlow, 1981), pp. 281–85.
50. Lockyer, *Buckingham*, pp. 392–403; Gardiner, *History of England*, vi, pp. 195–200; Birch, *Court of Charles I*, i, pp. 285, 291; *CSPV, 1626–28*, p. 447.
51. Birch, *Court of Charles I*, i, pp. 285, 367–68; *CSPV, 1628–29*, p. 157; C. Carlton, *Charles I: The Personal Monarch* (London, 1983), pp. 97–98.
52. *CSPD, 1627–28*, pp. 280, 313; *CSPV, 1625–26*, p. 462, *1626–28*, pp. 499, 519.
53. Birch, *Court of Charles I*, i, pp. 163, 191.
54. *CSPD, 1625–26*, p. 275; *CSPV, 1625–26*, pp. 365–68; J. Rushworth, *Historical Collections* (8 vols, London, 1721), i, pp. 216, 222.
55. P. Lake, 'Anti-Popery: The Structure of a Prejudice', in R. Cust and A. Hughes (eds), *Conflict in Early Stuart England* (Harlow, 1989), pp. 84–86; R. Cust, *The Forced Loan and English Politics, 1626–28* (Oxford, 1987), pp. 17–23. Jonathan Scott, *England's Troubles* (Cambridge, 2000), pp. 109–10 and elsewhere, discusses this 'Presbyterian Plot' and treats it not only as a perception but as a reality.
56. S. R. Gardiner, *Constitutional Documents of the Puritan Revolution* (3rd edn, Oxford, 1951), pp. 93–95.
57. Birch, *Court of Charles I*, i, pp. 177, 208, 319, 323, 439; R. Cust, 'News and Politics in Early Seventeenth-Century England', *P & P*, 112 (1986), pp. 72–73.
58. Rushworth, *Historical Collections*, i, p. 225; J. P. Kenyon, *The Stuart Constitution* (Cambridge, 1966), pp. 50–51; *CSPV, 1625–26*, pp. 319, 385.
59. See R. Cust, 'Charles I, the Privy Council and the Forced Loan', *JBS*, 24 (1985), pp. 208–35.
60. *CSPV, 1625–26*, p. 528; *1626–28*, p. 306.
61. Kenyon, *Stuart Constitution*, pp. 14–16; Cust, *The Forced Loan and English Politics*, pp. 62–67.

62. Gardiner, *History of England*, vi, pp. 124–25, 156–57; *CSPD, 1625–26*, pp. 354, 369; Cust, 'Charles I, the Privy Council and the Forced Loan', p. 220. See also *CSPD, 1627–28*, p. 555.

63. Gardiner, *History of England*, v, pp. 223–25, 231; Birch, *Court of Charles I*, i, pp. 360–61. See also C. Russell, *Parliaments and English Politics, 1621–9* (Oxford, 1979), ch. 6, which gives a picture of Charles (at this stage) more favourable than the one given here.

64. *CSPD, 1628–29*, p. 153.

65. Gardiner, *Constitutional Documents*, pp. 73–74; Birch, *Court of Charles I*, i, pp. 366, 401.

66. Birch, *Court of Charles I*, i, pp. 372–75; *CSPD, 1628–29*, p. 268; *CSPV, 1628–29*, p. 283; Clarendon, *History of the Rebellion*, i, p. 37; Gardiner, *History of England*, vi, pp. 353–55.

67. Gardiner, *Constitutional Documents*, pp. 95, 97–99; Rushworth, *Historical Collections*, ii, p. 3; *CSPD, 1628–29*, p. 504.

68. *CSPV, 1625–26*, p. 508, *1626–28*, pp. 305–6; BT 63, bishop of Mende to Richelieu, 27 April and 6 June 1626 NS; BT 65, Dumoulin to Herbault, 3 April 1627 NS.

69. *CSPV, 1628–29*, p. 589.

70. Sharpe, *Personal Rule*, pp. 585–94.

71. K. Fincham, 'The Judges' Decision on Ship Money: The Reaction of Kent', *BIHR*, 57 (1984), pp. 230–37; J. S. Morrill, *Revolt in the Provinces: The People of England and the Tragedies of War, 1630–48* (Harlow, 1999), pp. 181–83.

72. See Sharpe, *Personal Rule*, ch. 11.

73. Clarendon, *History of the Rebellion*, i, p. 93.

74. G. Parry, *The Golden Age Restor'd: The Culture of the Stuart Court, 1603–42* (Manchester, 1981), ch. 9, especially pp. 199–202; Carlton, *Charles I: The Personal Monarch*, pp. 147–53 .

75. T. G. Barnes, *Somerset, 1625–40* (Oxford, 1961), p. 239.

76. Russell, *Fall of the British Monarchies*, p. 82; Gardiner, *History of England*, ix, pp. 25–26, 269–70.

77. Russell, *Fall of the British Monarchies*, p. 68.

78. Clarendon, *History of the Rebellion*, i, pp. 163–64; V. Stater, *Noble Government: The Stuart Lord Lieutenancy and the Transformation of English Politics* (Athens, Georgia, 1994), pp. 54–60.

79. Ashton, *The City and the Court*, pp. 198–99.

80. Russell, *Fall of the British Monarchies*, pp. 87–89.

81. Gardiner, *History of England*, ix, pp. 158–63, 172–73, 176–77.

82. Russell, *Fall of the British Monarchies*, pp. 168–69, 171–74.

83. Gardiner, *History of England*, ix, p. 285.

84. Russell, *Fall of the British Monarchies*, ch. 4; Gardiner, *History of England*, x, p. 6.

85. Gardiner, *History of England*, ix, pp. 122, 229.

86. Gardiner, *History of England*, ix, p. 123 and n.

87. Gardiner, *History of England*, ix, pp. 255–56, 290, 323, 344–46.

88. Gardiner, *History of England*, ix, pp. 119, 178–79, 231–33; Clarendon, *History of the Rebellion*, i, p. 222.

89. Gardiner, *History of England*, ix, pp. 364–69; Clarendon, *History of the Rebellion*, i, pp. 337–40.

90. Clarendon, *History of the Rebellion*, i, pp. 318–21, 333–35; B. Manning, 'The Aristocracy and the Downfall of Charles I', in Manning (ed.), *Politics, Religion and the English Civil War* (London, 1973), ch. 2.

91. Gardiner, *History of England*, ix, p. 367.

92. Gardiner, *History of England*, ix, pp. 348–49.

93. Clarendon, *History of the Rebellion*, i, pp. 322–30, 352–54; *CSPV, 1640–42*, pp. 142, 149; C. Russell, 'The First Army Plot of 1641', *TRHS*, 5th series, 38 (1988), pp. 85–106.

94. Clarendon, *History of the Rebellion*, i, p. 388; Gardiner, *History of England*, ix, p. 376; x, pp. 29, 136; BT 65, Dumoulin to Herbault, 2 May 1627 NS; *CSPD, 1628–29*, p. 81.

95. Clarendon, *History of the Rebellion*, i, pp. 431–32.

96. Gardiner, *Constitutional Documents*, pp. 250–51; S. D'Ewes, *Journal from the First Recess of the Long Parliament to the Withdrawal of the King*, ed. W. H. Coates (New Haven, 1942), p. 362n.

97. Gardiner, *History of England*, ix, p. 401.

98. Gardiner, *History of England*, x, pp. 28–29.

99. *CSPV, 1640–42*, p. 232; Russell, *Fall of the British Monarchies*, pp. 322–28.

100. Russell, *Fall of the British Monarchies*, ch. 10.

101. B. Fitzpatrick, *Seventeenth-Century Ireland* (Dublin, 1988), ch. 6.

102. Gardiner, *History of England*, x, pp. 56–58.

103. Gardiner, *Constitutional Documents*, p. 229.

104. *CSPV, 1640–42*, p. 272; Gardiner, *History of England*, x, pp. 71–72; J. S. Morrill, *The Nature of the English Revolution* (Harlow, 1993), ch. 4. According to Gardiner, *History of England*, x, p. 118, the attack on Westminster Abbey was beaten off.

105. A. Fletcher, *The Outbreak of the English Civil War* (London, 1981), pp. xxvi–xxx, ch. 3.

106. D. Cressy, 'The Protestation Protested', *HJ*, 45 (2002), pp. 251–80.

107. K. J. Lindley, 'The Popular Fear of Catholics during the English Revolution', *P & P*, 51 (1971), pp. 23–55; J. Walter, *Understanding Popular Violence*

in the English Revolution: The Colchester Plunderers (Cambridge, 1999), ch. 6 and passim.

108. Gardiner, *History of England*, ix, p. 413; x, pp. 103, 110.

109. Clarendon, *History of the Rebellion*, i, pp. 399–400.

110. Clarendon, *History of the Rebellion*, i, pp. 402–3.

111. Clarendon, *History of the Rebellion*, i, p. 443; *CSPV, 1640–42*, pp. 242, 263.

112. Gardiner, *History of England*, x, p. 118. See also Gardiner, *History of England*, ix, p. 361; Clarendon, *History of the Rebellion*, i, p. 413n.; *CSPV, 1640–42*, p. 264.

113. BT 73, La Ferté Imbault to ?, 9 January 1642 NS.

114. Gardiner, *History of England*, x, pp. 136–37; Clarendon, *History of the Rebellion*, i, p. 484; BT 73, La Ferté Imbault, 16 January 1642 NS.

115. Gardiner, *History of England*, x, pp. 128–29, 136.

116. Clarendon, *History of the Rebellion*, i, p. 485; *CSPV, 1640–42*, pp. 280, 505.

117. See V. Pearl, *London and the Outbreak of the Puritan Revolution* (Oxford, 1961), pp. 139–44.

118. Gardiner, *History of England*, x, pp. 147–49.

119. Gardiner, *Constitutional Documents*, p. 237.

120. D. H. Pennington, 'The Rebels of 1642', in R. H. Parry (ed.), *The English Civil War and After* (London, 1970), ch. 2.

121. Kenyon, *Stuart Constitution*, pp. 22–23.

122. R. Hutton, *The Royalist War Effort, 1642–6* (London, 1982), chs 1–2.

123. C. Carlton, 'The Impact of the Fighting', in J. S. Morrill (ed.), *The Impact of the English Civil War* (London, 1991), ch. 1, especially pp. 20–21.

124. M. Braddick, *Parliamentary Taxation in Seventeenth-Century England* (Woodbridge, 1994), chs 3, 4 and 6, especially pp. 274–75.

125. Gardiner, *Constitutional Documents*, p. 268.

126. Morrill, *Nature of the English Revolution*, p. 152. Many acted as if episcopacy had been abolished earlier: Kenyon, *Stuart Constitution*, p. 257 and n. 3.

127. Carlton, *Charles I: The Personal Monarch*, p. 252.

128. Hutton, *Royalist War Effort*, pp. 105–9.

129. See Hutton, *Royalist War Effort*; Morrill, *Revolt in the Provinces*, ch. 3.

130. See Hibbard, *Charles I and the Popish Plot*.

131. *NHI*, iii, pp. 315–19.

132. Carlton, *Charles I: The Personal Monarch*, p. 289.

133. D. Scott, 'The "Northern Gentlemen", the Parliamentary Independents and Anglo-Scottish Relations in the Long Parliament', *HJ*, 42 (1999), pp. 347–75, especially pp. 365–70.

134. Sharpe, 'Charles I and Conscience', pp. 658–59; J. Bruce (ed.), *Charles I in 1646*, Camden Society (1856).

135. R. Ashton, 'From Cavalier to Roundhead Tyranny', in Morrill (ed.), *Reactions to the English Civil War*, ch. 8.

136. Kenyon, *Stuart Constitution*, pp. 295–301. Among the very rich literature on the army, perhaps the most important single work is I. Gentles, *The New Model Army in England, Scotland and Ireland, 1645–53* (Oxford, 1993).

137. Carlton, *Charles I: The Personal Monarch*, pp. 311–12.

138. I. Gentles, 'The Struggle for London in the Second Civil War', *HJ*, 26 (1983), pp. 276–305.

139. P. Crawford, 'Charles Stuart: That Man of Blood', *JBS*, 16 (1977), pp. 41–61.

140. O. Cromwell, *Letters and Speeches*, compiled by T. Carlyle, ed. S. C. Lomas (3 vols, London, 1904), i, p. 343.

141. Much new light will be shed on the trial and the regicide by a series of forthcoming works by Sean Kelsey.

Notes to Chapter 4: The Interregnum

1. S. R. Gardiner, *Constitutional Documents of the Puritan Revolution* (Oxford, 1951), pp. 384–88.

2. D. Underdown, *Royalist Conspiracy in England, 1649–60* (New Haven, 1960).

3. O. Cromwell, *Letters and Speeches*, compiled by T. Carlyle, ed. S. C. Lomas (3 vols, London, 1904), iii, p. 71.

4. See A. Woolrych, 'The Cromwellian Protectorate: A Military Dictatorship?', *History*, 75 (1990), pp. 207–31.

5. See C. Durston, *Cromwell's Major Generals* (Manchester, 2001).

6. I. Gentles, *New Model Army* (Oxford, 1993), pp. 357–72.

7. Gentles, *New Model Army*, pp. 373–80.

8. Gentles, *New Model Army*, pp. 365, 381.

9. Cromwell, *Letters and Speeches*, ii, p. 79.

10. K. Brown, *Kingdom or Province? Scotland the Royal Union, 1603–1707* (London, 1992), pp. 140, 147. I owe the point about indebtedness to a seminar paper by David Menarry.

11. Brown, *Kingdom or Province?*, pp. 138–40.

12. Gentles, *New Model Army*, p. 367.

13. Cromwell, *Letters and Speeches*, ii, pp. 7, 11.

14. Cromwell, *Letters and Speeches*, ii, pp. 14–16; *NHI*, iii, pp. 344–45.

15. K. S. Bottigheimer, *English Money and Irish Land* (Oxford, 1971); *NHI*, iii, pp. 360–61.

16. The best account of the confiscations is that by P. J. Corish in *NHI*, iii, pp. 357–75.

17. See T. C. Barnard, 'Crises of Identity among Irish Protestants, 1641–85', *P & P*, 127 (1990), pp. 58–68.

18. T. C. Barnard, *Cromwellian Ireland* (Oxford, 2000), ch. 5 and pp. 171–82.

19. See J. Miller, *Charles II* (London, 1991), pp. 15–30.

20. J. Evelyn, *Diary*, ed. E. S. de Beer (6 vols, Oxford, 1955), iii, p. 246.

21. *Lords Journals*, xi, p. 174.

22. R. Hutton, *The Restoration* (Oxford, 1985), p. 134.

23. J. P. Kenyon, *The Stuart Constitution* (Cambridge, 1966), p. 368.

24. *HMC Ormond*, new series, iii, p. 306.

25. For Taunton, see R. Clifton, *The Last Popular Rebellion* (London, 1984), pp. 27–31, 38–40, 43–45; *CSPD, Jan. – June 1683*, pp. 250, 278, 286–87.

26. *HMC, 5th Report*, pp. 184, 194.

27. Edward Hyde, earl of Clarendon, *History of the Rebellion*, ed. W. D. Macray (6 vols, Oxford, 1888), i, pp. 5, 399–400, 428–31 and passim; K. G. Feiling, *History of the Tory Party, 1640–1714* (Oxford, 1924), pp. 364, 372. Lawrence Hyde, earl of Rochester, should not be confused with John Wilmot, earl of Rochester by an earlier creation, who was a poet and notorious libertine.

28. But would the Tudors ever have *needed* to do so?

29. G. H. Jenkins, *The Foundations of Modern Wales, 1642–1780* (Oxford, 1993), p. 30.

30. See Morrill, *Revolt in the Provinces*, ch. 3.

31. J. H. Hexter, 'Presbyterians, Independents and Puritans: A Voice from the Past', *P & P*, 47 (1970), p. 135.

32. For hundreds of examples of attacks on Quakers, see J. Besse, *A Collection of the Sufferings of the People Called Quakers* (2 vols, London, 1753).

33. D. Underdown, 'Settlement in the Counties', in G. E. Aylmer (ed.), *The Interregnum* (London, 1972), ch. 7; G. E. Aylmer, 'Crisis and Regrouping in the Political Elites', in J. G. A. Pocock (ed.), *Three British Revolutions* (Princeton, 1980), pp. 147–60; A. Hughes, *Politics, Religion and Civil War in Warwickshire, 1620–60* (Cambridge, 1987), pp. 300–2, 333–37, 342–43.

34. M. A. Judson, *The Crisis of the Constitution, 1603–45* (New Brunswick, New Jersey, 1949) remains one of the best introductions to the political and constitutional thought of this period.

35. J. S. Morrill, *The Nature of the English Revolution* (Harlow, 1993), ch. 15

36. J. W. Gough, *Fundamental Law in English Constitutional History* (Oxford, 1955); A. Cromartie, 'The Constitutionalist Revolution', *P & P*, 163 (1999).

37. A. Sharp, *Political Ideas of the English Civil War, 1641–49* (Harlow, 1983), pp. 67–68, 140–43.

38. D. Wootton, 'From Rebellion to Revolution: The Crisis of the Winter of

1642–3 and the Origins of Civil War Radicalism', *EHR*, 105 (1990), pp. 654–69.

39. See for example, Kenyon, *Stuart Constitution*, pp. 296–301; W. Haller and G. Davies (eds), *The Leveller Tracts, 1647–53* (New York, 1944), p. 149.

40. B. Worden, *Roundhead Reputations: The English Civil Wars and the Passions of Posterity* (London, 2001), ch. 12, especially p. 327.

41. J. N. Figgis, *The Divine Right of Kings*, ed. G. R. Elton (New York, 1965), chs 7–9.

42. K. Thomas, *Religion and the Decline of Magic* (London, 1971), especially pp. 510–14, 790.

43. See W. M. Lamont, *Godly Rule* (London, 1969); W. Haller, *Liberty and Reformation in the Puritan Revolution* (New York, 1955); J. F. McGregor and B. Reay, *Radical Religion in the English Revolution* (Oxford, 1984).

44. G. C. Bolam et al., *The English Presbyterians* (London, 1968), pp. 38–45.

45. B. Worden, 'Cromwell and Toleration', in W. J. Sheils (ed.), *Persecution and Toleration* (Oxford, 1984), pp. 199–233.

46. D. Hirst, 'The Failure of Godly Rule in the English Republic', *P & P*, 132 (1991), pp. 33–66; A. Hughes, 'The Frustrations of the Godly', in J. Morrill (ed.), *Revolution and Restoration* (London, 1992), pp. 70–90.

47. See J. S. Wheeler, *The Making of a World Power* (Stroud, 1999); G. E. Aylmer, *The State's Servants: The Civil Service of the English Republic* (London, 1973); J. S. Wheeler, 'Navy Finance, 1649–60', *HJ*, 39 (1996), pp. 457–66.

Notes to Chapter 5: Charles II

1. For this paragraph and the next, see J. Miller, *The Restoration and the England of Charles II* (2nd edn, Harlow, 1997), chs 2–3.

2. J. P. Kenyon, *The Stuart Constitution* (Cambridge, 1966), p. 374.

3. J. Miller, 'The Crown and the Borough Charters in the Reign of Charles II', *EHR*, 100 (1985), pp. 59–63; P. Halliday, *Dismembering the Body Politic: Partisan Politics in England's Towns, 1650–1730* (Cambridge, 1998), pp. 85–92.

4. See C. D. Chandaman, *The English Public Revenue, 1660–88* (Oxford, 1975).

5. C. Roberts, 'The Impeachment of the Earl of Clarendon', *Cambridge Historical Journal*, 13 (1957), pp. 1–18.

6. George Savile, marquis of Halifax, *Works*, ed. J. P. Kenyon (Harmondsworth, 1969), p. 255.

7. BL, Stowe MS 214, fol. 154.

8. Halifax, *Works*, p. 256.

9. J. Miller, *Charles II* (London, 1991), pp. 3–4, 55–64, 161 and passim.

10. J. Miller, *After the Civil Wars: English Politics and Government in the Reign of Charles II* (Harlow, 2000), pp. 174–81; P. Seaward, *The Cavalier Parliament and the Reconstruction of the Old Regime, 1661–67* (Cambridge, 1989), ch. 7.

11. See J. Spurr, *The Restoration Church of England* (New Haven, 1991).

12. A. Browning (ed.), *English Historical Documents, 1660–1714* (London, 1953), pp. 384–86.

13. A. Marvell, *Poems and Letters*, ed. H. M. Margoliouth and E. Duncan Jones (3rd edn, 2 vols, Oxford, 1971), ii, p. 314.

14. A. Fletcher, 'The Enforcement of the Conventicle Acts 1664–79', in W. J. Sheils (ed.), *Persecution and Toleration* (Oxford, 1984), pp. 235–46.

15. Marvell, *Poems and Letters*, ii, p. 315; E. Berwick (ed.), *Rawdon Papers* (London, 1819), p. 138.

16. See Miller, *After the Civil Wars*, ch. 10.

17. T. C. Barnard, 'Scotland and Ireland in the Later Stewart Monarchy' in S. Ellis and S. Barber (eds), *Conquest and Union* (Harlow, 1995), pp. 270–72.

18. H. M. Scott and C. Storrs, 'Introduction: The Consolidation of Noble Power in Europe, 1600–1800', in Scott (ed), *The European Nobilities in the Seventeenth and Eighteenth Centuries*, i, *Western Europe* (Harlow, 1995), ch. 1 (especially pp. 35–44) and passim.

19. Barnard, 'Scotland and Ireland' in Ellis and Barber (eds), *Conquest and Union*, p. 270.

20. K. Brown, *Kingdom or province?* (London, 1992), pp. 40–45, 145, 168; M. A. Goldie, 'Divergence and Union: Scotland and England, 1660–1707', in B. Bradshaw and J. Morrill (eds), *The British Problem* (Basingstoke, 1996), pp. 227–28.

21. T. C. Smout, *History of the Scottish People* (London, 1972), p. 108; M. A. Goldie, 'Divergence and Union', in Bradshaw and Morrill (eds), *British Problem*, p. 227.

22. Brown, *Kingdom or Province?*, p. 40; Smout, *History of the Scottish People*, p. 109.

23. J. Buckroyd, *Church and State in Scotland, 1660–81* (Edinburgh, 1980), pp. 81–82.

24. Barnard, 'Scotland and Ireland' in Ellis and Barber (eds), *Conquest and Union*, p. 262.

25. See Buckroyd, *Church and State in Scotland*.

26. A. Clarke, '1659 and the Road to Restoration', in J. Ohlmeyer (ed.), *Ireland from Independence to Occupation, 1641–60* (Cambridge, 1995), ch. 12.

27. *NHI*, iii, pp. 429–30; J. C. Beckett, *The Making of Modern Ireland, 1603–1923* (London, 1966) , p. 126; Bodleian Library, Carte MS 47, fol.48.

28. Barnard, 'Scotland and Ireland', in Ellis and Barber (eds), *Conquest and Union*, p. 264.

29. Beckett, *Making of Modern Ireland*, p. 120. For Protestant anxieties, see Barnard, 'Conclusion', in Ohlmeyer (ed.), *From Independence to Occupation*, pp. 266–68, 272–77.

30. *NHI*, iii, pp. 422–29; Beckett, *Making of Modern Ireland*, pp. 118–21; Barnard, 'Conclusion', in Ohlmeyer (ed.), *From Independence to Occupation*, pp. 269–72.

31. W. King, *The State of the Protestants under the Late King James's Government* (London, 1691), pp. 31–33.

32. *CSPD, 1673–75*, pp. 38, 62; *NHI*, iii, p. 448; S. J. Connolly, *Religion, Law and Power: The Making of Protestant Ireland 1660–1760* (Oxford, 1992), pp. 203–09.

33. W. Petty, *The Political Anatomy of Ireland* (London, 1691), pp. 38–40. I am grateful to James McGuire for this reference.

34. Barnard, 'Conclusion', in Ohlmeyer (ed.) *From Independence to Occupation*, pp. 277–78.

35. C. Dalton, *Irish Army Lists, 1661–85* (London, 1907), pp. 77, 85. A commission was drawn up for a third Catholic, Alexander Macdonnell, but apparently never issued: ibid., p. 90. The king claimed that there was only one papist in the army: *Essex Papers*, ed. O. Airy, Camden Society (2 vols, 1890, 1913), i, p. 75.

36. Beckett, *Making of Modern Ireland*, pp. 133–34; *Essex Papers*, i, pp. 135, 222–23.

37. Petty, *Political Anatomy of Ireland*, pp. 27–29 (quotation from p. 27).

38. Barnard, 'Conclusion', in Ohlmeyer (ed.) *From Independence to Occupation*, pp. 269–72, 278–81; Barnard, 'Scotland and Ireland', in Ellis and Barber (eds), *Conquest and Union*, p. 271; *NHI*, iii, p. 441.

39. *HMC Ormond*, new series, iv, pp. 35–36; v, p. 155.

40. See Chandaman, *English Public Revenue*.

41. See A. F. Havighurst, 'The Judiciary and Politics in the Reign of Charles II', *Law Quarterly Review*, 66 (1950), pp. 62–78, 229–52.

42. See J. Childs, *The Army of Charles II* (London, 1976).

43. S. Pepys, *Diary*, ed. R. C. Latham and W. Matthews (11 vols, London, 1971–83), viii, p. 282.

44. The standard biography of Shaftesbury is K. H. D. Haley, *The First Earl of Shaftesbury* (Oxford, 1968).

45. G. Burnet, *Supplement to the History of My Own Time*, ed. H. C. Foxcroft (Oxford, 1902), p. 64.

46. See Miller, *After the Civil Wars*, pp. 198–211.

47. E. Newton, *The House of Lyme* (London, 1917), pp. 242–43, 252.

48. S. Pincus, 'From Butterboxes to Wooden Shoes: The Shift in English Popular Sentiment from Anti-Dutch to Anti-French in the 1670s', *HJ* 38 (1995), pp. 333–61.

49. BL, Add. MS 65138, no. 24.

50. T. Brown (ed.), *Miscellanea Aulica* (London, 1702), p. 66.

51. Browning, *English Historical Documents*, p. 387.

52. G. Burnet, *History of My Own Time* (6 vols, Oxford, 1823), i, p. 558, ii, p. 1; E. Dering, *Diaries and Papers*, ed. M. Bond (London, 1976), pp. 125–26.

53. A. Browning, *Thomas, Earl of Danby* (3 vols, Glasgow, 1951), ii, pp. 63–71.

54. Miller, *After the Civil Wars*, pp. 217–25.

55. J. Miller, *Popery and Politics in England, 1660–88* (Cambridge, 1973), pp. 155–59; J. P. Kenyon, *The Popish Plot* (London, 1972).

56. J. Miller, 'The Correspondence of Edward Coleman, 1674–8', *Recusant History*, 14 (1978), pp. 261–75.

57. For a cogent argument that it involved considerably more than exclusion, see M. Knights, *Politics and Opinion in Crisis, 1678–81* (Cambridge, 1994) chs 1–4.

58. J. Childs, 'The Army and the Oxford Parliament of 1681', *EHR*, 94 (1979), pp. 580–87; R. L. Greaves, *Secrets of the Kingdom: British Radicals from the Popish Plot to the Revolution of 1688–9* (Stanford, California, 1992), pp. 130–31.

59. See D. Allen, 'The Role of the London Trained Bands in the Exclusion Crisis', *EHR*, 87 (1972), pp. 287–303.

60. Miller, *Popery and Politics*, pp. 182–88; Browning, *Thomas, Earl of Danby*, ii, pp. 379–80.

61. Greaves, *Secrets of the Kingdom*, p. 106.

62. Bodleian, Carte MS 70, fol. 564.

63. See the judicious discussion in Greaves, *Secrets of the Kingdom*, ch. 4.

64. T. Dineley, *The Account of the Official Progress of the Duke of Beaufort through Wales in 1684* (London, 1888); M. McClain, 'The Duke of Beaufort's Tory Progress through Wales, 1684', *Welsh Historical Review*, 18 (1997), pp. 592–620.

65. Miller, *After the Civil Wars*, p. 283.

66. Dr Williams's Library, MS 31P, p. 436.

67. Goldie, 'Divergence and Union', in Bradshaw and Morrill (eds), *The British Problem*, p. 225; Brown, *Kingdom or Province?*, p. 165.

68. Miller, 'The Crown and the Borough Charters', pp. 70–84; Halliday, *Dismembering the Body Politic*, ch. 6.

69. Kenyon, *Stuart Constitution*, pp. 471–74.

70. Knights, *Politics and Opinion in Crisis*, ch. 10.

71. T. Harris, 'Was the Tory Reaction Popular? Attitudes of Londoners to the Prosecution of Dissent, 1681–6', *London Journal*, 13 (1987–88), pp. 106–20; T. Harris, *London Crowds in the Reign of Charles II* (London, 1987), chs 6–7.

72. The quotation is from Sir W. Temple, *Memoirs, 1672–79* (London, 1692), p. 154.

73. Halifax, *Works*, p 265.

74. Ibid., pp. 266–67.

Notes to Chapter 6: James II

1. S. Pepys, *Diary*, ed. R. C. Latham and W. Matthews (11 vols, London, 1971–83), v, p. 60; viii, p. 68.

2. D. McKie, 'James, Duke of York, FRS', *Notes and Records of the Royal Society*, 13 (1958), pp. 8–15.

3. G. Burnet, *History of My Own Time* (6 vols, Oxford, 1823), ii, p. 24.

4. H. Townshend, *Diary*, ed. J. W. Willis Bund, Worcestershire Historical Society (4 vols, 1915–20), i, p. 72.

5. A. Browning, *English Historical Documents, 1660–1714* (London, 1953), p. 395.

6. *HMC Dartmouth*, i, p. 36.

7. J. Gutch, *Collectanea Curiosa* (2 vols, London, 1781), i, p. 436; A. F. Havighurst, 'James II and the Twelve Men in Scarlet', *Law Quarterly Review*, 69 (1953), pp. 522–46.

8. BL, Egerton MS 2543, fol. 270.

9. Public Record Office, PC 2/71, p. 1.

10. Burnet, *History of My Own Time*, ii, p. 27.

11. M. Goldie, 'The Political Thought of the Anglican Revolution', in R. Beddard (ed.), *The Revolutions of 1688* (Oxford, 1991), ch. 2, especially pp. 112–16, 121–24.

12. See the first paragraph of the declaration of indulgence: Browning, *English Historical Documents*, p. 395.

13. J. Miller, *James II* (revised edn, New Haven, 2000), p. 126.

14. See J. P. Kenyon, 'The Commission for Ecclesiastical Causes, 1686–8: A Reconsideration', *HJ*, 34 (1991), pp. 727–36.

15. The best study of Monmouth is Clifton, *The Last Popular Rebellion*. See also P. Earle, *Monmouth's Rebels* (London, 1977).

16. J. Miller, 'The Immediate Impact of the Revocation in England', in C. E. J. Caldicott, H. Gough and J-P. Pittion (eds), *The Hugueots and Ireland* (Dublin, 1987), pp. 161–74. (The quotation, on p. 166, is from BL, Add. MS 52279, fol. 10.)

17. J. Lingard, *History of England* (6th edn, 10 vols, London, 1855), x, p. 203.

18. Miller, *James II*, pp. 170, 128.

19. See J. Miller, 'The Earl of Tyrconnell and James II's Irish Policy, 1685–8', *HJ*, 20 (1977), pp. 803–23.

20. Ibid., pp. 809–10.

21. K. Brown, *Kingdom or Province? Scotland and the Regal Union* (London, 1992), p. 167; J. Miller, 'The Militia and the Army in the Reign of James II', *HJ*, 16 (1973), pp. 662–63. For the 1650s, see Hirst, 'The English Republic and the Meaning of Britain', in Bradshaw and Morrill (eds), *The British Problem*, p. 218.

22. Browning, *English Historical Documents*, pp. 395–97.

23. Marquis of Halifax, *Works* (Harmondsworth, 1969), p. 106.

24. M. Goldie, 'James II and the Dissenters' Revenge: The Commission of Enquiry of 1688', *Historical Research*, 66 (1993), pp. 54–78.

25. J. R. Jones, *The Revolution of 1688 in England* (London, 1972), ch. 6; M. J. Short, 'The Corporation of Hull and the Government of James II', *Historical Research*, 71 (1998), pp. 172–95.

26. Halliday, *Dismembering the Body Politic*, ch. 7; J. Childs, *The Army, James II and the Glorious Revolution* (Manchester, 1980), pp. 109–11.

27. Halifax, *Works*, pp. 338–39.

28. Kenyon, *Stuart Constitution*, pp. 441–42.

29. R. Thomas, 'The Seven Bishops and their Petition', *Journal of Ecclesiastical History*, 12 (1961), pp. 56–70, especially pp. 66–67; G. V. Bennett, 'The Seven Bishops: A Reconsideration', in D. Baker (ed.), *Religious Motivation* (Oxford, 1978), pp. 267–87, especially p. 283.

30. Gutch, *Collectanea Curiosa*, i, pp. 338–40.

31. E. N. Williams, *The Eighteenth-Century Constitution* (Cambridge, 1960), pp. 8–10.

32. J. Miller, '"Proto-Jacobitism?": The Tories in the Revolution of 1688–89', in E. Cruickshanks and J. Black (eds), *The Jacobite Challenge* (Edinburgh, 1988), ch. 1.

33. J. I. Israel, 'The Dutch Role in the Glorious Revolution', in Israel (ed.), *The Anglo-Dutch Moment: Essays on the Glorious Revolution and its World Impact* (Cambridge, 1991), pp. 105–9, 121–22, 125–26.

34. Williams, *Eighteenth-Century Constitution*, pp. 10–16.

35. T. Harris, 'London Crowds and the Revolution of 1688', in E. Cruickshanks (ed.), *By Force or by Default? The Revolution of 1688–9* (Edinburgh, 1989), ch. 4.

36. T. Bruce, earl of Ailesbury, *Memoirs*, ed. W. E. Buckley, Roxburgh Club (2 vols, 1890), i, p. 224.

Notes to Chapter 7: William and Mary

1. G. Burnet, *History of My Own Time* (6 vols, Oxford, 1823), iv, p. 553.
2. Ibid., iv, p. 548–49.
3. Ibid., iii, pp. 129–31.
4. J. Israel, *The Anglo-Dutch Moment* (Cambridge, 1991), pp. 2, 125–29.
5. Miller, 'Proto-Jacobitism?', in E. Cruickshanks and J. Black (eds), *The Jacobite Challenge* (Edinburgh, 1988), pp. 12–19.
6. See J. P. Kenyon, 'The Revolution of 1688: Resistance and Contract', in N. McKendrick (ed.), *Historical Perspectives: Studies in English Thought and Society in Honour of J. H. Plumb* (London, 1974), ch. 3.
7. P. Yorke, earl of Hardwicke, *Miscellaneous State Papers* (2 vols, London, 1778), ii, pp. 406–10, 413; A. Grey, *Debates in the House of Commons, 1667–94* (10 vols, London, 1763), ix, pp. 12, 26.
8. J. Miller, 'The Glorious Revolution: "Contract" and "Abdication" Reconsidered', *HJ*, 25 (1982), pp. 543–47.
9. Grey, *Debates*, ix, p. 15. See also ibid., p. 62; Burnet, *History of My Own Time*, iii, pp. 362–63.
10. Burnet, *History of My Own Time*, iii, p. 374.
11. Burnet, *History of My Own Time*, iii, pp. 372–76; J. Miller, *The Glorious Revolution* (2nd edn, Harlow, 1997), ch. 2.
12. Grey, *Debates*, ix, p. 57; Hardwicke, *State Papers*, ii, p. 418.
13. W. Cobbett (ed.), *The Parliamentary History of England* (London, 1806–12), v, p. 89; Grey, *Debates*, ix, p. 13.
14. *Commons Journals*, x, p. 15.
15. H. Horwitz, '1689 (and All That)', *Parliamentary History*, 6 (1987), pp. 29–30.
16. W. Ferguson, *Scotland: 1689 to the Present* (Edinburgh, 1968), pp. 102–8; K. Brown, *Kingdom or Province? Scotland and the Regal Union* (London, 1992), pp. 176–78; T. C. Smout, *History of the Scottish People* (London, 1972), p. 479–80; M. Goldie, 'Divergence and Union', in B. Bradshaw and J. Morrill (eds) *The British Problem* (Basingstoke, 1996), p. 232.
17. J. R. Young, 'The Scottish Parliament and the Covenanting Heritage of Constitutional Reform', in A. I. Macinnes and J. Ohlmeyer (eds), *The Stuart Kingdoms in the Seventeenth Century: Awkward Neighbours* (Dublin, 2002), pp. 226–42.
18. T. Barnard, 'Conclusion', in J. Ohlmeyer (ed.), *From Independence to Occupation* (Cambridge, 1995), p. 282; W. King, *The State of the Protestants* (London, 1691), pp. 125–27, '178–79' (recte 186–87).
19. *HMC, House of Lords, 1689–90*, p. 182. On the war in general, see

J. G. Simms, *Jacobite Ireland, 1685–91* (London, 1969); J. Miller, *James II* (New Haven, 2000), ch. 15.

20. *Analecta Hibernica*, xxi, pp. 147, 167.

21. E. Ò Ciardha, *Ireland and the Jacobite Cause, 1685–1766* (Dublin, 2002), pp. 68–72.

22. J. T. Gilbert (ed.), *A Jacobite Narrative of the Wars in Ireland* (Dublin, 1971), p. 63.

23. See Miller, *James II*, ch. 16.

24. Nottingham University Library, MS PwA 1330.

25. Ò Ciardha, *Ireland and the Jacobite Cause*, pp. 68–76.

26. Simms, *Jacobite Ireland*, chs 11–15; J. Miller, 'William III: The English View', in B. Whelan (ed.), *The Last of the Great Wars* (Limerick, 1995), pp. 11–15.

27. Miller, 'William III: The English View', in Whelan (ed.), *Last of the Great Wars*, pp. 27, 35–38.

28. A. Browning, *English Historical Documents, 1660–1714* (London, 1953), pp. 765–69.

29. J. Israel, 'Introduction', in O. Grell, J. Israel and N. Tyacke (eds), *From Persecution to Toleration* (Oxford, 1991), pp. 17–18.

30. *NHI*, iii, pp. 505–8, iv, pp. 2–3.

31. *NHI*, iv, pp. 12–13, 16–21; E. M. Johnston, *Ireland in the Eighteenth Century* (Dublin, 1974), pp. 17–29; C. I. McGrath, 'Securing the Protestant Interest: The Origins and Purpose of the Penal Laws of 1695', *Irish Historical Studies*, 30 (1996) pp. 25–46.

32. The fullest discussion of the declaration is L. G. Schwoerer, *The Declaration of Rights, 1689* (Baltimore, 1981). Professor Schwoerer sees the declaration as more novel and radical than I do.

33. Williams, *The Eighteenth-Century Constitution* (Cambridge, 1960), pp. 34–36.

34. Grey, *Debates*, ix, p. 56; Israel, *Anglo-Dutch Moment*, p. 3.

35. E. N. Williams, *Eighteenth-Century Constitution*, pp. 60–62.

36. Grey, *Debates*, ix, p. 36.

37. Grey, *Debates*, ix, p. 33.

38. Grey, *Debates*, ix, p. 177.

39. C. Roberts, 'The Constitutional Significance of the Financial Settlement of 1690', *HJ*, 20 (1977), pp. 59–76.

40. E. A. Reitan, 'From Revenue to Civil List, 1689–1702', *HJ*, 13 (1970), pp. 571–88.

41. Williams, *Eighteenth-Century Constitution*, pp. 56–60.

42. See B. Kemp, *King and Commons, 1660–1832* (London, 1957).

43. H. Horwitz, *Parliament, Policy and Politics in the Reign of William III* (Manchester, 1977), pp. 175–76.

44. G. V. Bennett, 'Conflict in the Church', in G. Holmes (ed.), *Britain after the Glorious Revolution* (London, 1969), ch. 7; J. Spurr, 'The Church of England, Comprehension and the Toleration Act of 1689', *EHR*, 104 (1989), pp. 937–46; Horwitz, *Parliament, Policy and Politics*, pp. 23–26.

45. Williams, *Eighteenth-Century Constitution*, pp. 60, 62.

46. Williams, *Eighteenth-Century Constitution*, pp. 61, 63; Miller, 'William III: The English View', in Whelan (ed.), *Last of the Great Wars*, pp. 19–21.

47. Horwitz, *Parliament, Policy and Politics*, pp. 42, 73–75, 201.

48. J. A. Downie, 'The Commission of Public Accounts and the Formation of the Country Party', *EHR*, 91 (1976), pp. 33–51.

49. S. B. Baxter, *William III* (London, 1966), ch. 20. This is a scholarly biography, but tends to see everything from William's point of view.

50. Williams, *Eighteenth-Century Constitution*, p. 61.

51. G. C. Gibbs, 'The Revolution and Foreign Policy', in Holmes (ed.), *Britain after the Glorious Revolution*, pp. 67–72; G. C. Gibbs, 'Laying Treaties Before Parliament in the Eighteenth Century', in R. M. Hatton and M. S. Anderson (eds), *Essays in Diplomatic History in Honour of D. B. Horn* (London, 1970), ch. 7.

52. Burnet, *History of My Own Time*, iv, p. 553.

Notes to Chapter 8: Anne

1. J. R. Young, 'The Scottish Parliament and the Covenanting Heritage of Constitutional Reform', in A. I. Macinnes and J. Ohlmeyer (eds), *The Stuart Kingdoms in the Seventeenth Century* (Dublin, 2002), pp. 242–49.

2. T. C. Smout, 'The Road to Union', in G. Holmes (ed.), *Britain after the Glorious Revolution* (London, 1969), ch. 8; D. W. Hayton, 'Constitutional Experiments and Political Expediency', in S. Ellis and S. Barber (eds), *Conquest and Union* (Harlow, 1995), pp. 276–78; M. Goldie, 'Divergence and Union', in B. Bradshaw and J. Morrill (eds), *The British Problem* (Basingstoke, 1996), pp. 230, 242–45; C. Whatley, 'England, Scotland and the "Golden Ball": The Union of 1707', *The Historian*, 51 (1996); P. W. J. Riley, *The Union of England and Scotland* (Manchester, 1979).

3. See for example E. Cregeen, 'The Changing Face of the House of Argyll in the Scottish Highlands', in N. Phillipson and R. Mitchison (eds), *Scotland in the Age of Improvement* (Edinburgh, 1970), pp. 8–10.

4. Goldie, 'Divergence and Union', in Bradshaw and Morrill (eds), *The British Problem*, p. 222.

5. T. C. Smout, *History of the Scottish People* (London, 1972), pp. 226–27, 355–56.

6. See L. Colley, *Britons: Forging the Nation, 1707–1837* (New Haven, 1992), chs 1–3.

7. *NHI*, iv, pp. 33–34; J. C. Beckett, *The Making of Modern Ireland* (London, 1966), p. 176; E. M. Johnston, *Ireland in the Eighteenth Century* (Dublin, 1974), p. 19.

8. E. Ò Ciardha, *Ireland and the Jacobite Cause* (Dublin, 2002), pp. 85–86, 89–93, 131–34.

9. Ibid., pp. 29–30 and passim.

10. Hayton, 'Constitutional Experiments and Political Expediency', in Ellis and Barber (eds), *Conquest and Union*, p. 304; *NHI*, iv, p. 39.

11. Barnard, 'Scotland and Ireland in the Late Stewart Monarchy', in Ellis and Barber (eds), *Conquest and Union*, p. 262.

12. Johnston, *Ireland in the Eighteenth Century*, pp. 29–31; J. Smyth, 'The Communities of Ireland and the British State, 1660–1707', in Bradshaw and Morrill (eds), *The British Problem*, pp. 253–55; S. J. Connolly, *Religion, Law and Power* (Oxford, 1992), p. 118.

13. T. Barnard, 'Crises of Irish Protestant Identity', *P & P*, 127 (1990), pp. 46–47, 39–42.

14. Johnston, *Ireland in the Eighteenth Century*, ch. 3; Smyth, 'Communities of Ireland', in Bradshaw and Morrill (eds), *The British Problem*, pp. 247–49; *NHI*, iv, pp. 110–12.

15. C. I. McGrath, *The Making of the Eighteenth-Century Irish Constitution: Government, Parliament and the Revenue, 1692–1714* (Dublin, 2000), passim.

16. Johnston, *Ireland in the Eighteenth Century*, pp. 71–73. The former Parliament House now houses the Bank of Ireland.

17. The very rich literature on party includes G. Holmes, *British Politics in the Age of Anne* (London, 1987); J. H. Plumb, *The Growth of Political Stability in England* (London, 1967), ch. 5; J. P. Kenyon, *Revolution Principles: The Politics of Party, 1689–1720* (Cambridge, 1977); and T. Harris, *Politics under the Later Stuarts* (Harlow, 1993).

18. W. C. Costin and J. S. Watson (eds), *The Law and Working of the Constitution* (2 vols, London, 1952), i, p. 376.

19. E. Gregg, *Queen Anne* (London, 1980), p. 133. This is much the best biography.

20. Gregg, *Queen Anne*, p. 134.

21. Gregg, *Queen Anne*, p. 223.

22. A. McInnes, *Robert Harley: Puritan Politician* (London, 1970), p. 109.

23. Gregg, *Queen Anne*, pp. 258–59.

24. G. Holmes, 'Harley, St John and the Death of the Tory Party, 1710–4', in Holmes (ed.), *Britain after the Glorious Revolution*, ch. 10; G. Holmes and W. A. Speck (eds), *The Divided Society: Parties and Politics in England, 1694–1716* (London, 1967), pp. 141–42.

25. Gregg, *Queen Anne*, pp. 234–39 and passim; F. Harris, *A Passion for Government: The Life of Sarah, Duchess of Marlborough* (Oxford, 1991), an excellent biography.

26. H. Roseveare, *The Financial Revolution, 1660–1760* (Harlow, 1991), ch. 2.

27. James I, *Letters*, ed. Akrigg, p. 294; J. Chamberlain, *Letters*, ed. N. McClure, i, p. 579.

28. See Roseveare, *Financial Revolution*, ch. 4; P. G. M. Dickson, *The Financial Revolution, 1688–1756* (London, 1967); J. Brewer, *The Sinews of Power: War, Money and the English State, 1689–1783* (London, 1989).

29. See Plumb, *Growth of Political Stability*, ch. 3; L. Colley, *In Defiance of Oligarchy: The Tory Party, 1714–60* (Cambridge, 1982).

30. G. Holmes, *The Electorate and the National Will in the First Age of Party* (Lancaster, 1975), pp. 23–24; J. H. Plumb, 'The Growth of the Electorate in England, 1600–1715', *P & P*, 45 (1969), p. 111; W. A. Speck, *Tory and Whig: The Struggle in the Constituencies, 1701–15* (London, 1970), p. 16.

31. See above all Holmes, *British Politics in the Age of Anne*.

32. Holmes and Speck (eds), *The Divided Society*, pp. 135–36.

33. G. Holmes, *The Trial of Dr Sacheverell* (London, 1973), pp. 61–75.

34. Holmes, *Trial of Sacheverell*, ch. 7; G. Holmes, 'The Sacheverell Riots', *P & P*, 72 (1976), pp. 55–85.

35. *Norwich Gazette*, 17–24 June 1710.

36. Gregg, *Queen Anne*, pp. 392–98.

37. Colley, *Britons*, ch. 5.

38. The best studies of Jacobitism are, for England, P. K. Monod, *Jacobitism and the English People, 1688–1788* (Cambridge, 1989); and, for Scotland, B. Lenman, *The Jacobite Risings in Britain, 1689–1746* (London, 1980). For the fairies, see Lenman, *Jacobite Risings*, p. 58.

Bibliography

Ashton, R., *James I by his Contemporaries* (London, 1969).

Barnard, T., 'Crises of Identity among Irish Protestants, 1641–85', *P & P*, 127 (1990).

Barnard, T., *Cromwellian Ireland* (2nd edn, Oxford, 2000).

Beckett, J. C., *The Making of Modern Ireland, 1603–1923* (London 1966).

Birch, T., *The Court and Times of Charles I* (2 vols, London, 1848).

Birch, T., *The Court and Times of James I* (2 vols, London, 1849).

Braddick, M. J., *The Nerves of State: Taxation and the Financing of the English State, 1558–1714* (Manchester, 1996).

Bradshaw, B. and Morrill, J. (eds), *The British Problem, c. 1534–1707* (Basingstoke, 1996).

Brewer, J., *The Sinews of Power: War, Money and the English State, 1688–1783* (London, 1989).

Brown, K., *Kingdom or Province? Scotland and the Royal Union, 1603–1707* (London, 1992).

Browning, A. (ed.), *English Historical Documents, 1660–1714* (London, 1953).

Burnet, G., *History of My Own Time* (6 vols, Oxford, 1823).

Canny, N., *Making Ireland British, 1580–1650* (Oxford, 2001).

Chamberlain, J., *Letters*, ed. N. McClure (2 vols, Philadelphia, 1939).

Clarendon, Edward Hyde, earl of, *History of the Rebellion*, ed. W. D. Macray (6 vols, Oxford, 1888).

Colley, L., *Britons: Forging the Nation, 1707–1837* (New Haven, 1992).

Connolly, S. J., *Religion, Law and Power: The Making of Protestant Ireland, 1660–1760* (Oxford, 1992).

Cromartie, A., 'The Constitutionalist Revolution: The Transformation of Political Culture in Early Stuart England', *P & P*, 163 (1999).

Cromwell, O., *Letters and Speeches*, compiled by T. Carlyle, ed. S. C. Lomas (3 vols, London, 1904).

Cust, R., *The Forced Loan and English Politics, 1626–28* (Oxford, 1987).

Ellis, S. G., *Tudor Ireland* (Harlow, 1985).

Ellis, S. G. and Barber, S. (eds), *Conquest and Union: Fashioning a British State, 1475–1725* (Harlow, 1995).

Fincham, K (ed.), *The Early Stuart Church* (Basingstoke, 1993).

Fletcher, A., *The Outbreak of the English Civil War* (London, 1981).

Gardiner, S. R., *Constitutional Documents of the Puritan Revolution* (3rd edn, Oxford, 1951).

Gardiner, S. R., *History of England, 1603–42* (10 vols, London, 1883–84).

Gentles, I., *The New Model Army* (Oxford, 1992).

Goodman, G., *The Court of King James*, ed. J. S. Brewer (2 vols, London 1839).

Gregg, E., *Queen Anne* (London, 1980).

Grell, O., Israel, J. and Tyacke, N. (eds), *From Persecution to Toleration* (Oxford, 1991).

Grey, A., *Debates in the House of Commons, 1667–94* (10 vols, London, 1769).

Halifax, George Savile, marquis of, *Works*, ed. J. P. Kenyon (Harmondsworth, 1969).

Halliday, Paul, *Dismembering the Body Politic: Partisan Politics in England's Towns, 1650–1730* (Cambridge, 1998).

Harington, J., *Nugae Antiquae*, ed. T. Park (2 vols, London, 1804).

Harris, T., *Politics under the Later Stuarts, 1660–1714* (Harlow, 1993).

Hexter, J. H., *Reappraisals in History* (London, 1961).

Holmes, G (ed.), *Britain after the Glorious Revolution, 1689–1714* (London, 1969).

Holmes, G., *British Politics in the Age of Anne* (revised edn, London, 1987).

Holmes, G., *The Trial of Dr Sacheverell* (London, 1973).

Horwitz, H., *Parliament, Policy and Politics in the Reign of William III* (Manchester, 1977).

Hutton, R., *The Royalist War Effort* (London, 1982).

Israel, J. (ed.), *The Anglo-Dutch Moment: Essays on the Glorious Revolution and its World Impact* (Cambridge, 1991).

James I, *Letters*, ed. G. P. V. Akrigg (Berkeley, California, 1984).

James, M. E., *Society, Politics and Culture: Studies in Early Modern England* (Cambridge, 1986).

Johnston, E. M., *Ireland in the Eighteenth Century* (Dublin, 1974).

Jones, W. J., *Politics and the Bench: The Judges and the English Civil War* (London, 1971).

Kenyon, J. P., *Revolution Principles: The Politics of Party, 1689–1720* (Cambridge, 1977).

Kenyon, J. P., *Robert Spencer, Earl of Sunderland* (London, 1958).

Kenyon, J. P., *The Stuart Constitution* (Cambridge, 1966).

Kenyon, J. P., *The Stuarts* (London, 1958).

King, W., *The State of the Protestants in Ireland under the Late King James* (London, 1691).

Knights, M., *Politics and Opinion in Crisis, 1678–81* (Cambridge, 1994).

Lake, P., 'Anti-Popery: The Structure of a Prejudice', in R. Cust and A. Hughes (eds), *Conflict in Early Stuart England* (Harlow, 1989).

Lockyer, R., *Buckingham* (London, 1981).

Miller, J., *After the Civil Wars: English Politics and Government in the Reign of Charles II* (Harlow, 2000).

Miller, J., *Charles II* (London, 1991).

Miller, J., *James II* (revised edn, New Haven, 2000).

Miller, J., *Popery and Politics in England, 1660–88* (Cambridge, 1973).

Morrill, J., *The Nature of the English Revolution* (Harlow, 1993).

Morrill, J. (ed.), *Reactions to the English Civil War* (London, 1982).

Morrill, J., *Revolt in the Provinces: The People of England and the Tragedies of War, 1630–48* (Harlow, 1999).

Ò Ciardha, E., *Ireland and the Jacobite Cause, 1685–1766* (Dublin, 2002).

Ohlmeyer, J. (ed.), *Ireland from Independence to Occupation, 1641–60* (Cambridge, 1995).

Pepys, S., *Diary*, ed. R. C. Latham and W. Matthews (11 vols, London, 1971–83).

Roseveare, H., *The Financial Revolution, 1660–1760* (Harlow, 1990).

Rushworth, J., *Historical Collections* (8 vols, London, 1721).

Russell, C., 'Parliamentary History in Perspective, 1604–29', *History*, 61 (1976).

Russell, C., *The Causes of the English Civil War* (Oxford, 1990).

Russell, C., *The Crisis of Parliament: English History, 1509–1660* (Oxford, 1971).

Russell, C., *The Fall of the British Monarchies, 1637–42* (Oxford, 1991).

Scott, Sir W. (ed.), *Secret History of the Court of James I* (2 vols, Edinburgh, 1811).

Sharpe, K., *The Personal Rule of Charles I* (New Haven, 1992).

Smout, T. C., *A History of the Scottish People, 1560–1830* (London, 1972).

Stone, L., *The Crisis of the Aristocracy, 1558–1641* (Oxford, 1965).

Underdown, D., *Revel, Riot and Rebellion: Popular Politics and Culture in England, 1603–60* (Oxford, 1985).

Williams, E. N., *The Eighteenth-Century Constitution* (Cambridge, 1960).

Williams, G., *Religion, Language and Nationality in Wales* (Cardiff, 1979).

Willson, D. H., *James VI and I* (London, 1956).

Wilson, A., *The History of Great Britain: Being the Life and Reign of King James* (London, 1653).

Wormald, J., 'James VI and I: Two Kings or One?', *History*, 68 (1983).

Index

Abbot, George, archbishop of
  Canterbury, 39
Amicable Grant (1525), 9, 13
Ancient Constitution 105, 132–33,
  156
Anne of Austria, queen of France,
  114
Anne of Denmark, queen of England
  and Scotland, 39–40
Anne, queen of England and
  Scotland, 44, 187, 200, 206,
  210–11, 225–30, 233, 235–39,
  242–4, 246, 247, 249, 250
Anti-popery, 26, 54–55, 68, 70–71,
  72, 83, 98–99, 101, 105, 164–65,
  167, 168–69, 170, 184–85, 224,
  232
Argyll, Archibald Campbell, duke of,
  248
Argyll, Archibald Campbell, earl of,
  189
Arlington, Henry Bennet, earl of,
  157, 162, 163, 165, 167
Arminians, 32–35, 53–54, 69–72, 84,
  85, 86, 96
Army (English), 84, 86, 88–89,
  93–94, 96, 100, 141, 155, 164–65,
  168, 171, 187, 190, 193, 198–200,
  217, 221, 222, 242; see also New
  Model Army
Army (in Ireland), 24–26, 81, 90–91,
  94, 118, 154, 191–92, 198,
  213–16, 233

Army (Scottish), 89–90, 91, 94, 149,
  151, 193
Articles, Lords of the, 19, 42, 150,
  151, 212
Arundell of Wardour, Henry, lord,
  162
Ashley, lord, see Shaftesbury, earl of
Assessment, 103, 136
Association, Bond of (1584), 12–13,
  46, 219
Association (1696), 219
Aston, Sir Arthur, 119
Attainder, 91, 96, 97, 189, 214
Aubrey, John, 128

Bacon, Francis, 51, 83
Balmerino, James Elphinstone, lord,
  77
Bank of England, 240–41, 245
Baptists, 135, 145, 193
Barbon, Praise-God, 116
Bate's case, 29–30, 76
Beaufort, Henry Somerset, duke of,
  174
Bedford, Francis Russell, fourth earl
  of, 92, 93
Bernini, Gianlorenzo, 67
Berwick, Pacification of, 88
Bishops (English), 4, 10, 19, 89–90,
  97, 100, 101, 104, 106–7, 108,
  140, 146, 158, 188, 226, 238
Bishops (Scottish), 42, 79–81,
  150–51, 211–12

Boleyn, Anne, queen of England, 17

Bolingbroke, Henry St John, viscount, 238

Borrowing, government, 239–41

Bothwell Brig (1679), 171, 175, 188

Boyne, battle of the, 215

Bradshaw, John, 128

Breda, Declaration of (1660), 127, 128

Broghill, Roger Boyle, Baron, later earl of Orrery, 122, 151, 152, 153

Buckingham, George Villiers, first duke of, 37–39, 41, 50–51, 56–59, 65, 68, 81–85, 86, 118

Buckingham, George Villiers, second duke of, 157–58, 163, 167, 183

Burgess, Daniel, 245

Burghley, William Cecil, Baron, 29, 46

Burnet, Gilbert, 158, 167, 182, 186, 203, 205, 206–7, 224

Bute, John Stuart, earl of, 232

Cabal, the, 156–58, 167

Cade, Jack, 7

Cadiz, 81

Carlisle, James Hay, earl of, 50, 52

Carlisle, Lucy Hay, countess of, 93, 100

Carlos II, king of Spain 160–61, 223

Castlemaine, Barbara Palmer, Lady, 156

Catherine of Braganza, 144, 165

Catholics (English), 10, 30, 32, 58, 60, 72, 78, 88, 97, 99, 100, 105, 121, 162, 164, 165, 168–69, 170, 178, 184–85, 190, 193, 194–95, 196, 198, 220

Catholics (Irish), 22–26, 59–65, 77–78, 95–96, 105–6, 119, 122–25, 152–55, 212–17, 224, 232–34, 249

Cavalier Parliament, 139–43, 146–48, 154, 155–56, 158–59, 163, 165–69

Cecil, Robert, see Salisbury, earl of

Charles I, king of England and Scotland, xi, 38, 40–41, 48, 55–58, 63, 65–102, 104–11, 113, 115, 118, 130, 131, 132, 143, 156, 157, 170–71, 173, 185, 190, 196, 203, 212, 227, 246, 249

Charles II, king of England and Scotland, xi, 13, 44, 106, 113–14, 119–21, 127–30, 131–32, 136–37, 139–79, 181–84, 188–89, 191–92, 194, 206, 216, 218, 227, 239, 240, 246, 249, 250

Charles II, king of Spain, see Carlos II

Charles Edward, the Young Pretender ('Charles III' of England and Scotland), 232, 248

Christian IV, king of Denmark 40

Church of England, 3, 7, 19–21, 26, 28–9, 30–35, 49, 53–54, 89–90, 97, 115, 129, 145–47, 158, 170, 176, 185–86, 187–88, 190–91, 193, 194–95, 197, 219–21, 227–28, 237–38

Church of Ireland, 22, 64, 78–79, 125, 212, 233–34

Church of Scotland, 19–21, 26, 32, 42, 49, 79–81, 120–22, 149–50, 193, 211–12, 230–31, 232

Churchill, John, baron, see Marlborough, duke of

Clanricarde, Ulick de Burgh, earl of, 78

Clarendon, Edward Hyde, first earl of, 73, 75, 87, 120, 128, 130, 143–45, 156, 157, 158

Clarendon, Henry Hyde, second earl of, 191–92

Clifford, Thomas, lord, 157, 161–62, 163, 164, 165, 167

Cobbett, William, 14

Coke, Sir Edward, 45

Coleman, Edward, 169, 171

Common Prayer, Book of, *see* Prayer Book (English)

Compton, Henry, 188, 197, 225, 228

Confederate Catholics, *see* Kilkenny, Confederation of

Congregationalists, 135, 145; *see also* Gathered churches

Conventicle Acts (1664 and 1670), 148, 159, 164

Convention (1660), 127–29, 139, 141

Convention (1689), 208–11, 217–18

Convocation, 79

Cork, Richard Boyle, earl of, 24

Cornbury, Edward Hyde, viscount, 200

Corporation Act (1661), 141, 175, 219, 220

Covenant, 80, 88, 104, 129, 141, 147, 150; *see also* Solemn League and Covenant)

Cranfield, Lionel, *see* Middlesex, earl of

Cromwell, Oliver, lord protector, 24, 68, 102, 110, 115–23, 125–26, 128, 131, 142, 149, 157, 203, 215

Cromwell, Richard, lord protector, 126, 131

Culloden, 248

Cumberland, William Augustus, duke of, 248

Danby, Thomas Osborne, earl of, 167–69, 170, 178, 190, 197, 199

Darien, 212

David I, king of Scotland, 15

David II, king of Scotland, 15

Defoe, Daniel, 232

Derry (or Londonderry), siege of, 213–14

Dissenters, 135–36, 145, 146, 147–48, 158–59, 163–64, 168, 174–75, 190, 193, 194–95, 196, 197, 198, 219–20, 226, 227, 238, 244, 245, 247

Dover, Secret Treaty of (1670), 162–63, 166, 178

Drake, Sir Francis, 2, 81

Drogheda, 24, 119

Dryden, John, 157

Dunbar (1650), 120, 121, 125

Dundee, John Graham, viscount, 211

Dunkirk, 118, 161

Dutch Wars, 118, 136–37, 156, 159, 161, 163–67, 239

Ecclesiastical Commission, 187–88

Edgehill, 102

Edward I, king of England, 15, 121

Edward VI, king of England, 1, 10, 16, 28–29

Eikon Basilike, 67

Elections, parliamentary, 89, 127, 169, 172–73, 176, 196, 198, 200, 208, 217, 243–44

Elizabeth I, queen of England, xi–xii, 1–2, 6, 10, 12–13, 17, 19, 23–25, 28–29, 30–32, 33, 45–48, 60, 70, 135, 178, 229, 249

Elizabeth, Electress Palatine and 'Winter Queen' of Bohemia, 40, 54–55, 102, 227

Engagement (1647), 108–9
Essex, Arthur Capel, earl of, 143, 154, 174
Essex, Robert Devereux, third earl of, 92
Essex, Walter Devereux, second earl of, 25, 46
Evelyn, John, 128
Excise, 103, 136
Exclusion, 169–71, 173, 183, 208, 210, 235, 244
Explanation, Act of (Irish, 1665), 152, 214

Fairfax, Sir Thomas, 127
Farmer, Anthony, 191
Felton, John, 85
Ferdinand II, holy roman emperor, 54–55
Feversham, Louis Duras, earl of, 189
Fitzalan, Walter, 15
Five Articles of Perth, 42
Five Members, 100–1
Fleetwood, Charles, 126
Forced loan (1626–27), 73, 74, 83–84
Forest laws, 75
Francis II, king of France, 16
Frederick, Elector Palatine, 40, 54–55, 58, 102
Fronde, 113, 130

Gathered churches, 97, 107, 108–9, 117–18
General assembly (of the Church of Scotland), 20–21, 42, 80–81, 88, 211–12
George I, king of Great Britain, 227, 228, 233, 246–47

George II, king of Great Britain, 236, 248
George III, king of Great Britain, 232, 247
George of Denmark, prince, 187, 226, 238
Ginkel, Frederick Christian, 216
Glamorgan, Edward Somerset, earl of, 106
Glencoe, 212
Gloucester, Henry, duke of (d. 1660), 113, 144
Gloucester, William Henry, duke of (1689–1700), 210, 221, 226
Godden versus Hales (1686), 194
Godfrey, Sir Edmund Berry, 169
Godolphin, Sidney, Baron, 236–38
Goodman, Godfrey, 40
Gordon, George Gordon, duke of, 208
Graces, the, 78, 95
Grand Remonstrance, 96–97
Great Contract, 52
Grey, Lady Jane, 9
Gunpowder Plot, 51, 60
Gustavus Adolphus, king of Sweden, 86

Halifax, George Savile, marquis of, 143, 178–79, 191, 195
Hampden, John, 74, 76, 87
Harbord, William, 218
Harley, Robert, 237–38, 239, 240
Heads of the Proposals, 108
Henrietta Maria, queen of England and Scotland 67–68, 72, 81, 85, 87, 91, 93, 106, 107, 113, 120, 142, 143, 165, 225
Henriette, duchess of Orleans ('Madame'), 162, 225

Henry, prince of Wales, 40, 41
Henry IV, king of France, 142, 162, 182
Henry VI, king of England, 5, 9, 18
Henry VIII, king of England, xi, 1, 2, 3, 5, 6, 10, 17, 22, 28–29, 45, 62, 68, 249
Heritable jurisdictions, 14, 17, 41, 122, 149
Hertford, Edward, earl of (later duke of Somerset), 15
Huddleston, John, 178
Huguenots, 54, 58, 81–82, 151, 187, 190, 193, 204, 206, 221, 225
Hume, David, 232
Hyde, Edward, see Clarendon, earl of
Hyde, Anne, duchess of York, 144, 165, 181, 183

Impeachment, 51, 58, 83, 90, 91, 100, 173
Impositions, 29–30, 73–74, 76, 92
'Incident', the, 94, 96
Indemnity, Act of (1660), 128–29, 139
Indulgence, declaration of (1672), 163–65, 167
Indulgence, declaration of (1687), 193–94, 197
Indulgence, declaration of (Scottish, 1687), 193, 198
Instrument of Government, 116, 117
Ireland, xii–xiii, 13–14, 15, 19, 21–27, 59–65, 72, 77–79, 90–91, 95–96, 105–6, 118–19, 122–25, 151–55, 165, 171, 175, 191–92, 198, 208, 212–17, 224, 232–35, 247, 249
Ireton, Henry, 128

Jacobites, 211, 213–16, 227–28, 229–32, 233, 247–48
Jamaica, 118
James I (James VI of Scotland and James I of England), xii, 1–3, 8, 16, 17, 26–27, 29–30, 32–35, 37–65, 70, 86, 142, 144, 145, 157, 166, 181, 185, 204, 227, 250; as king of Scotland, 16, 18–21, 40, 41–43, 49
James II (James II of England and James VII of Scotland), as duke of York, 113, 114, 152, 154, 161–62, 164, 165–66, 167, 168–69, 169–71, 173, 175, 177–78; as king, 181–201, 203, 206–11, 213–15, 217–18, 221, 225, 226, 227–28, 233, 236–37, 240, 246, 249
James IV of Scotland, 1, 15
James V of Scotland, 1, 15, 16
James VI of Scotland, see James I
James VII of Scotland, see James II
James Francis Edward, the Old Pretender ('James III' of England and 'James VIII' of Scotland), 197–98, 199, 200, 208, 219, 223, 226, 227–28, 232, 240, 247–48
Johnson, Dr Samuel, 44

Keppel, Arnold van, 222
Ket, Robert, 7, 8
Kilkenny, Confederation of, 95, 105–6, 118, 119, 122, 123, 152
Killiecrankie, 211
King, William, 153, 212–13
King's Evil, see Royal Touch
Kirk, see Church of Scotland

Lairds, 19, 41, 42

Lamb, Dr John, 82

Lambert, John, 116, 117

La Rochelle, 81–82, 84, 85

Laud, William, 69–72, 73, 78–79, 91, 147

Lauderdale, John Maitland, earl and duke of, 150–51, 157, 163, 167, 175

Laudians, see Arminians

Law (English), 3–4, 5, 6, 12, 13, 22, 23, 26, 27–28, 29–30, 44–45, 47–48, 62–64, 73–77, 87, 92, 115, 155, 171, 174, 176, 185, 217

Law (Irish), 13–14, 23, 25, 26, 27, 62–64, 77–78

Law (Scottish), 13–14, 41, 49, 149, 230

Leopold I, holy roman emperor, 163

Leslie, David, 89, 120

Levellers, 133–34

Licensing Act, see Press censorship

Limerick, treaty of (1691), 216–17, 232

Locke, John, 220–21

London, City of, 61, 75–76, 78, 88, 100–1, 103, 126, 130, 171, 176

Lords, House of, 91, 96, 99, 100, 101, 113, 115, 140, 141

Louis XIII, king of France, 67, 81–82

Louis XIV, king of France, 113, 151, 159–64, 166–69, 187, 190, 192, 196, 198, 201, 203, 204, 205, 213, 215, 223, 229, 237, 240, 241

'Madame', see Henriette

Magdalen College, 185, 188, 191

Major generals, 118, 131

Mandeville, Edward Montagu, viscount, 100

Mansfeld, Ernst von, 59

Mantegna, Andrea, 68, 116

Mar, John Erskine, earl of, 247–48

Margaret Tudor, 15

Maria, infanta of Spain, 55–57

Marlborough, John Churchill, duke of, 200, 222, 223, 228–29, 236–38

Marlborough, Sarah Churchill, duchess of, 228–29, 239

Marston Moor (1644), 104, 105

Martial Law, 84, 141, 217

Marvell, Andrew, 148

Mary I, queen of England, 1, 154, 193, 207

Mary II, queen of England and Scotland, 168, 186–87, 188, 195, 196, 205–7, 209–10, 217, 222, 224, 225, 226, 228, 246, 249

Mary, princess of Orange, wife of William II, prince of Orange, 114, 144, 196

Mary, queen of Scots, 1, 2, 10, 12–13, 16–17, 31–32, 45, 246

Mary Beatrice of Modena, queen of England and Scotland, 165–66, 181, 186, 196–97, 205, 207, 225–26

Masham, Abigail, 239

Mazarin, Jules, cardinal, 114

Melville, Andrew, 20, 41

Middlesex, Lionel Cranfield, earl of, 58, 83

Militia Bill (1641), 96, 99, 101

Militia (English), 2, 6, 10, 11, 88, 101, 139, 140, 155, 171, 173–74, 189, 193, 199

Militia (Irish), 154, 192, 193, 233

Militia (Scottish), 149, 151, 159, 193

Monk, George, 122, 126–27

Monmouth, James Scott, duke of,
    144, 171, 188–90, 206
Monopolies, 46, 48, 50–51, 56, 57,
    76, 92
Montagu, Ralph, 169
Mountjoy, Charles Blount, baron,
    25, 59
Mountnorris, Francis Annesley, lord,
    77

Naseby, 105, 106
Navy, 103, 118, 136–37, 155, 171,
    196, 209, 222
New English (in Ireland), 23–26,
    59–65, 78–79, 81, 90, 125, 151–55
Newburn (1640), 89
New Model Army, 105, 106, 108–11,
    114–15, 117–21, 123, 125–27,
    131, 137, 139, 141
Nijmegen, peace of (1679), 168, 204
Nine Years War, 25–26, 59
Nobility (English), 4, 5–6, 9, 10, 14,
    51, 87, 89, 101, 198, 200, 222
Nobility (Irish), 13–14, 23, 24,
    62–64, 153
Nobility (Scottish), 13–14, 15, 16,
    17–18, 41–43, 77, 79–80, 122,
    149, 151, 175, 211–12
Nonconformists, see Dissenters

Oates, Titus, 168–69, 170, 173
Occasional conformity, 220, 221,
    237, 238, 244
O'Doherty, Sir Cahir, 61
Old English (in Ireland), 21–22,
    24–25, 59, 62–64, 77–78, 81, 95
O'Neill, Sir Phelim, 96, 123
Orange Order, 224
Orleans, Philippe, duke of
    ('Monsieur'), 162

Ormond, James Butler, first duke of,
    62, 105–6, 118, 123, 129, 145,
    152–54, 158, 171, 172, 175, 191
Orrery, earl of, see Broghill, lord

Papacy, 2, 17, 21, 22, 38, 105–6, 197,
    233
Parliament (English), 3, 4–5, 6,
    27–30, 44–53, 56–58, 65, 73–74,
    77, 81–86, 88–110, 116–18, 129,
    133–34, 169–73, 188, 190, 194,
    196, 207, 218–21, 234–43, 250;
    see also Cavalier Parliament;
    Convention; Lords, House of;
    Rump
Parliament (Irish), 22, 25, 64, 152,
    154, 214, 216–17, 234–35
Parliament of Saints, 116
Parliament (Scottish), 19, 42, 77, 80,
    88, 89, 94, 96, 149, 151, 211–12,
    229–31
'Parliamentary tyranny', 107, 131,
    133
Parties, 106, 130, 168, 172–73, 221;
    see also Tories; Whigs
Patents, 46, 48, 50–51
Penn, William, 193
Pepys, Samuel, 156, 181
Percy family, 4, 6
Petition of Right, 84–85
Petty, Sir William, 153, 154
Philip II, king of Spain, 17, 25, 160,
    207
Philip IV, king of Spain, 55, 160
Philip V, king of Spain, 223, 237
Plantations (in Ireland), 24–25,
    60–63, 77–78, 123–25
Plunkett, Oliver, 173
Pope, see Papacy
Pope-burnings, 166, 170, 172

Popular disorder, 7–10, 12, 13, 87, 91, 96, 97–99, 134, 172, 198, 199, 200, 245–46, 247

Portland, Hans Willem Bentinck, earl of, 222, 223

Poynings' Law, 22, 214, 235

Prayer book (English), 3, 30–31, 71, 97, 135, 146–47

Prayer Book (Scottish), 79–80

Prerogatives, royal, 93–94, 96–98, 106–7, 127, 140, 217–19, 237–38

Presbyterians (English), 116–17, 127, 131–32, 135–36, 146, 164, 221, 245

Press censorship, 45, 86–87, 98, 140, 170, 177, 220–21

Preston (1648), 109, 110

Pretender, Old, see James Francis Edward

Pretender, Young, see Charles Edward

Pride's Purge, 110, 116, 127, 131

Pride, Thomas, 110

Protectorate, 116–18

Protestation (1641), 98–99

Providentialism, 109–10, 115–16, 135–36, 184, 186, 203, 215

Puritans, 30–35, 52, 53–54, 70–72, 83, 90, 135–36, 145, 146

Pym, John, 91, 92, 93, 96, 99, 100–1, 143

Quakers, 117, 131, 135, 136, 145, 148, 174, 193

Raleigh, Walter, 24

Rapparees, 213, 215–16, 233, 247

Rebellion, see Popular disorder

Recusancy laws, 25, 60, 64, 72

Remonstrance, the (Irish), 152

Richelieu, cardinal, 67

Right, Claim of (1689), 211

Rights, Bill of (1689), 210

Rights, Declaration of (1689), 211, 217–18

Rinuccini, Giovanni Battista, 105, 118–19

Riot, see Popular disorder

Robert I, king of Scotland, 15

Robert II, king of Scotland, 15, 16

Rochester, Lawrence Hyde, earl of, 130, 191

Royal Touch, 43–44, 134, 189, 222, 227, 247

Royalists, 97–100, 101–6, 110, 113, 114–15, 118, 121, 127, 129

Rubens, Peter Paul, 68, 86, 111

Rump, 110, 113, 114, 115–16, 119–20, 121, 123–24, 126–27

Rupert, prince, 102, 105

Russell, William, lord, 172, 174

Rye House Plot, 174, 176, 188

Sacheverell, Henry, 244–46

Salisbury, Robert Cecil, first earl of, 46, 50, 52

Salisbury, William Cecil, second earl of, 75

Schomberg, Friedrich Schomberg, duke of, 214

Scotland, xii–xiii, 3, 5, 13–22, 26–27, 30, 37, 49, 62, 63, 65, 72, 77, 79–81, 88–90, 94–95, 97, 104, 106, 108–9, 110, 113, 118, 119–22, 126, 148–51, 171, 175, 192–93, 198, 208, 211–12, 227, 229–32, 242, 247–48, 249–50

Separatists, see Gathered churches

Settlement, Act of (Irish, 1662), 152, 214

Settlement, Act of (English, 1701), 210, 212, 219, 221, 229, 242

Seven Bishops, 197

Shaftesbury, Anthony Ashley Cooper, earl of, 157, 158, 163, 167, 170, 171, 173, 176

Shakespeare, William, xii, 16

Sheldon, Gilbert, archbishop of Canterbury, 146

Ship money, 74, 76, 87–88, 92, 140

Sidney, Algernon, 174

Smith, Adam, 232

Solemn League and Covenant, 104, 109

Somerset, Robert Carr, earl of, 38–39, 50

Sophia, electress of Hanover, 210–11, 227

South Sea Bubble, 247

Spanish match, 55–57, 82

Spenser, Edmund, 23

Star Chamber, 41, 44, 73, 86–87, 92, 140, 155, 174

Strafford, Thomas Wentworth, earl of, 77–79, 81, 90–92, 93, 95, 96, 104, 115, 132, 170

Stuart, Esmé, 39

Subsidies, 29, 87

Tacking, 221, 237, 238

Talbot, Peter, 191

Taxation and revenue, 9–10, 28–30, 44, 52, 56, 58, 73–76, 83, 86, 87, 89, 92, 103, 136, 139, 141–42, 155, 160, 188, 218–19, 237, 239–41

Test Acts (1673 and 1678), 165, 188, 194–95, 220

Thirty-Nine Articles, 34, 79

Toleration Act, 220, 226, 244, 245

Tonnage and poundage, 28, 73–74, 83, 85, 92

Tories (English political party), 130, 172–77, 186, 190–91, 196, 198–99, 201, 208–11, 218–21, 227–28, 235–46

Tories (Irish bandits), 153, 154, 172

Triennial Act (1641), 92, 142; (1694), 219, 242

Tumultuous Petitioning, Act against (1661), 140

Turenne, Henri de la Tour d'Auvergne, vicomte de, 162, 182

Tyler, Wat, 7

Tyrconnell, Richard Talbot, earl of, 191–93, 198, 212–13

Tyrconnell, Rory O'Donnell, earl of, 59–61

Tyrone, Hugh O'Neill, earl of, 25, 59–61

Ulster Scots, 61, 79, 154, 233

Uniformity, Act of (1662), 146–47, 148, 164

Union, Act of (1707), xii, 229–32, 250

Ussher, James, archbishop of Armagh, 79

Van Dyck, Sir Anthony, 67, 68

Villiers, Elizabeth, 205, 206

Wales, xii–xiii, 3, 5, 22, 24, 249

Walpole, Sir Robert, 243

Walter, Lucy, 144, 188

Wardship, 28

Warwick, Robert Rich, earl of, 92

Watt, James, 232

Weldon, Sir Anthony, 37, 38, 39, 65

Wentworth, Sir Thomas, *see* Strafford, earl of
Westminster Assembly of Divines, 104, 135
Wexford, 24, 118, 123
Wharton, Philip, baron, 175
Wharton, Thomas, earl of, 238
Whigs, 130, 172–77, 188–89, 208–10, 218–21, 227, 235–46, 248
White, John, 34
William I, king of England, 75
William II, prince of Orange, 114

William III, prince of Orange and king of England, 160, 166, 168, 178, 187, 188, 189, 195, 196–201, 203–12, 214–19, 221–24, 227, 228–29, 233, 236–37, 242–43, 246, 250
Worcester (1651), 121, 125, 178
Worcester House Declaration (1660), 146
Wren, Matthew, 71

York, duke of, *see* James II